AN INSIDER'S GUIDE
TO LOW-PRICED WINES

BOOKS BY WILLIAM EDMAN MASSEE

WINES AND SPIRITS

WINE-FOOD INDEX

WINE HANDBOOK

WINES OF FRANCE
(*in collaboration with Alexis Lichine*)

THE ART OF COMFORT

PASTA PRONTO

An Insider's Guide
to
Low-Priced Wines

BY
WILLIAM EDMAN MASSEE

DOLPHIN BOOKS
DOUBLEDAY & COMPANY, INC.
GARDEN CITY, NEW YORK
1974

ISBN: 0-385-08308-4
Library of Congress Catalog Card Number 72–84932
Copyright © 1974 by WILLIAM EDMAN MASSEE
All Rights Reserved
Printed in the United States of America
First Edition

CONTENTS

Wines in General — 1
    INTRODUCTION — 2
    LOOKING FOR WINES — 7
    DISCOVERING WINES — 15

Common Wines — 21
    JUG WINES — 22
    POP WINES — 30
    REGIONAL WINES — 36

District and Township Wines — 49
    ITALY — 53
    FRANCE AND NORTH AFRICA — 58
    GERMANY — 79
    SWITZERLAND, AUSTRIA, AND MIDDLE EUROPE — 86
    SPAIN AND PORTUGAL — 93
    THE EASTERN MEDITERRANEAN — 101
    CALIFORNIA — 105
    NEW YORK AND THE EAST — 119
    LATIN AMERICA — 126

The Wine Trade		129
	SHIPPERS	130
	IMPORTERS	155
	OTHER ELEMENTS OF THE TRADE	184
Appendix		199
	WINE TASTINGS	200
	TOP BORDEAUX CHÂTEAUX	205
	STOCKING A SMALL CELLAR	208
	THE COUNTRY WINES OF FRANCE	213
	VDQS	215
	SWEET WINES	217
	EXPANDED LIST OF SHIPPERS	218
Index		222

AUTHOR'S NOTE

This book is full of lists—of wines by the hundreds, of growers, shippers, importers. The lists are intended to lead you to the best buys on the shelves and to avoid those that are poor values at any price.

AN INSIDER'S GUIDE
TO LOW-PRICED WINES

Wines in General

INTRODUCTION
LOOKING FOR WINES
DISCOVERING WINES

INTRODUCTION

Wine prices have trebled during the past decade, and yet there are more low-priced wines on the market than ever before. Both conditions occurred because America is becoming a wine-drinking country, at least in the cities, where demand is constantly threatening supply. Just when you discover a good bottle at a low price, the price goes up or the wine disappears from the market. The search begins again—through the new vintages, the strange labels. Word gets around that districts once ignored are producing good wines, thanks to improved techniques, but a quick browse of the shelves shows a choice too wide to sample before the good ones disappear.

A new technique of wine buying is needed today, along with a new attitude about wine drinking. Lucky is anybody discovering wines for the first time, because there are no old rules to forget, no prejudices to set aside. Now it's possible to start from scratch in the new world of wines and drink well from the first sip. What you start with may be no great wonder, but it should taste good.

Price comes first in today's market, wines whose names are famous or familiar being generally overpriced, as are those in short supply. There are exceptions: wines that are out of fashion or so familiar or plentiful that they are overlooked. We might as well begin with a list, so you can run right out and buy some of the best bargains on the market today.

Best Wine Bargains of The Seventies:

Sauternes or Barsac—Sweet white wines from twin districts in France's Bordeaux region. Drink your dessert, well chilled, or serve with fruits or pastry.

Sylvaner or Traminer—Flowery dry white wines from France's Rhineland province of Alsace. Chilled, with fowl or fish.

Zinfandel—Fruity dry red from California's Napa, Sonoma, and Monterey valleys. Cool, with stews and roasts.

INTRODUCTION

Côtes-du-Rhône Rouge—Fruity dry red from the Rhône Valley of France. Cool slightly, to serve with beef or lamb.

Finos or Manzanillas—Dry Sherries from Spain. Serve chilled or on the rocks instead of cocktails, or with cold seafood such as shrimp or lobster.

There are other good values—the many wines from unfamiliar Bordeaux districts, for example, or those with brand names—but a local shop may have one or two from a list that includes dozens. Good examples of those listed above, however, can be found in every store.

There are hundreds to choose from, none of which should cost more than two or three dollars, although prize specimens may soar above four. You may have to develop a taste for these wines because they are unfamiliar, but they offer best value for the money. The price is right too, because it is half what you might spend for spirits. A useful rule of thumb is to average spending for wines half what you spend for liquor, based on the idea that you get something like sixteen drinks from a fifth of spirits and about eight drinks from a bottle of wine, which is about the same size. Wines you drink casually, in the course of an ordinary day, should cost less than $4 a bottle.

Neophytes may consider $2 a bottle too much, remembering the liters of wine around Europe costing well under a dollar. Closest we can come to such prices are jug wines, those sold by the gallon and half gallon. There are several quite good ones from California and some coming in from Spain, Portugal, and Italy, with many more in the offing—from France and Central Europe, from Mexico and South America. To get you started, here are a few to try. Cost works out to fifteen cents a glass or so, less than fake orange juice or soda pop, even less than coffee, tea, or milk at the nearest lunch counter.

Best Buys Among the Jug Wines

Whites
The Christian Brothers Rhine Wine—Good, winelike taste.
Gallo Chablis Blanc—Nice enough, and soft.
Charles Krug Chablis—Clean and light.

Reds
The Christian Brothers Burgundy—Light and nice, fruity.
Charles Krug Claret—Pleasing, light, and dry.
Louis Martini Mountain Claret—Light, clean, and very good.
Gallo Hearty Burgundy—Very light, but something there.

Price comes first for the new wine buyer who just wants something drinkable and cares not a bit about the loose borrowing of the names of European wine regions. The wines may bear little resemblance to the traditional European wines, but the names may give some hint of what the wines are supposed to imitate, although they rarely do. These names of a type, *generic* wines, really serve to indicate the lowest common denominator of wines on the market. Only a few of them are worth buying.

The next step up are wines bearing brand names, such as Gallo Paisano or Drouhin's Soleil Blanc. Brand names are easy to buy, as are those bearing the names of various shippers and importers; they will be found throughout the book. More confusing are wines bearing place names and grape names, the time-honored way to identify wines. Most such wines are expensive.

Quality comes first, followed by fame, in writings about wine, one often being confused with the other. Wines have always been known by the places from which they come, beginning with the region, then its districts and townships. The more specific the name, logically, the better the wine, except that the term "regionals" is generally used for all wines not coming from a specific vineyard. That's confusing to start with.

Designations are used more precisely here: A regional wine is a blend from lesser vineyards, a fact honored by French law, for example, where a wine labeled Bordeaux Supérieur meets more rigid standards than a regional simply labeled Bordeaux.

A district wine meets still higher standards, the Bordeaux district of Haut Médoc being a district wine supposedly better than a regional. Within the district are townships or communes such as Margaux and Saint Estèphe, one not necessarily better than another, but different because of soil and climate. Actually the differences are minor—the merest shadings—but these "town wines" are generally of greater distinction than district or regional wines.

In most places around the world, the district name is enough to ensure a superior wine. Only in a few districts—in the three great regions of Bordeaux, Burgundy, and the Rhine—do township names truly indicate significant differences in wine.

The best and most expensive wines are marketed under vineyard names, generally called *crus,* meaning "growths," in France. The best of the vineyard wines are bottled by the owner of the vineyard, a practice called château-bottling in Bordeaux, estate-bottling elsewhere. This is a guarantee of authenticity, protected by law, but not a guarantee of excellence.

All the distinctions of naming, from broad to specific are merely assurance that the wine is genuine and from the place indicated on the label. They should be familiar to the buyer who is willing to pay for expensive wines that develop with aging. For anybody concentrating on wines under four dollars, the district name is enough.

All this can be bypassed by knowing the names of the grapes that produce the best wines. Grape names are used to identify fine bottles from such diverse places as California, Chile, and Alsace. These are called *varietal* wines; they are sold under grape names such as Cabernet and Pinot Noir, Riesling and Chardonnay. Lists appear where appropriate.

For best values at reasonable prices, however, it is much more important to know about the shippers in the major wine-producing regions. Shippers provide three bottles out of four that come from any particular region, wines ranging from ordinary and less to extraordinary and more. Some shippers focus on home markets, dumping surplus abroad, while other do just the reverse. They supply almost all of the inexpensive wines—those costing under $3 a bottle—selling in large volume.

A sensible buyer new to wine is wise to concentrate on the big shippers, who have a reputation to protect. They buy wines and blend them to a taste that does not vary much from year to year, producing fair to good wines for everyday drinking.

An old hand at buying inexpensive wines can be as confused as the neophyte. Books and buffs dismiss generic wines, brand names, and regionals of the shippers as undistinguished blends—overfiltered, sweetened, pasteurized—and that's what they were a decade ago. One reason for this was that wines had to be so made that they could stand poor handling and would stay in drinkable condition for as much as a year on store shelves. Now wines move faster through trade channels, so fresher wines can be bottled. A buyer, though, hesitates to buy brands and regionals that he was once warned against, unaware that they have improved.

The old hand stuck to the traditional vineyard ratings, however outdated, moving down the lists as prices went up, ignoring the fact that people in wine-drinking countries drink young, simple wines most of the time—something he rarely got a chance to do. Now he does have the chance to drink what the rest of the world does, young wines ready to drink a year or two after the vintage. Hundreds of them are on the market, low in price because they need not bear the cost of long storing. Such wines are now made all over the world, thanks to improved wine-making techniques.

Many of the new techniques were developed in California, which accounts for the improved quality of those wines. Only the largest shippers abroad have been able to take advantage of the developments or been willing to make the investment. Small shippers have been hampered by tradition, insufficient capital, or limited markets, so changes come slowly in many regions. A buyer reaching a tentative hand toward a bottle on a shelf will be safe in choosing one from a well-known shipper.

The same lack of daring will stand him in good stead when it comes to importers. Those that have been in business a long time generally provide a range of wines better than the newcomers. Their wines may receive more careful handling and storage, for instance. Small shipments of little-known importers may be manhandled during shipment, or appear infrequently on the market. The safe way is to buy from established shippers and their importers, and to buy from well-known local shops that stock their wines.

Daring does enter into wine buying, however, and that comes when buying wines unknown.

LOOKING FOR WINES

One day in Florence, after driving through the hill towns, we found a restaurant where the prices looked all right. We ordered carefully—osso bucco and risotto—then asked for local wine. The waiter grinned, laid a finger at the corner of his eye to let us know he thought us wise, and ran off, leaving us alarmed. When a waiter approves, half the time you've played into his hands and ordered something expensive. He rushed back with a cradle on wheels tortured out of thick black wire and holding a bottle that looked two feet high. Plunking it on the table, he grabbed the neck of the bottle and lowered it like a boom over a handful of glasses, grinning at us as the red wine gurgled into them. "It's too much," I protested, "we can't drink all that." He handed me a glass. "Chianti," he said, leering like a satyr. "Drink only what you want. Taste it." Cool, fruity, sharp, light, delicious. Three hours later, of course, we'd drunk it all, and Florence was the greatest city on earth.

But we forgot the name of the wine. And we couldn't find the restaurant again. For the rest of our days in Florence we tried to find that Chianti, but all the others were too heavy or tasted of the cask or were almost sweetish rather than fruity. I suppose we've tasted Chianti a hundred times since; now and then there was a hint of the lightness and the fruitiness, but that's all; maybe the first sip's best, but if we'd remembered the name we might have been able to repeat the delight.

The first rule in looking for wines, perhaps, is to remember the name. We've lost track of more wines because we've forgotten the names. Maybe we'd remember the district, but we'd forget the shipper or the importer or the grower. You lose a lot of wines before you realize that the only sure way is to jot down all the details—even where and when you drank it—so you can recapture past joys. The mark of an expert wine taster is a good memory, it's said, for tastes as well as names, but the best of them all, Frank Schoonmaker, always carries a notebook to record details of every wine he tastes. That annual collection of notes, spanning half a century of wine tasting, is the most valuable source of wine information in the world today. This book, is a similar selection of inexpensive wines, from more than two decades of tasting.

You can never be sure just what note is going to be most helpful in tracking down a lost wine. In the past, low-priced wines were notorious for inconsistency. A grower might plant new vines, or change his wine-making method, or try a different blending, or change the name to match new regulations. Knowing where his vineyards are, you can track down the bottlings from his neighbors' vines. Location of a vineyard can make all the difference in a wine, and geography is a first tool for finding the classic wines from traditional districts. Most wine lore since Herodotus has been set down to give a sense of the land, in the form of journeys through the vineyards. By tasting the wines as they are presented in such accounts, you can make your own voyage of discovery.

Many growers sell their wines to shippers, a major part of the trade, for a wine's life in cask and bottle is as important as it's life in the vineyards and the fermenting vats. A particular bottling may be quickly gone, but a similar one may be as satisfactory. You may like what the English call "the style" of wines from a particular shipper, tempting you to try other wines from the same source, leading to your own discoveries. Shippers have long-term contracts with growers—many own vineyards and do all the bottling themselves—and wonders can be found by searching through their lists. Similarly importers have long-term and often exclusive arrangements with suppliers, and their names can be important in finding lost wines. Contracts do end, however, and wines you've lost may appear on other lists. Some importers may have only regional distribution, so that a wine you like in New Orleans may come from a different importer in New York; you can track down such wines when you know the name of the shipper or the grower. Experts attach much importance to the names of shipper or grower, and always seem to be talking about them, taking such details as vintage or vineyard for granted. It's the men who make the wines and market them that are important, not just the famous wine names.

A newcomer to wines can bypass all that, not yet having lost any wines. All he really needs to know is the name of the grape—those few varieties called noble vines. Of course, you already have to know a lot about wines before you realize that the grapes are so important. Most people first taste wines without knowing anything about them—on holidays, at parties, on trips. Outside of California, few Americans drink wines regularly, as a part of everyday living. You don't start watching out for wines until you've tasted a really good one, and then it's natural to buy the famous names and famous vintages, which seem always to be expensive. It's quite natural to consider wines a luxury, but such a conclusion can lead one astray. The way to avoid that is to know your grapes.

Imitation is the best policy when new vineyards are being planted. The noble vines of Burgundy, Bordeaux, and the Rhineland have gone around the world. They are called shy bearers, because they don't produce many grapes, but the quality of wine made from them is generally high, so interest in world markets—and in books—generally focuses on wines of these celebrated varieties. Other wines, from lesser grapes, can be fresh and fruity when well made, ready to drink a few months after the vintage and meant to be drunk up within a couple of years. These secondary varieties can produce enormous quantities of wine, most of which was drunk in the country where they were produced in the days when the time from vineyard to table was long. With today's quick distribution and growing interest, wines that are quickly ready are now being shipped around the world. Knowing the grapes, you can look for the wines.

The grapes in the following lists are in order of importance, more or less, and wines from them are generally available. Note that the red-wine grapes of Bordeaux are listed together because they are planted together in the vineyards and fermented together, one grape complementing another; this practice is slowly being followed elsewhere.

Red-Wine Grapes

Cabernet Sauvignon—Produces a dry, light red wine that takes five years and longer to round out. This great grape of Bordeaux does well in California, where it produces the best wine of the state. Also produces distinctive wines elsewhere, and the best rosés from the Loire, which round out in two years.

Cabernet Franc—Produces a light and softer wine in Bordeaux and elsewhere than its relative and matures a little quicker, often in four years. The predominating grape in Saint Émilion, where it is called Bouchet.

Merlot—Produces a soft, fruity wine that begins to round out after four years. Planted in Bordeaux with the Cabernets, in northern Italy, and elsewhere.

Malbec—Produces a quickly maturing, well-balanced wine. It is planted with the other Bordeaux grapes to lighten them, and is the grape of the Cahors district, in southern France. Often called the Cot or Pressac.

Pinot Noir—The great grape of Burgundy, which does well in California and elsewhere when the climate is not too mild. Takes three years and longer to develop.

Gamay—Produces fruity, quickly maturing wines, particularly Beaujolais. There are several varieties, the Gamay Noir au Jus Blanc being the most distinguished; its California cousin is called Napa Gamay. (In California, what's called Gamay Beaujolais is now thought to be a variety of Pinot.) In Burgundy, blends of Pinot Noir and Gamay are called Passe-tous-Grains, drinkable when young, and now exported as Pinot Noir Gamay.

Nebbiolo—The great grape of the Italian Piedmont and Lombardy, producing a fruity, balanced wine after three years or longer.

Barbera—Another Piedmont grape, producing soft and fruity wines ready in three years. Does even better in California.

Petit Syrah—The great grape of Hermitage and Côte Rôtie, on the Rhône, where it produces deep-red wines taking six years and longer to mature. A grape called Petit Sirah in California is considered to be a different variety, although it makes full, fruity wines there.

San Gioveto—The main grape of Chianti, producing light, fresh wines when not much more than a year old, but with slightly different vinification producing full wines that take four years to mature. Also called San Giovese.

Zinfandel—Produces wines that taste like those from the San Gioveto, to which it may be related. Planted only in California.

These European grapes and their cousins produce the best red table wines of the world. Other varieties native to various localities, hybrids, and blends from these add many more distinctive wines to the roster, most of which are ready to drink when put on the market.

Rosé-Wine Grapes

Any red-wine grape can be made into a pink wine, simply by removing the fermenting juice from the skins when the desired color is reached. Perhaps the best grape for pink wines is the Grenache of Tavel; the district is considered to produce the best French rosé. The grape does equally well in California, and acceptably wherever it is grown. Light reds are also made from it, and sweet dessert wines.

White-Wine Grapes

Chardonnay or Pinot Chardonnay—The grape that produces all the great white Burgundies. Dry, full, and fruity, the wines may take three years to develop when from a great vineyard such as Montrachet or Corton Charlemagne, but are ready to drink in the second year when from a district such as Chablis or Pouilly-Fuissé. This grape produces the best dry white of California and distinguished wines elsewhere. No longer considered to be a Pinot variety, it is coming to be called simply Chardonnay. Pinot Blanc—A Burgundy grape second only to Chardonnay, producing superior whites. Considered to do better in California than in Burgundy.

Riesling—The great grape of the Rhineland, called Johannisberg Riesling or White Riesling in California, to distinguish it from various hybrids and misnamed wines. ("California Riesling" is usually Sylvaner.) The wines range from flowery to fruity, and types made from late-picked grapes are sweet.

Sauvignon Blanc—The great grape of Bordeaux, particularly in Graves; in Sauternes it is planted with Semillon to make sweet wines. Also planted on the upper Loire, where it makes the dry, crisp wines of Pouilly-Fumé and Sancerre. In California the wines tend to be softer and sometimes flowery; today's practice in Bordeaux is to make extremely dry and not very flowery wines from it.

Semillon—The second Bordeaux grape, producing softer, less-distinguished wines than its vineyard companion.

Chenin Blanc—Produces a fresh and flowery dry wine, particularly in the middle Loire, where it is called Pineau de la Loire. In California it is often called White Pinot, and buyers confuse it with Pinot Blanc.

Folle Blanche—Produces a light, fresh dry wine on the lower Loire, where it is also called Picpoul or Gros Plant and imported as such. Does well in California, producing one of the best dry whites.

Sylvaner—Produces a soft, flowery wine, particularly in Alsace, Franconia, and the Rheinhessen. Often called the Franken Riesling in Germany and often called Riesling in California, where it is so marketed.

Traminer—Produces a spicy, full wine in Alsace and elsewhere. A special strain called Gewürztraminer is particularly spicy and is becoming the one most widely marketed. Does excellently in California.

Many other white-wine grapes are planted, particularly to make sweet wines, perhaps the most important being the various Muscat varieties of France and Italy. People in wine countries don't have to give grapes a thought, because a plentiful supply of fresh, young, inexpensive bottlings is as common as bread and cheese. Wine is drunk without fuss or fancy, and when one palls there's another to have instead. Those drunk every day may cost about a dollar, and a special bottle for a dinner party may cost no more than two or three; only a grand occasion like Christmas or an anniversary calls for a fine old bottle that may cost five dollars or so.

Americans aren't so casual about wines, because few of us drink them every day, nor are we so lucky as to have a large and constant supply available. We drink a couple of gallons a year, on the average, compared to the French or Italian consumption of thirty gallons, so we pay a premium for wines in a still-restricted market. Demand is far ahead of supply, importers hesitating to bring in good but unknown wines that may languish on the shelves. A case of European wines may cost five dollars to ship, including duties; both importers and wholesalers add mark-ups of 25 per cent, and the retailer may charge double his cost, so that these charges add to the price of each bottle. A quick thinker might conclude that California, which provides three of every four bottles drunk in this country, is a possible source of reasonably priced wines, but high vineyard and labor costs keep prices up. Until wine production in this country doubles, which will take a decade, Americans will have to search for good wines at low prices.

The quickest way to get the best buys around is to buy a dozen bottles of anything new that's available, a mixed case, and drink them during the following week or so, making notes. Good times to do this are during sales, which occur in January (after the holidays and before inventory), in May (when stocks are cleared), and in October (before the new vintages arrive for the holidays). These are also the times to pick up odd lots and bargains.

But this is all too sensible. Most people find a couple of wines they like and stick to them until the supply runs out. To escape the drought and extend the range, the trick is to follow the expert's way of tasting. To do so, check first to see that the wine is clear (there's always something wrong with a wine that's cloudy) and that there is nothing wrong with the smell or taste. This is done by swirling the wine in the glass, then sniffing.

Alcohol evaporates on contact with air. Swirling the glass increases the action, releasing the various smells in a wine, those flowery and fruity esters that come into being when simple alcohols break down into what's called higher alcohols. The same thing occurs when you take a sip—about a spoonful of wine—then suck in air so that the wine bounces around inside your mouth.

By thus whistling in, you taste at least twice as much as when you just swig and swallow. While you're doing all this, being careful not to choke and not worrying about the noise you are making, you take note of the various qualities of the wine.

Terms for tastes are couched in a sort of shorthand that sounds precious, but has quite specific meanings that are hard to explain because we have few ordinary words to describe tastes and smells. But this vocabulary, and the awareness it signifies, is of little concern when all we are seeking is a good wine to drink. There are really only a few things to watch out for:

>Nothing bad.
>Nothing blah.
>Something good.
>Something distinctive.

Everybody knows what these vague phrases mean, more or less. They indicate a progression, a series of impressions—a discovery. All you have to do is taste.

DISCOVERING WINES

As with children and dogs and other good things, a person needs a way with wines. The best attitude is one of hope. There's no point going around expecting cheap wines to be nasty and expensive ones to be overrated, which is the suspicious way of most people at wine tastings. Some find the least expensive wines to be sour or bitter, sweetish or watery, while the most expensive seem to be dry or full, rich or light-bodied, depending on whether they think they ought to like them or not. Merchants and importers present what they have at tastings—costly wines not ready to drink, low-priced wines rarely better than they should be—of two minds about putting prices on the wines. The high-priced ones are always drunk up and inexpensive ones passed over (the merchants never speak of cheap wines), even though the least wine may be most ready to drink. Hopefully a person can find something to like at a tasting, preferably low-priced.

Drinking isn't a bit like tasting. In wine countries, every inn and cafe seems to have delicious bottles for fifty cents or so. Even adding a dollar for transportation, why can't we have the same thing here? Well, we can, and we do, for our jug wines from California are of equal quality and usually better—but the style is different. Most of our jug wines are made to taste soft and bland and sweetish—the producers call them "mellow"—because that's what sells. The roughness, coarseness, and sharpness, the bite of the ordinary wine of Europe, is worked out of our cheap wines. At a tasting, maybe we'd hate them.

Cheap wines taste best when drunk with meals. At tastings, there's a tendency to look for flaws. You can't expect too much from a bottle costing less than two dollars or assume that a bottle costing twice as much will be twice as good. But both will probably taste good with meals. It may take some time to discover the good ones that go well with daily fare, but at tastings, three bottles out of four may seem unsatisfactory. To find the good ones quickly, a comparative tasting may be the only way, always hoping that most of the wines will taste good.

That's the positive thing to look for: a good-tasting wine that doesn't have anything much unpleasant about it. There are three bad things to watch out for, and two not-so-bad.

Most wines are judged by smell, which is confirmed by taste. Looks count, but most wines look all right, so long as they are clear. Without going into the subtleties of the taster's terms, here are some broad ones to consider that will indicate whether a wine is fit to drink, with or without food.

1) Vegetable Stench

Some wines smell of the swamp, with the rank odor of a frog pond or a stagnant pool or of the water in a vase where flowers have been kept too long. In its less unpleasant forms, the smell may be reminiscent of skunk cabbage or wet straw, of limp carrots or bruised celery. The smell may come from rotten or from unripe grapes, from stems, or from poor vinification.

2) Chemical Stink

Wines can smell like a school laboratory or a crammed medicine chest, of burning rubber or a paper factory, or an oil-cracking plant. New Yorkers might find in some the odors of the Jersey Flats. In its less unpleasant forms, the smell may be like a print shop or a hardware store or a painter's loft. The stink comes from chemicals used too freely in making the wine or from badly controlled chemical changes in the vinification process.

3) Barnyard Reek

This is the smell of the hen house or the cow shed or the pig sty, a sharp and acrid odor that stings the nose. In its less unpleasant form, it may remind one of a drying marsh or a root cellar—a sharp version of vegetable stench, with perhaps a touch of chemical stink. It is the result of sloppy wine-making practice, and may come from stems, rotten grapes, or fermentation that is too quick or too slow.

These are not very nice in a wine. Sometimes you can't smell the wine for the off odors. When there's just a trace of them, you might scarcely notice. But they are the basic bad smells of wine. Mild versions may occur naturally when the wine changes as it ages, disappearing as the wine reaches maturity. In most cases when the odors are sharply noticeable, the wine will remain flawed.

There are two other smells that can be unpleasant when pronounced, although both may wane when the bottle has been open to the air for a few minutes. Even when pronounced, the following smells are not unpleasant to some people:

4) *Cask Odor*

Woodiness, in both smell and taste, comes from too long a time in vat or cask, and can predominate over the wine itself. When the wood has not been scrubbed down, or when it is moldy, this wet-lumber smell can be unpleasing. In mild forms, the smell is of freshly cut oak, or of a new house or a paneled room.

5) *Cellar Taint*

A moldy cellar or an excessively damp one may impart the smell of concrete or wet stone to a wine. This is not the same as an earth smell, which comes from grapes grown in heavy soils. Only when the taint masks the other characteristics of a wine can it be considered unpleasant.

These are the most obnoxious things to look for in a wine. If none are present, or scarcely noticeable, the wine is drinkable. Absence of bad qualities is considered more important than the presence of good ones, to some.

People who drink a lot of cheap wines can even tolerate these unpleasantnesses, for however strange in the beginning, one quickly gets used to them. But there are certain unexpected tastes in wines that surprise drinkers, this unfamiliarity often breeding unwarranted contempt. Many people tasting a dry table wine for the first time are apt to say it is sour. That's the taste of fruit acids. A truly sour wine is one that's been turned to vinegar (*vin aigre* in French) by the action of acetic acid, and is a wine that has spoiled. Acid is a bad word in English generally, but when it comes to wines the word is taken to suggest freshness and a pleasant sharpness, almost the taste of a green twig or of some delicious fruit.

People say a wine tastes "bitter," and they really mean bitter. That comes from tannin in the wine, picked up from stems, seeds, and the cask. It is not noticeable when the fruit acids of the wines are pronounced enough to balance the bitterness. Tannin is essential to hold the wine together as it matures. The bitterness lessens gradually as the tannin becomes tartrates, which drop to the bottom of the bottle to become sediment. Bitterness disappears with age, and when it declines at the same rate as the fruit acids, the wine stays drinkable. Many great wines go through periods when the fruit and tannin are out of balance.

Lots of people drink dry wines and call them sweet. A sensation of sweetness may come from the glycerine that is part of every wine, from the various flowery alcohols, from the fruit acids. When there is also a freshness from acid, the wine is quite pleasing. But many cheap wines have their fermentation stopped so that grape sugar remains in the wine. This residual sugar serves to mask too much acid or tannin, but makes the wine taste bland. So does pasteurization, or too much filtration.

The most distorting taste in a dry wine comes from chaptalization, the process of adding sugar to the fermenting juice to increase the alcoholic content of the wine. Building up the alcohol in this way helps preserve the wine but changes its nature and gives it a vapid quality. A wine built up to more than twelve per cent alcohol will be much less interesting than a natural wine that is a degree or so less in alcohol.

Let's say that the wine tastes pleasant enough to you and adequately dry. What makes it distinctive? We are now ready for some tasters' terms: fullness, body, bouquet, roundness. There are many more, but these will do.

Fullness has to do with the taste of wine in a wine, as opposed to the taste of water. A full wine won't taste watery.

Body is much the same thing. A wine light in body may taste watery or thin, as if it has been diluted or watered down. If the wine has plenty of fruit—the taste of fruit—or plenty of sharpness (the fresh taste that comes from fruit acids), you will not mind the watery quality, the lightness. A full-bodied wine, with no watery taste at all, may simply be too much to swallow; so you sip it. Fullness of body comes from lots of alcohol, lots of fruit acids, lots of tannin—and the wine may be better if you add a little water or some soda, or an ice cube. This might be sacrilege for a wine costing more than four dollars. It's good sense to adjust an inexpensive wine to your taste.

Bouquet is the term used to describe all the flowery and fruity odors from the alcohols and acids in the wine. Some wines have enormous bouquets: you can smell an open bottle of Sherry across a room. Some wines have light bouquets—flowery smells scarcely noticeable.

Roundness in a wine suggests a balance of qualities, a certain development, a wine that doesn't lack anything essential, that doesn't taste empty or vapid. Hard to explain, it's easy to taste, and the taste is good, pleasant, satisfying.

These good things that stand out in a wine are what make it distinctive. Over all, a wine may taste light or full, flowery or fruity, have a quality that appeals, not readily put in words: like a young girl, perhaps, or a happy woman, like a cheerful tune or a soaring symphony, like a spring morning or a summer afternoon. A distinctive wine will have a character all its own. You'll discover it in the tasting.

Common Wines

JUG WINES
POP WINES
REGIONAL WINES

JUG WINES

Peaceful revolutions are best, and a wine drinker takes part in one every time he opens a bottle. No wine is produced the way it was twenty years ago, and every purchase is a vote for the revolution or against it, shaping the change while it is going on. No vote is stronger than the one cast when a drinker buys a jug of wine, which can be an indeterminate sweetish mess or something not bad at all. Those afraid of change stick to regular bottles at prices they're used to, never knowing what they're missing.

Jug wines are ordinary wines bottled by the gallon or half gallon and many sizes in between. They are a way to get a lot of wine without much fuss or expense, perfectly suited to the casual or even indifferent American who likes wines sometimes instead of beer or soda pop or water. For those who regularly have a glass with dinner, jug wines should sensibly account for one purchase out of two, many of them being better than the *vin ordinaire* a Frenchman drinks every day, the kind he buys in a grocery store or across the zinc in his favorite bistro.

The gallon size is too big for refrigerators and cabinets in most kitchens, so the twenty-glass or half-gallon jug, holding 64 ounces, is beginning to take over the market. Once opened, a jug is apt to be around awhile; some producers overstabilize the wines so they won't sour, or sweeten them so much you won't notice if they do. These are wines to vote against—by not buying them. Some cost as little as three dollars a gallon and aren't worth that.

Other producers don't compromise, bottling fresh wines treated as little as possible, counting on you to drink them up while they're good, within a couple of days. When you don't expect to drink so much, the thing to do is to fill smaller bottles as full as possible when you open the jug, then seal them tightly. The wine will keep for months without refrigeration. Screw tops and half bottles are both handy.

Revolutionary jug wines are cheaper by the gallon—the trade likes to call them "popular priced," because that's supposed to sound better—and good ones can cost seven or eight dollars. This seems like a lot when you're standing in the store and see others costing half that. But a gallon jug fills five ordinary bottles, the jug wine often being better than wines costing $2 and more in standard sizes.

The European counterpart of jug wines is *vin ordinaire,* common wine of the previous vintage. It's also called *vin courant,* open wine, because there are still places where you can go to get your bottle filled, or where you can watch wine drawn from the cask into demijohns, some of them holding five gallons and more. The wine is meant to be drunk promptly, and there's pleasure in noting the changes from day to day, some excitement in racing to the bottom of the bottle before all the freshness fades.

Wines that last longer than a season or two, that are bottled not merely for ease of handling but because they improve with time in glass, are called *grands vins.* Any wine that improves in bottle is a grand wine, althought not necessarily a great one, a distinction lost on innocent buyers.

Our jug wines generally lack the freshness and the changing fruitiness of *vin ordinaire,* being stabilized by filtration to a degree of pleasantness. They are often 12 per cent or more in alcohol, a strength our producers feel Americans prefer, and which keeps the wine from changing. The ordinary wine of Europe may be a degree or so less in alcohol, shortening its life. The only truly young wine on the American market is new Beaujolais, arriving here in the December after the vintage. It's so popular that Rhône producers and the makers of white wine from such regions as Alsace are beginning to market extremely young wines here, bottlings that must be drunk up by the following spring. This interest in young wines may encourage our jug-wine producers to try the same thing.

As of now, our jug wines are generally of two types: blends that follow what are considered to be traditional styles, and "mellow" wines, which are softened with sugar. Sugar masks flaws, and mellow wines are bland and without much character, if any, meant to be drunk by those who don't really like wines but like the idea of them. Generally, the more you pay and the drier the wine, the better the blend.

White wines are harder to make than reds, any flaws being more easily detectable in their less-pronounced tastes, so the best buys in jug wines are usually red. In California, "Burgundy" usually means a fruity red, "Claret" means one that is thinner and lighter and perhaps somewhat drier. "Chianti," or one with another Italianate name means one like "Burgundy." "Rhine Wine" means one that's sort of flowery and not sharp, "Chablis" means one that's sort of dry, without sweetness, and "Sauterne" means one that's kind of sweet. You shouldn't be discouraged if you can't see much difference. Just ignore any off tastes of the cellar or of damp straw, or anything that reminds you of a swamp in spring or a medicine chest.

The best jug wines, though, are clean in taste, fine for parties and day-to-day drinking, good for making into punches by adding the juice of a lemon or an orange, or both, a dollop of brandy or liqueur, perhaps a sprinkle of sugar, and lots of ice. They make good long drinks, with ice and soda, and they are good for cooking. Some think that even the reds taste best chilled, or with an ice cube in the glass.

The best way to buy jug wines is by starting out with half bottles, the size the trade calls tenths. To become familiar with what's available, you can buy a dozen tenths of those wines you think you may like by the gallon, at the same time building up a small supply of bottles that can be used for leftover wines.

Personally, I avoid the cheapest wines, as being so bland as to be uninteresting. Some of the Italianate types just mentioned may appeal, though. The following producers put out the best jug wines, to my mind, although all the growers from the California North Coast and South Bay counties market respectable wines. Those from the Central Valley—Gallo, Franzia, Petri—are worth exploring. Gallo Hearty Burgundy is a good example; it contains 14% alcohol.

California Jug Wines

Charles Krug—Particularly for whites
Louis M. Martini—Mountain Red
The Christian Brothers—Claret and Chablis
Inglenook—Zinfandel
Almaden—Mountain Red and Grenache Rosé

Paul Masson—Rhine Wine
Villa Armando—Vino Rustico
Beringer—Mountain Rosé

European Jug Wines

Producers abroad market a bewildering variety of wines in various sizes, using the standard liter jugs (equal to about a quart) and others containing 48 ounces and more. They are used mostly for ordinary wines that will be quickly drunk. A favorite size is the double bottle, or magnum, which contains up to 51 ounces; it was once reserved exclusively for expensive wines, the consideration being that the larger quantity of wine would mature more slowly and evenly than in bottles of regular size. These double bottles are now being used for wines meant to be drunk young, and their purchase may mean some small saving. When there is no saving, the standard bottle (24 ounces in most regions) is the most practical size.

Italy

Straw-covered bottles of Chianti holding one or two quarts created the market for jug wines in the United States, and no Italian restaurant can operate without them. The producing region in the countryside around Florence is enormous, and the wines vary from good to indifferent. In general, the major houses produce drinkable wines that are widely available, often adding white Soave and Orvieto to their lines. Other regions north and south have been successful with their regular bottlings and have only recently begun exporting in large bottles. (For Chianti, see comments on major houses in that section.)

Segesta—Sicilian reds and whites bottled from the Rallo estates. The reds are fruity, the whites pleasantly dry. Imported by Banfi, New York.

Marino—A Roman firm that bottles white Frascati and red Castelli Romani in 68-ounce sizes, both worth trying. The house also produces a line of "Mellow Roman Country Wines" in 60-ounce bottles that are low in price. Imported by Banfi, New York.

Riunite—The group of co-operatives in Reggio Emilia, Cantina Coop. Riunite di Reggio Emilia, bottles a particularly fruity red wine for about $4. Imported by Banfi, New York.

Rovere Barbera—The Piedmont produces a hundred million gallons in a year, and much of it should be made available in jugs. Marchesini della Rovere markets a 68-ounce bottle of light Barbera and a less-distinguished wine called Piemonte, of the sort you might call a perfectly good glass of wine. Selling for about three dollars, the wines are beginning to find a market. Imported by Winegate, New York.

Frascati—Cantina Sociale Coop. di Marino is marketing a good white wine from Frascati that has some character. (The firm's red wines may be considered thin.) A little over $3 for 68 ounces. Imported by Banfi, New York.

Verona—One of the best white-wine buys on the market is the Soave from a co-operative, the Cantina Sociale di Soave, which also offers drinkable Bardolino and Valpolicella, for less than $4 for 68 ounces. It is imported by one of the large makers of Concord grape wines through an import division called Tudor Arms Imports, New York.

Spain

For the past few years, Spanish jug wines have drawn the attention of knowing wine drinkers who have found themselves priced out of the market for Burgundy and Bordeaux—those people who drink a bottle or so a day, with meals and as apéritifs, in the European fashion. The best of them can be assumed to be those from Rioja and the other northern districts, such as Panadés and Alella, but others from Tarragona and Valdepeñas and Valencia attract attention when sold at four or five dollars a gallon. They pall after a time, having little more freshness than those from California, and not being of as good quality as The Christian Brothers and Inglenook jugs, for example. By switching from one to another, overfamiliarity can be avoided, or at least ignored, and any cloying taste can be muted by adding an ice cube or a little soda to the glass. Rejoice if you can find a particularly acid red or white in a regular bottle; by blending this into the jug wine, you can sharpen the flavor a little. A bottle of acid white wine mixed into a jug of red sometimes produces something quite refreshing. Spanish jug wines are generally high in alcohol, often 14%, and can stand dilution with ice or sharpening with a squeeze of lemon, particularly the whites; the reds become duller with chilling, a quality not so apparent when they are drunk with food.

Like Californians, the Spanish insist on calling their reds "Burgundy" or "Claret," also a general practice in Portugal and Chile and Argentina. Unfortunately, those that do not masquerade under borrowed French names do not represent higher standards. The wines vary from shipment to shipment, cause for amused surprise rather than alarm. You might do comparative tastings from time to time, but it is much less discouraging to switch brands when one you have selected falls off.

Juan Hernández—Bottled in Valencia and called "Spanish Burgundy," this red has more fruit and freshness than many. Imported by Wine Imports of America, Hawthorne, N.J.

Bertrán—Bottled in Tarragona, the red is quite heavy and the white has a certain sharpness. Either is improved by adding an ice cube to the glass. Imported by Monarch Wine, New York.

Yago—The red is called "Burgundy" and generally ranks fairly high in comparative tastings. It seems light-bodied for a Rioja. The white has a tendency to be bland. Imported by Monsieur Henri, New York.

Age—Bottled by Bodegas Unidas in Rioja, the red is generally fruity, but the white is bland. Imported by Classic Imports, New York.

Cepa Negra—Simply called "Red Wine" on the label, it is bottled by Bodegas Bravo in Barcelona. It often has some freshness. Imported by Joseph Victori, New York.

Portugal

Portugal has plenty of wine from the north and from vineyards around Lisbon, but the overseas market has focused mainly on rosés, in bottles and crocks. Jugs might develop a substantial market here, particularly if the wines were bottled young to preserve a fruity freshness in the reds, a pleasing acidity in the whites. A few come in, most imitations of Spanish jug wines.

Latada—From Cavenal, Caves Nacionals Limitada, in Lisbon, the red is often quite fruity. There are also a white and a rosé. Imported by Monsieur Henri, New York.

France

The French were the first to make a great success abroad with wines in bottle rather than cask, beginning with the best vintages of Bordeaux, Burgundy, and Champagne. Until the turn of the century, most of the other French wines were shipped in cask, and when bottlings of Loires and Rhônes and Rhines became accepted, more or less standard bottles of 75 centiliters, about 26 ounces, were used, each region adopting distinctive shapes that might vary by an ounce or so. For great wines, the double bottle, or magnum, was used, wines maturing more slowly therein; for convenience, half bottles came into being.

Today, many wines meant to be drunk young are appearing in big bottles—mostly magnums—but they generally command a premium. In the wine districts, good ordinary wines are sold in demijohns and small casks, but these are not exported. The French have little considered exporting low-priced wines in jugs. It is a good thing for other wine-producing areas that they have not. Jugs of dry white Bordeaux, Alsatian Sylvaner or Zwicker, Côtes-du-Rhône reds or Anjou rosés would sweep the market.

There is a stirring now among bulk producers of wines from the Midi. Half-gallon jugs are beginning to appear. If the wines are fresh in taste and pleasantly fruity, they will be quickly bought up, proving so popular that other producers of jug wines will begin to put sprightlier wines in their jugs; and well before the end of the decade, such wines from various countries will be fighting for the market. We will then have plentiful supplies of young wines at last, at something like a dollar a quart. The secret of success will be to bottle the wines promptly and move them quickly through the channels of trade so that they are drunk within a month or so of the bottling. Chances are that California's Napa Valley producers will be first on the market, followed by the giants in the

Central Valley, but don't discount the importers of Italian wines, importers from Spain and Portugal, or Argentina or Chile. There is an enormous quantity of wine in North Africa, in Algeria and Morocco, most of which now goes to the Russian satellite countries. And there are Yugoslavia, Bulgaria, Hungary, even Romania and Greece—all producing large quantities of wine. There is Germany. And there is the rest of France. Prospects are looking up.

French producers of *vin ordinaire* are eying the American market, as are the large shippers who have vast stocks of inexpensive wines. The wine's no problem, but weight of bottles is; a good bump during shipment might break a big jug. One company experimented with a plastic bag with an air valve that worked on the principle of a baby's bottle, so that air could get out when part of the wine was withdrawn. The idea was to fit a five-gallon bag in a permanent wooden cask, so that a restaurant could tap the wine in the same way they handle draught beer; the company was ahead of its time, but is beginning to generate enough restaurant interest to warrant marketing costs.

Plastic bottles are now being introduced—a company called Margnat is offering 48 ounces of red or rosé for about $3—which halves the shipping cost. Putting wines in cans would also cut shipping costs and make it possible to deliver wines to the market so that they would taste as if they were just drawn from the cask. Canned wines meet sales resistance, even in France, although Parisians have accepted wines in cartons like those for milk. Price savings will ensure acceptance of plastic bottles, eventually.

Côteaux du Languedoc—Vineyards of the Languedoc, lying back from the Mediterranean and near the foothills of the Pyrenees, are rated as VDQS, *Vins Délimités de Qualité Supérieur.* Georges Bonfils is one of the larger shippers, and its light but fruity red wine is one of the best jug wines presently available, the 67-ounce bottle retailing for about $5. Imported by Austin Nichols, New York (Liggett & Myers Division).

Mâcon Rouge—A typical and inexpensive magnum of red from Mâcon, 48 ounces for under $5, bottled by Louis Aumont. Imported by Winegate, New York.

POP WINES

A soda-pop culture garnished with hamburgers and french fries makes little room for wines. In the transition from soft drinks to hard, as the young go from the cold fizz of coke to the sour froth of beer, the common bubble and the chill ease the shock of changing tastes. Sweetness soothes the change from spiked orange or grapefruit or pineapple juice to the sour of Daiquiris and the bitter of gin and tonic. Their elders evaded the taste of hard liquor by making the move from soda fountain to cocktail lounge via the Bloody Mary and the Tom Collins, but a new potable was needed to suit the drive-in and the transistor on the grass. Pop wines have come to be the answer.

Sweeten a common wine with fruit essences, sharpen it with flavorings, even sparkle it with bubbles, pick a striking name. Presto! You have a pop wine, made to be drunk instead of soft drinks or beer, anywhere, anyhow, anytime. Short for "popular," producers don't like the name, because it's so like the drink it is intended to replace, somehow belittling. They hold contests to find a catchy euphemism better than "fun wines" or "mod wines." Calling them "appetizer wines" smacks of the dietary. "Apéritifs" is too Frenchy. "Cocktail wines" suggest alcohol, not the exciting, new taste thrill promised by the commercials. Pop wines they are, and they account for most of the increase in wine drinking of the past decade. They replace the port-sherry-muscatel "dessert wine" category—commonly known as Sneaky Pete—the cheapest form of alcohol, now happily losing favor.

Wine-based drinks are as old as vineyards. The chief factotum at a Grecian banquet was the man who mixed the wine with honey and spices, cooling it with snow brought from the mountain by runners. When bottles became common, two thousand years later, he became the butler, whose first job was to bottle wines from the cask and make punches and toddies of them. Long after the Romans, wine was used to make water palatable, only recent generations being lucky enough to have wines that are good to drink without flavoring or dilution. Because sweetness masks off tastes, most of the early wines were made to be sweet, even then calling for "sophistication" with spices, a word that continues in the trade to identify any meddling at all with the fermentation of freshly squeezed grapes.

To combat the necessary sweetness, bitter roots and flowers and herbs—rue, artemisia or absinthe or wormwood—were added to wines. The latter was developed into Vermouth, the first widely accepted aromatic wine, popular in the eighteenth century. French apéritifs soon followed. Those made bitter with quinine or cinchona bark, such as Dubonnet and Byrrh, were the drinks of fashion in the bistros and sidewalk cafes of the past century. In one form or another, pop wines have always been popular.

Every country has evolved its own wine drinks, starting by spiking the punch bowl or sprinkling it with spring blossoms. Simplest of all may be the German Spritzer—a glass of white wine topped with soda and maybe a slice of lemon or some ice. Spring along the Rhine is heralded with *Mai Wein,* made by steeping the herb woodruff in new wine for hours or days. Strawberries replace the woodruff when they come in, then raspberries. Most appealing of all may be the *Pfirsich-bowle,* sliced fresh peaches, sugared and brandied, added to a pitcher of white wine; sometimes the flavor is corrected with a little sugar and brandy or liqueur, and a bottle of sparkling wine or soda is added; perhaps some mint is tossed in; slices of lemon or orange or cucumber are floated on top for decoration.

The Spanish make Sangria, adding to a pitcher of red wine (sometimes white is used) the juice and long peel from an orange and a lemon, with a little sugar, if necessary. As the seasons turn, other fruits may be added, and sometimes a sprinkling of cinnamon or nutmeg or clove, or a dash of brandy. Every Mediterranean country has a version of this, so common or casual as to scarcely warrant a recipe—just something added to the wine, with ice, to make a refreshing drink in hot weather.

In Burgundy, soda added to a glass of white wine is called *rince cochon,* pig rinse, the drink being a comfort during a hangover. The named used to be applied to a glass of white Burgundy into which has been stirred a dollop of Cassis, the currant liqueur that is a specialty of Dijon; this drink came to be known as Kir, after a beloved wartime mayor of the town. In winter, *vin chaud* is a standby of the bistros, in its simplest form only a glass of heated red wine. A sugar cube is sometimes simmered with the wine, to which a clove or two, a cinnamon stick, or a little grated nutmeg may be added. Sometimes the sugar cube is simply dropped into the glass before the hot wine is poured, the glass being served with a cinnamon stick for stirring. Fancy places may add a slice of lemon. The drink may be lightened with water or strengthened with brandy.

The aromatic wines popular first in the cafes and later as part of cocktails in the Roaring Twenties were generally as strong as fortified wines such as Sherry and Port, somewhere between 14% and 20% alcohol. Diluted with ice or fruit, the various bowls were generally less than that. Today's pop wines are merely premixed versions of these wine drinks, usually less than 14% if only to avoid taxes.

New versions have come out every year for the past couple of decades, formulas changing with fashion. Those launched in the fifties were mostly like Vermouth, one of the first being Thunderbird, followed by a slightly more lemony Silver Satin. With the Seventies, fruit flavors came in, Bali Hai being reminiscent of pineapples, for instance. Many were less-sweet and thinner versions of the blackberry and gooseberry and elderberry wines of our grandfathers. Then came Cold Duck.

Kalte Ente is the original, a Rhineland name for a bowl of white still wine charged with soda or sparkling wine, with fruits. Michigan growers decided to carbonate their wine from Concord grapes, a glut on the market, and dubbed it Cold Duck. The first ones tasted like the grape juice of our childhood with bubbles. The best of them still do, but now the flavor range is wide, and there are things like Cold Turkey and Cold Bear on the market, not to mention Kalte Ente, imported from Germany.

Cold Duck was invented for the mass market. Any product for the mass market must appeal to the lowest common denominator, its price containing a large percentage for packaging, advertising, and distribution. Americans know this better than anybody. Our bread is the worst in the world. Our grandmothers used to be able to buy milk from Guernsey herds, or Jerseys, or Ayrshires; now all we have is various grades of a chalky liquid, thin and blue. Tomatoes are available year around, consistently inedible. Butter is stored for months before being sold, eggs are tasteless, hams are pumped full of water. Carrots, oranges, and other produce are dyed to hide the fact that they are grown from inferior strains picked before ripeness so they can withstand the trip to market. The dirge is endless. Until now, only wines have resisted the fawning attentions of the mass marketeer out to make a buck.

Or have they?

The taste has long since gone from Vermouth, watered down and bleached to meet the fashion for a dry Martini. The names of Port and Sherry, Champagne and Cognac, even Sauternes and Beaujolais have been borrowed and bastardized so that cheap imitations bear no resemblance at all to the originals. Pop wines—bland, full of sugar, tasting of chemicals—are the first mass-market products from the world of wines. Their success is already inspiring imitators among table-wine producers, who now market those "mellow" reds and whites that are sweetened with sugar, variously called Burgundy and Chianti, Pink Chablis and Rhine Wine, produced mostly in California. At a time when North Coast and South Bay producers are coming up with marvels, pop wines and mellow ones are flooding the market to confuse buyers. Pop wines are, of course, the soda-fountain concoctions of our day, with alcohol replacing the ice cream.

There is no point at all in listing the names of pop wines that make up the current craze. Like Moxie, they will be gone tomorrow. The pet of the moment is apple wine—not a hard cider, the best of the fermented juices, preferable to perry from pears—which is stabilized apple juice with alcohol, some now made sparkling.

A few of them may live, to become as popular as Vermouth or one of the French apéritifs. One might almost describe a perfect one . . .

Not too sweet, almost tart, in fact, to be made sharper with a twist of lemon or lime if you like. A distinctive taste—reminiscent of meadows, perhaps, or the sea, or a mountain glade. Light and fresh, capable of being strengthened with a jigger of brandy or vodka, but delicious by itself, with ice, and even better when sparkled with soda. A drink whose taste you remember and wish to try again. Familiar, but somehow haunting. The ads almost write themselves.

None has appeared yet, perhaps because so much is in the mind. Few of us are familiar with all the kinds there are, still novelties, so we haven't had time to cloak them in nostalgia. One has to find them for oneself.

Some of them aren't all that bad, one is expected to add, with a false air of fairness. It's true. They are not that bad. They are merely worthless, a joke, like those pairs of cupcakes wrapped in cellophane for the grade school trade. Pop wines are designed for the high school trade, those daring youths who jauntily puff pot and swig the flavored alcohol as a way of thumbing their noses at parental culture. They are the victims of mass marketing with every swig, of course, of the ads written by their fathers, and the networks that run the ads, and the experts who devise the pop wines. Pop wines are adult vengeance on the rebellious young.

Maybe one of the pop wines will turn out to be good. Spiked Concord grape juice can be refreshing when it's not too sweet. Good lemon essences are available, and all those herbs, spices, and roots. Wines for a base are plentiful. And the market's always there.

The answer has been around all the time, and Gallo stumbled on it with a concoction called Boone's Apple Wine, alcoholic apple juice. It's liquid applesauce with a kick, perhaps reminding drinkers of the baby foods spooned into them in their high-chair days. The nostalgia's there, and there's also a long tradition behind it. Countries that don't grow wine grapes make wines of other fruits. Gallo thought of marketing a wine, which is grown-up, with the fruit flavors of childhood.

Most fruit wines are thick and sweet, like Danish cherry wines or the kosher wines that are mostly made from Concords, which are eating grapes, not wine grapes. Fruit wines are drunk between meals or as dessert. They are a social substitute for a nice cup of tea, for coffee and cake. Our farmer ancestors, if they weren't too puritanical, made wine from any fruits and berries at hand, just as they made jams and jellies, cordials and liqueurs. Much of this craft died out with commercialization, but particularly the English managed to keep the tradition of fruit wines alive.

Even today an English householder will set out berry bushes and fruit trees with homemade wines in mind—gooseberries, elderberries, greengage plums. Cider is still a popular drink, mead made from honey is still available, echoes from the old days, when their ancestors made heather wines. Some of the English fruit wines made commercially are scarcely sweet at all, possessing a tang and natural taste that brings to mind gardens and orchards and fields, sunlight and brooks and the freshness after rain. They are wines not for mealtime but for casual drinking, somehow outside the tight social form of the cocktail party or the highball at the bar. As people break away from the rigid patterns that bound our drinking, they begin to find pleasure in the new tastes.

The sidewalk cafe was in a way invented for the drinking of apéritifs, an outgrowth of the coffee houses, just as the bar was invented out of the pub and the saloon for whiskey drinking, just as the cocktail lounge evolved out of the speak-easy. Pot and rock music are creating an environment for pop wines—with no architecture as yet to go with it—but that may evolve when pop wines are better made. We can taste the future in the fruit wines of England, some of the best of them being those from Merrydown in Sussex, imported by Morgenstern of New York. By the end of the decade we may be drinking them in a modern version of the Bavarian beer garden or an alpine ski lodge or the country-club terrace dotted with umbrellas over round tables. My guess is that the architecture will be a version of the old-fashioned soda fountain, complete with wire chairs.

We know what the wines will be like, but until good ones are available under brand names, we'll just have to make our own.

REGIONAL WINES

The wine everybody knows can be the worst of buys. What you've heard of is what you get; better to be safe than sorry. All those strange labels on the shelves are suspect—why so many names, so many prices? Even the ads are suspicious, demanding trust, promising delight, assuring you that every wine goes with anything and the one you like is the one that's best. I don't know what I like, you mutter, so how can it be best? What's tried and true? What's the difference? I'll get . . . a Chianti?

The first wine I remember buying was a Graves, because a character in a novel I was reading said it was a glorious white wine. Went with fish, fowl, and eggs, all of which I liked. Cost was about two dollars, which seemed reasonable. We had it with chicken and it tasted fine but smelt like burning matches. Nothing much, I guessed, kind of sweet, but all right. The next few wines were much the same.

Cagy, even worldly wise, I never bought the cheapest, going up a dime or two, sometimes as much as a dollar, over the lowest price on the shelf. Beaujolais, Liebfraumilch, Châteauneuf-du-Pape. I read that James Joyce liked the driest whites he could find and that his favorite was Neuchâtel. Tried that too. So so. Like the rest. Nothing to get excited about.

Then, late one night, I had dinner with a wine buyer in a restaurant just off the Champs Élysées. We went there because they had a good Pouilly-Fuissé. We had it with oysters on the half shell, Marennes. I swallowed an oyster and took a sip from my glass. That one taste taught me what wines were all about. Names, vintage, price—all that was by the way. A good wine tastes marvelous. Forget all about wines that aren't wonderful, search out all the ones that are good. All you have to do is taste.

Brought up on brand names, one easily assumes that all Beaujolais is alike, for example; some slight differences as the price goes up, maybe, but who can tell the difference? Not thinking there was any, I had consistently bought regional wines at average prices, skipping from one to another, never finding one above a common level of adequacy. Most people coming upon wines do the same thing.

Regional wines are blends from a particular area, brought to a standard, but they are by no means brands. Price reflects popularity, availability, distribution, matters having little to do with excellence. The broader the name—the larger the area that uses a common name—the more varied the wine. In the market place, this operates in several ways.

The best-known regional names all mean different things. They probably account for nine bottles out of ten on the international market—for most of the wines we drink. There are good buys—and good bottles—in every one.

Chianti

The most familiar name in the world of wines, Chianti comes from a region around Florence, in Tuscany, a province that produces more than one hundred million gallons a year. Half of this is Chianti, most of which is red wine marketed in the round straw-colored bottles called *fiaschi*. Cheap, fresh, and a little sharp, it is made mostly from San Gioveto and Canaiolo grapes in proportions introduced a century ago by Barone Ricasoli. He is also credited with developing the *governo* system, which gives Chianti its prickly quality. This is the matter of drying some of the grapes on straw mats to concentrate their sugar, then adding their rich fermenting juice to the already fermented regular crushing. The system produces a young wine of surprising freshness, but is used less or not at all for Chiantis meant to be aged, which are sold in regular wine bottles.

In the thirties, a couple of hundred square miles of vineyard between Florence and Siena was designated as Chianti Classico, to be identified by a neck label showing a black rooster on a gold circle. Chianti Classico is often considered to be the best wine of the district, for located there are the Brolio estates of the Ricasolis, as well as vineyards of other leading houses such as Antinori and Serristori. There is a special grouping of outstanding producers with vineyards near the Classico area, whose bottles are marketed with a white cherub, or *putto,* on the neck label.

A putto neck label is also used for the good wines from vineyards right around Florence, **Colli Fiorentini,** and for full wines meant to be drunk young from the district of **Rufina.** Often ranked high are the fruity Chiantis from **Montalbano,** from vineyards toward Pistoia and bearing neck labels showing the towers of the town. From the hills around Pisa, **Colline Pisane,** come a few good wines with a centaur on the neck label. In between, from around Empoli and with a neck label showing a bunch of grapes, are wines considered coarser than the Classicos, **Chianti dei Colli Empolesi.**

Wines with much smaller reputations come from vineyards near Siena, **Colli Senesi,** the neck label showing Romulus and Remus being suckled by the she-wolf. Similarly undistinguished are sharp-tasting Chiantis from hills to the east around Arezzo, **Colli Aretini,** whose neck label bears a chimera. These last two are the ones most widely distributed abroad. Expectedly, wines vary widely in each area, but a buyer new to Chiantis rightly puts his faith in neck labels, looking for roosters, cherubs, towers, and grapes, but being cautious about she-wolves and chimeras.

The buyer is also wise to make sure that wines in straw-covered bottles are as young as possible, preferably from the preceding year, and that wine in regular bottles are four years old.

Any list of the best Chiantis would include the following, with regular bottlings costing under four dollars, older Riservas costing perhaps a dollar more, best grades of younger wines in straw-covered fiaschi costing a dollar less.

Brolio Riserva, from Ricasoli, aged five years in wood before bottling.

Castello di Meleto, from Ricasoli, less full and not aged as long in wood.

Nipozzano, from Frescobaldi, particularly long-lived; full, balanced, and soft.

Riserva Ducale, from Ruffino, a balanced, rounded wine.

Stravecchio Melini, made outside the Classico district, but considered by the house of Melini to be a classic example of what Chianti should be. They don't put the Florentine putto on their labels, because the wine is more Classico than Fiorentino.

Villa Antinori, a distinguished Classico noted for balance.

There are more than sixty Chiantis on the market. Others worth noting are Nozzole, Pagni, Bertolli, Suali, Cantina del Papa, Boccaccio, and Orfevi. For a low-priced Chianti to use as a standard, I would suggest the Chianti Putto of Serristori, brought in by Frank Schoonmaker, available by the half gallon for a little more than four dollars.

Beaujolais

Of the good wines in the world meant to be drunk young, Beaujolais is the best. There are perhaps twenty million gallons in a good year, a scant fifth of Chianti production. The district lies in southern Burgundy, but only wines from specific areas in the northern parts are considered true Burgundies. Nine areas—about a quarter of the district's 40,000 acres—are allowed to put their names on the bottle. The large areas are Brouilly and Côtes de Brouilly, Morgon and Moulin-à-Vent, Fleurie, and Juliénas. Smaller quantities of wine come from Chiroubles, Saint-Amour, and Chénas. Wines from some forty other places go to market as Beaujolais-Villages, and these can be delicious. District blends from the south are sold as Beaujolais Supérieur or just plain Beaujolais; they can be good.

Much of the lesser Beaujolais is at its best right after fermentation. Fresh, fruity, tingly—it can be among the most delightful tastes in the world of wines. There's a rush each year to get the first of this new Beaujolais to Paris, some growers picking early and fermenting extra fast. To curb too much haste, this *Beaujolais nouveau* is allowed to get to Paris only after the middle of November. The first to arrive on the market is called *Beaujolais Primeur,* and some of it is flown to the States in time for Christmas.

Most of the better vineyards allow their wines to ferment for about a week, then let them settle down until after the first of the year, when they are bottled. This is *Beaujolais de l'Année,* and the wine of the year continues to develop and change delightfully through the spring and into summer. Beaujolais of the year is a fruity joy to drink, usually arriving in New York sometime in April.

Beaujolais that is entitled to an area name is usually held in cask through the spring following the vintage, many of the wines being kept in cask for a full year. These are the fullest of the Beaujolais and the best, picking up depth and roundness from their short time in wood. They are still fruity and fresh, though, keeping that quality into the second year. **Morgon** takes the longest to round out; **Moulin-a-Vent** is generally the one that holds its fruit the longest, having a fullness that distinguishes the wines even three years after the vintage. The **Brouillys** are quickly ready and remarkably fruity, at their best during the second year; **Côte de Brouilly** is fuller than its companion, but as short-lived. **Fleurie** has a special fragrance, **Juliénas** a lightness that makes it attractive. **Chiroubles** is the first of the wines to be ready and the first to fade, perhaps the most refreshing of all, and the darling of Paris. **Chénas** and **Saint-Amour** are light and quickly ready. All these wines are best in the second year after the vintage, shortly after bottling, only Morgon and Moulin-à-Vent seeming to develop much in bottle. All of them should be drunk before they are four years old, most of them before they are three.

Like Chiantis, they are best when cool, at what used to be called cellar temperature, perhaps fifty or fifty-five degrees. There is a tendency to make them heavy in alcohol, twelve per cent and more, but they seem at their best when they are only 10 or 11%.

The popularity of Beaujolais has influenced owners in the Rhône to consider quick fermentation and prompt bottling, so that young Rhônes are beginning to find their way to Paris during the winter following the vintage. They, too, have a fine freshness and fruit and have begun to appear on the American market.

There are hundreds of Beaujolais on the market, including some whites that are worth buying only when price is not much over two dollars. The Beaujolais from one major importer is not likely to be much different from another's, although low-priced lots simply called "Beaujolais" may be nondescript and scarcely distinguishable from any other cheap wine. Beaujolais Supérieur, Beaujolais-Villages, and those bearing an area name should be progressively better—fresher and fruitier. Best buying advice is to try each new shipment as it comes in, from shops that have a

REGIONAL WINES 41

reputation for stocking good wines, a general rule for all wine buying. Generally, the younger the Beaujolais the better.

Under $3
Beaujolais Nouveau
Beaujolais Supérieur

Around $3
Beaujolais-Villages

Over $3

Chiroubles
Saint-Amour
Chénas
Juliénas
Fleurie

Brouilly
Côte de Brouilly
Moulin-à-Vent
Morgon

NOTE: There are 18 co-operatives in Beaujolais, maintaining a baker's dozen of tasting rooms and 22 cellars also offering tastings that are maintained by other groups. A tour of a few is the best way to get to know Beaujolais.

A representative Beaujolais for purposes of comparison might well be the Beaujolais Supérieur of Louis Latour, imported by Wildman, New York.

Zinfandel

Not one of the world's best-known wines, but quickly becoming one of the best-known here, this California wine shares the quality of Beaujolais and Chianti, particularly in that the wine is delicious when young. Like Chianti, it also develops with age into quite a different wine. It is now believed to derive from an Italian grape, perhaps the San Gioveto or the Nebbiolo, so this is not surprising.

NOTE: Every major producer in the North Coast and South Bay counties around San Francisco markets a Zinfandel. A representative Zinfandel for comparative tastings might be the Mountain Zinfandel of Louis Martini.

Châteauneuf-du-Pape

Some wines seem to become popular because the name sounds nice, and most people seem to feel that way about wines from the new castle of the pope, built as a summer place when the papacy was in Avignon. A big red wine, sturdy, nothing particularly distinguished in the taste. Heavy, even. Made from a dozen varieties of grapes, none of which stands out, bigger than other southern wines, often as much as 14% alcohol, it's ready to drink within four years of the vintage and usually fades away after seven years or so. Not very exciting.

That's exactly what most Châteauneuf-du-Pape is, consistently better than ordinary, at three dollars a bottle. But not that much better. And then you get one that's estate bottled, by the vineyard owner. It's delicious—a discovery. Such discoveries can be made in every region and every district, of course, but it's surprising here.

Better Rhône wines come from Hermitage and Côte Rôtie. But somehow Châteauneuf has caught the fancy of the world and it outshines them. A hearty wine for hearty foods, it is what everybody thinks a Burgundy should be, when actually the great wines of Burgundy are lighter and more subtle.

Perhaps its popularity stems from the fact that it is exactly what you expect in a red wine, and better than many. A stalwart wine, like a good friend.

The Châteauneufs from the big producers and importers now cost over four dollars a bottle for typical big, full, rounded wines four or five years old. Younger wines, lighter wines, those from small or unknown producers, and direct imports may cost a dollar less. Low-priced wines are usually blends of poor years. The wines are pricing themselves out of the market.

Over $3
A. Ogier & Fils
Domaine de Beaucastel
Château de la Gardine

Over $4
Château Fortia
Chapoutier La Marcelle
Saint Patrice
Rochette & Cie.
Domaine de Mont Redon

NOTE: For comparative tastings, try the fine Châteauneuf of Rochette imported by Kobrand, New York.

Bordeaux Supérieur

Bordeaux is the world's greatest wine region, its fame resting on some one hundred Classed Growths that produce the most distinguished of red wines, plus a couple of hundred vineyards loosely called Petits Châteaux that are often distinguished. The *Crus Classés* come from four main districts—Haut Médoc, Graves, Saint Émilion, and Pomerol—while great sweet white wines are produced in the twin districts of Sauternes and Barsac. Around these are a galaxy of lesser districts, producing many good reds and some good white wines, both dry and sweet. Most of them are marketed as Bordeaux rouge and Bordeaux blanc; they are rarely more than ordinary. Slightly better wines are blended by the great shipping firms into reds and whites marketed as Bordeaux Supérieur; many of these are excellent.

The best regionals are blends of wines from the districts and their communes, also marketed under the names of the shippers. As Haut Médoc and Saint Émilion, they may be the best low-priced wines generally available. Graves, which produces both reds and whites, are out of fashion for no good reason, and are also excellent. Pomerol, the smallest of the great districts, markets most of its wines from the individual châteaux. The reds may cost five dollars or so, are ready to drink four years after the vintage, and many continue to improve. The whites cost a little less and are ready in two years.

In the past decade, various co-operatives and some of the larger shippers have taken over the wine making or have begun to supervise it closely, which has improved the quality of the wines. The demand for fresh, young, inexpensive wines has encouraged the trend for quick vinification and for the planting of grapes such as the Cabernet Franc and the Merlot, whose wines mature more quickly than do wines from the Cabernet Sauvignon. As a result, wines from lesser districts will become available, to broaden the range.

Bordeaux makes much more white wine than red. Much of it was sweet, imitating Sauternes, in past decades, when those were the most popular of wines. Today dry wines are being made, marketed as Blanc de Blancs, a phrase that people like, or under brand names or those of the shippers. The wines of Graves, once soft and flowery and as sweet as possible, are now being made as simple dry wines and are slowly developing a market. All the new whites tend to be dry, fresh, and flowery, reminding people of those from the Loire, where many are made from Bordeaux varieties.

For the time being, the names of the great shippers are the best lead to the wines. Those particularly well represented on the American market are listed in the chapter on shippers.

Burgundy

Burgundy, which produces the greatest of dry whites and some of the greatest reds, is divided in three: Chablis, the Côte d'Or, and southern Burgundy. Chablis lies to the north, a district whose name has come to mean dry white wine everywhere, producing a minuscule quantity of expensive wine. Burgundy's heart is the thirty-mile stretch called the Côte d'Or, nearly all of its wines now costing more than four dollars. Only the light reds and whites from southern Burgundy produced in substantial quantity are available for less. In the past, Burgundies have been known by the names of their districts, towns, and vineyards, never going to market with only the regional name on the bottle.

The name, though, became the one to use for hearty wines made anywhere. Some of California's best-selling wines are called Burgundy and Chablis, for instance. This was confusing to all and considered cheap trickery by many, so the use of grape names was encouraged. Pinot Noir and Chardonnay are the great Burgundy grapes, so these names came to be used to identify a goodly share of California's best wines. They also became popular. And the result is that a lot of regional blends from Burgundy are now being marketed here with grape names, a happy irony for the buyer, who can find excellent bottles for three dollars or so.

The Gamay is the grape of the southern Burgundy district of Beaujolais. Burgundy blends of Pinot Noir and Gamay, never thought much of in France, were officially dubbed *Bourgogne-Passe-Tout-Grains*. By making the grape names known, a market has been made here for blends called **Pinot Noir Gamay;** modern vinification methods result in passable wines. **Pinot Blanc** is used in secondary Burgundian vineyards, but the name is used in California and is now appearing on fair wines from Burgundy. **Aligoté** is another secondary Burgundy grape, a name little known here; this is now being offered as Blanc de Blancs, the phrase that simply means white wine from white grapes. These are good ordinary wines, for wine and soda, for punches, for lunches; at two dollars or so a bottle they are good buys. All the leading shippers and importers have begun to offer such wines, and even a few brand names are appearing. There's no need for a list; just keep an eye peeled for the wines.

Perhaps the best regionals, because the wines are plentiful and reasonable in price, are the reds and whites of the southern Burgundy district of Mâconnais. They are marketed as Mâcon Rouge or Mâcon Blanc, and there are whites offered as Pinot Chardonnay Mâcon. This is the name put on the wine when there is an excess of Pouilly-Fuissé, which is the best Mâcon district, with firm controls on production. In plentiful years, Pinot Chardonnay Mâcon may really be Pouilly-Fuissé or the wine of the twin districts, Pouilly-Vinzelles and Pouilly-Loché, as well as the new district Saint Véran.

Perhaps it's only fair that because the name of Burgundy was abused so long abroad, some correction of the abuse has created a fine market for Burgundy regionals, wines by other names, much better than the old ones.

Liebfraumilch

Originally an excellent wine from the churchyard vineyard of Worms cathedral, the name came to be used for any Sylvaner blends from the Rhineland district of Rheinhessen. The neighboring Rheinpfalz decided to use the name, and now the lesser wines of both districts go to market as Liebfraumilch. Some of them sell for a dollar and change in American shops and aren't worth it.

Rheinhessens have never been as popular abroad as wines from the Rheingau and the Moselle, however, so some of the best growers of the district take excellent vintages of Nierstein and Nackenheim and Oppenheim, and offer them as Liebfraumilch. Some of the leading shippers buy only the best wines for their Liebfraumilch label. One of these, the Blue Nun of Sichel, has become so popular that there is now a sister wine from the Moselle, Blue Nun Bernkasteler Riesling. These may cost four dollars and more, not at all the same wines as Liebfraumilch selling for two dollars or less.

Other German names identify similar regional wines: Moselblümchen, from the Moselle; Steinwein, from Franconia. Like Liebfraumilch, such wines from good shippers may be excellent in quality and reasonable in price when selling for three dollars; they are poor buys at low prices.

Portuguese Rosé

It's unusual for a country's name to become attached to a regional wine, the usual way being for a vineyard, township, or district to become the name for popular blends. Portugal is unique, the home of Porto, the incredible fortified red wine so imitated that it has changed its name from port, as well as the home of fresh and pleasing white wines and hearty reds. The only table wine that has found favor in the past is the pink wine of Portugal.

A carbonated rosé in brown crocks, Lancer's, caught the fancy of an older generation, and a still rosé in a squat round bottle, Mateus, caught the fancy of the younger. Mateus, commonly called ma-TOOS, but more properly mah-tay-oosh, is probably the largest-selling wine in the world. It is a fresh and pleasing wine, lightly sweet. Its success has encouraged importation of Portuguese reds and whites, not to say many other pink wines, most of them with brand names. At two or three dollars a bottle, all of them are pleasant enough to drink, typical of regional wines everywhere.

Sangria

The Spanish have never been internationally successful with their table wines. Rioja is the best region, the vineyards tended in the French fashion, but the many good wines have never been able to stand up to French and Italian competition. The great rise in French wine prices has helped the wines find a market in recent years. But the great Spanish success has been Sangria. It's really a pop wine.

For generations, the Spanish have made a cooling summer drink by adding oranges and lemons to red wines, with or without ice, and perhaps a dash of brandy to perk things up. Sangria is practically a national drink, quite easy to make, but scarcely a decade ago the import firm of Monsieur Henri decided to bring the drink to New York already mixed, at a low proof of not much more than 10 per cent so they could sell it cheaply. It was called Yago Sant' Gria. About the same time, the Spanish Pavilion became the hit of the New York World's Fair. Sangria made from scratch became the hit of the pavilion. Since then, it has swept the country, opening up the market for other flavored wines. Every importer of Spanish wines now offers a Sangria. It is a national drink, not a regional wine, but it now ranks in popularity with Chianti, Beaujolais, and Liebfraumilch, as well as Portuguese rosé, and deserves consideration with them. At two dollars or so, it is a good buy.

District and Township Wines

Nothing varies with the soil so much as wines, traditionally known by the places from which they come, so the more specific the name the better the wine is supposed to be. A district name on the label or even that of a township implies a progression to excellence, although all of them are called regionals by the trade. Confusion arises because some places have become famous, upsetting the logical order and leading to borrowings and imitations.

Once there was only Burgundy from the domain of the hearty dukes, but certain vineyards became so renowned that town fathers took to tacking the names of great vineyards to that of the township, hoping the aura of the great would cast a glow on the lesser wines. The Chambertin vineyards are the greatest in the town of Gevrey, so the town became Gevrey-Chambertin. Many's the innocent buyer who has been served an often-ordinary blend called Gevrey-Chambertin, from lesser vineyards in the town, deceived into believing that he was drinking wine from the great vineyard of Chambertin. There is one great Château Lafite in Bordeaux, but some fifty others vary the spelling or hyphenate similar names so that people will think they are getting the real thing. The more famous the name the broader its use.

The English would have none of it. There was too much fuss about wines altogether, so they anglicized the broadest possible names and let it go at that. Wine from the ducal vineyards was hearty, and that was Burgundy. Wine from Bordeaux was lighter, and that was claret. Rhine wines were hocks—short for Hochheimer. Fortified wine from Jerez, in southern Spain, was sherry, that from Portugal was port. That was that, and for five hundred years the British took vintages to the edge of empire, shaping the wines to their desires. He who has the markets holds the trade.

Wine growers were fit to be tied. There were differences, after all. Famous names had been abused, borrowed, or stolen, but they could be protected. The French began making lists, protecting the names by law, defining the regions, the districts, the towns, even delimiting the vineyards and prescribing what grapes could be planted, how they should be tended, how the wines should be made. French love of classification produced the most complex group of regulations the world has known. They are laughable at first glance, but finally quite simple.

The best wines are marketed under regulations called *Appellations d'Origine Contrôlées*, AOC, place-name control laws. On every label of such wines is the phrase *Appellation Contrôlée*, summing up all the complexity. A group of good but less prestigious wines has been denominated VDQS, a stamp bearing the initials appearing on the label and signifying *Vins Délimités de Qualité Supérieure*, delimited wines of superior quality. Less distinctive than these are the oceans of ordinary wines of France, sold by alcoholic percentage or brand name, rarely exported.

Every major wine country has controls that guarantee place of origin, indicated by stamps or phrases on the bottles. They are also guarantees that wines are of a certain standard, but confusion reigns just because there are too many names.

For most wines, the district name is enough to guarantee a distinctive wine, providing it comes from a reputable grower or shipper. Only in Burgundy, Bordeaux, and the Rhineland are the township names significant. Even there, the mere presence of the town name is not enough to indicate a superior wine. The presence of a vineyard name, perhaps even the name of the grower (an estate-bottling), usually indicates the best wine of all, and the most costly. Listed on the following pages are the main districts and townships of those regions whose wines are in general distribution in the United States.

ITALY

The Piedmont

Lombardy

Verona

*Other Districts,
Other Wines*

ITALY

Italy produces more wine—nearly two billion gallons—and drinks more—over thirty gallons per capita—than any other country. The best of them come under recent control laws (indicated on the label by DOC, *Denominazione di Origine Controllata*) patterned after those of the French. Perhaps a score of red wines are readily available from the provinces north of Rome. Half as many districts producing dry white wines have established markets abroad. Here are the best.

REDS

Piedmont	Lombardy	Verona	Emilia	Tuscany
Barolo	Valtellina	Bardolino	Lambrusco	Chianti
Gattinara		Valpolicella		
Barbaresco				
Barbera				
Freisa				

WHITES

Verona	Umbria	Marche	Latium	Campania
Soave	Orvieto	Verdicchio	Frascati	Lachryma
			Est! Est! Est!	Christi

The Piedmont

Running up to the mountains that form the borders with France and Switzerland are the foothill vineyards of the Piedmont, producing over one hundred million gallons a year, some of it Italy's best wine. Barolo and Gattinara are two full reds ranked highest, followed closely by the lighter Barbaresco. All are made from the Nebbiolo grape, and wines are sometimes marketed under the grape name, as are those made from Barbera, Freisa, and Grignolino. Those made from the Nebbiolo are like the best of the

Rhônes and, like a good Hermitage, can cost four or five dollars a bottle. Wines from other grapes are lower in price and the ones to look for. Importers also offer the white Cortese, the best of which comes from around Gavi; and invariably there is the sweetish and sparkling Asti Spumante. The wines are produced in large vineyards and there seems to be little difference between one shipper's Freisa and another's. It's hard to find out, because a store is likely to stock only a single Freisa or Grignolino, and perhaps not even that, whereas it might have several Hermitages or Châteauneufs. The Italians have never shown as much concern for distinctions as the French, partly because the wines rarely attain the high level of the greatest wines of Burgundy and Bordeaux, partly because every province produces local wine and the custom is to drink what's at hand. This casual approach might well be preserved, the wise buyer picking up this Piedmont wine or that instead of Chianti or similarly priced reds of California or France.

For comparative purposes, here is a check list of some of the shippers whose wines are being brought in by major importers:
Borgogno, imported by Banfi
Calissano & Figli, imported by Crosse & Blackwell
Franco Fiorina, imported by Dreyfus, Ashby
Antiche Cantina Tenuta Galarey, imported by Frank Schoonmaker
Marchese Villa Doria, imported by Winegate
Guido Giri, imported by Frederick Wildman.

Lombardy

Wines from the Nebbiolo that rank with those from the Piedmont come from the gorge of the Adda River, in Lombardy. The district is called Valtellina, but the wines are named for the hillsides they come from: Sassella, Grumello, and Inferno. These lie east of the town of Sondrio, along with two lesser hills whose wines are rarely seen: Grigioni and Fracia. Until recently, you didn't see much of the other three, either. They are dark, full wines, often taking a decade to round out, but like the Barolos and Gattinaras and Barbarescos of the Piedmont, they cost five dollars and more a bottle. The Nebbiolo is called Spanna or Chiaven-

ITALY

nasca in Lombardy, and often-good wines so named can sometimes be found for less than three dollars.

Verona

Bardolino and Valpolicella are two prizes of the land of Romeo and Juliet, light red wines that are delicious when drunk within a year or so of the vintage. Some of the Valpolicella is reserved and kept a year or longer in wood, then being entitled to be called Superiore; even so, it should be drunk when three or four years old. Bolla is the leading producer, but all the major Chianti firms market the Veronese wines.

The best wine of the area, often ranked as the best white wine of Italy, is Soave, which should also be drunk when it is young and fresh, within three years of the vintage. A large co-operative, the Cantina Sociale, markets a large portion of Soave production, as well as the other Veronese wines; imported by Frank Schoonmaker, all are good to use for comparison with others shipped from the district. Schoonmaker also offers a Rosso di Verona and a Bianco di Verona. The wines generally retail for three dollars a bottle.

Other Districts, Other Wines

A flood of Italian wines are coming on the market as a result of the great demand for and high prices of French wines. Already well established are such white wines as Verdicchio, Frascati, and Orvieto; such reds as Lambrusco, from Emilia-Romagna; such rosés as Chiaretto, from Garda. These, and the many others to come, are worth trying.

Verdicchio is a grape grown on the Adriatic side of the Appenines, the best of which comes from Castelli di Jesi. The wine is dry and light, best when young.

Frascati is the pet white wine of Rome because it comes from the Alban Hills, southeast of the city. Fairly full and quite dry, it is the best of the wines of Castelli Romani, widely exported.

Orvieto was the white companion of Chianti until that region began producing its own white wines. It is known here as a dry wine, but the popular version in Italy is somewhat sweet, *abbocato*. Many of the vines are still grown in the old fashion, between trees, over walls, in fields with other things, on trellises. The wine making was once as haphazard as the vines, but what's called *coltura promiscua* is beginning to disappear and wine-making methods are beginning to conform to modern techniques.

Of all the semi-sweet white wines of Italy, perhaps Est! Est! Est! is best known. It comes from the town of Montefiascone (flask mountain), north of Rome. The wine is overrated but can be pleasant enough when served with fruit.

The best white wine of the South is from the island of Ischia, near Capri, but little escapes to the mainland, let alone overseas. It is dry, good when young, and high in price when it can be found. Somewhat less dry is Lachryma Christi, from the flanks of Vesuvius, near Naples. The wine owes its popularity to the name and the stories about it. The commonest one is that when Christ returned to earth to see what was left of Paradise, which was the Bay of Naples, he wept when he saw the carryings on of the people. The falling tears became vines, and the wine of Vesuvius came into the world. The name has been borrowed for sparkling wine made all over Italy, of which most versions are usually as saccharine as the story.

A wine becoming popular is Lambrusco, lightly sweet and lightly sparkling (*frizzante*) red wine from vineyards near Bologna. When poured, it foams. This is a cheery sight, and the wine tastes good enough with dishes that have a sweet savor.

A typically Italian casual attitude should be brought to these and many of the other Italian wines coming on the market. The big shippers tend to make large lots of the most popular wines, using modern methods, attaining an acceptable level of quality with their methods, and producing something extraordinary when it comes to the best Chiantis and the reds of the Piedmont and Lombardy. Many small growers produce excellent wines, but these small lots scarcely warrant exporting and distribution in large foreign markets; most such wines are snapped up by restaurants, not only those in Italy but in Switzerland and the other countries of the Common Market. Many of the old-time distributors across the United States have Italian backgrounds and import directly from these small producers, so a wine buff traveling around the country may come upon unfamiliar wines worth trying. A price around three dollars a bottle is about right for such a wine, a price around two dollars a bottle probably indicates something better passed up.

FRANCE and NORTH AFRICA

Burgundy

Rhône

Bordeaux

The Loire

Alsace

Côtes de Provence

Arbois and Côtes du Jura

Savoie

The Midi and the Southwest

North Africa

FRANCE

The French, who produce something less than two billon gallons of wine in a good year and drink something less than thirty gallons per person every year, have set standards of excellence for centuries, not only for wines, but for cuisine, fashion, and perfumery, among other things. French logic accepts as a truism the fact that something good can always become something better and cost has nothing to do with it. The idea runs counter to the basic principles of the mass marketeer, who seeks to appeal to the many, not the few who seek the best, at a time when competence is raising what might be called the level of adequacy around the world. The conflict worries the French, who take pride in producing the best table wines in the world, as an example, but find themselves being priced out of world markets.

The resolution of the problem seems simple to the Frenchman, who eats excellent bread every day and can choose, from a myriad of cheeses and fresh vegetables and meat, fowl, and seafood, what he wishes to have for dinner that night. What you do is to make more of the good things at reasonable prices, patterned after the expensive best. This requires enormous capital investment, and while the French are hesitating about making it, other countries are adapting French techniques and improving on them, then offering acceptable products in the market. California wines and Wisconsin cheeses and Seventh Avenue fashions are only the most obvious examples. Noting them, the French are studying their wine business, particularly in Bordeaux.

There are about a quarter of a million acres of vineyards planted in Bordeaux, 25% less than were in bearing at the turn of the century. A third of these, well over a hundred square miles of vineland, produce ordinary wines, when they could be producing wines good enough to come under Appellation Contrôlée. These vineyards might well be replanted in noble vines, which would then produce perhaps ten million cases of fine wines. A similar amount of dry white wines could be produced simply by changing present vinification techniques. The changes would double production of those Bordeaux wines now so popular on world markets—and greatly lower price levels.

Similar changes are possible in other regions of France, the rest of Europe, and other parts of the world. Bordeaux, and the rest of France, may retain its pre-eminence in the world of wines. You can watch for evidence of this through the seventies by keeping an eye on the price for Bordeaux Supérieur. If it stays around three dollars, even dropping slightly while exports increase, this indicates that the French are matching production to demand; if the price jumps, demand is getting ahead of replanting; if prices collapse, that's a sign of overproduction. The French, and other producers of wine, can raise quality but need not raise prices. If the mass marketeers take command, quality will decline but prices won't. Only your taste will tell.

The Common Market, a French conception, may depend on the way the wine trade goes. Nobody wants a world where the things of day to day get progressively worse. The French know well how to make good things better. Drinking their wines, you can tell whether they are continuing to do so.

Burgundy

Burgundy, as stated earlier, is customarily divided into three parts: **Chablis, the Côte d'Or,** and **Southern Burgundy.**

The best **Chablis** vineyards are classed as Grand Cru and Premier Cru (Great Growth and First Growth, respectively), which are rare and expensive. Wines simply labeled Chablis come from lesser vineyards; those called Petit Chablis come from minor vineyards that produce light wines mostly drunk up within the year and not regularly exported, or worth the four dollars they might cost here.

The **Côte d'Or** is divided into the Côte de Nuits and the Côte de Beaune. Vineyards rated as Grand Cru and Premier Cru are invariably expensive, and even wines with township names are now high in price. For the record, the principal towns are:

FRANCE

Côte de Nuits	Côte de Beaune
Fixin	Aloxe-Corton
Gevrey-Chambertin	Beaune
Morey-Saint-Denis	Pommard
Chambolle-Musigny	Volnay
Clos de Vougeot	Meursault
Vosne-Romanée	Puligny-Montrachet
Nuits-Saint-Georges	Chassagne-Montrachet

Wines from flatland vineyards in the Côte de Nuits are planted in ordinary grapes that are permitted large yields, are blended, and should be called Gevrey or Morey or Chambolle or Nuits. They can be good buys at three dollars or less. When Premier Cru or a vineyard name, or both, is on the label, they are wines from the slope, made from Pinot Noir, and are good buys at five dollars. The Great Growths will have Grand Cru on the label and the name of the great vineyard and won't even have the name of the town; they cost six dollars and more.

What happens on the Côte de Nuits also happens on the southern half of the Côte d'Or, the Côte de Beaune. Townships with Grand Cru vineyards should be called, properly, Aloxe, Puligny, and Chassagne, and the great names of Corton and Montrachet should not be added to them. Nobody would pay a premium for their wines, of course. Names of vineyards also identify the best wines of Pommard, Volnay, Beaune, and Meursault, and such wines command a premium. Lesser towns, such as Savigny and Monthélie and Santenay, are content to sell most of their wines with the town name.

All the fuss about vineyard names also exists in Bordeaux and along the Rhine and Moselle, where each township has a few wines worth a premium, but such particularity is scarcely important anywhere else. One grower or another in other districts may make outstanding wines, but the grower will depend on his own reputation to market his bottlings. For wines under four dollars, the name of the town or district is more than enough in other wine regions of the world, where the shipper or importer must be tried and trusted.

Wines from little-known villages and communes can be found, however. Blends from them are marketed as Hautes-Côtes-de-Beaune and Hautes-Côtes-de-Nuits. Blends rated somewhat higher are wines marketed as Côte-de-Beaune-Villages or Côte-de-Nuits-Villages. Some of the best of these are exported under their commune names and are among the best buys in Burgundy today. They are listed below.

Savigny-les-Beaune	Monthélie
Auxey-Duresses	Santenay
Saint-Romain	Pernand-Vergelesses

Southern Burgundy is divided into three districts. Beaujolais is the best known, discussed under "Regional Wines," its popularity transcending even that of all the rest of Burgundy.

The Côte Chalonnaise lies just below the Côte d'Or, producing two distinctive red wines, from the communes of Mercurey and Givry, and two distinctive whites, from Rully and Montagny.

The Côte Mâconnaise, to the south, produces much wine, the most popular being Pouilly-Fuissé; the wines are now overpriced. Two neighboring white-wine townships, Pouilly-Vinzelles and Pouilly-Loché, offer wines perhaps lighter than those of their neighbor. Best buys, however are Mâcon Supérieur, both red and white. They are a degree higher in alcohol, and thus considered fuller, than Mâcon Rouge or Mâcon Blanc. Mâcon Blanc is also sold as Pinot-Chardonnay-Mâcon, the least of these. A new white-wine township has recently been denominated, near Pouilly-Fuissé, taking its name from the small commune of Saint-Vérand. The spelling is often simplified to Saint-Véran.

To get some idea of quantity—which gives an idea of price—about half a million gallons of wines sold as Pouilly are made; about two million gallons of Mâcon Supérieur, half of which is white; and almost another million gallons called simply Mâcon (mostly red) and Pinot-Chardonnay-Mâcon. Mâcon Supérieur at well under three dollars is the wine to look for.

Rhône

District names are enough to identify the good wines of the Rhône, exceptions being Hermitage and Côte Rôtie, whose wines are as expensive as Burgundies. Distinctions can also be made among the vineyards of Châteauneuf-du-Pape, where only the simple district name identifies a few wines that are under four dollars. There is only a small production of the two best whites, Condrieu and Château Grillet, all of it high in price.

But there are other districts to choose from, including one of the best buys in the world of wines, ten million cases of it. That is a blend from various townships marketed as Côtes-du-Rhône, a fairly full red wine that is ready to drink a couple of years after the vintage, continuing to improve for a year or two longer. Some of the towns prefer to use their own names for their best wines, rather than the over-all name; see the list below.

The district of Tavel is reputed to produce the best pink wine of France, from the Grenache grape, but only the most expensive seem to have much distinction. There are several small white-wine districts, perhaps the best being Seyssel. The Rhônes listed below should not cost much more than three dollars a bottle. Lesser wines are listed in the right-hand column.

REDS

Côtes-du-Rhône:
    Gigondas
    Chusclan
    Cairanne
Crozes-Hermitage
Cornas

Côtes-du-Rhône:
    Laudun
    Vacqueyras
    Vinsobres
Saint Joseph

WHITES

Seyssel
Clairette de Die
Hermitage Blanc
Mercurol-Crozes-Hermitage

Clairette du Languedoc
Clairette de Bellegarde
Palette
Saint Péray

ROSÉS

Tavel

Lirac

Bordeaux

The top wines of Bordeaux are the Classed Growths and château-bottlings from the main vineyard districts and their townships. The lowest ranks are the regional wines marketed as Bordeaux and Bordeaux Supérieur, discussed in the section on regional wines. As a reminder, here are the higher-ranking familiar names:

Haut Médoc:
 Margaux
 Saint Julien
 Pauillac
 Saint Estèphe

Graves
 Saint Émilion
 Pomerol
 Sauternes and Barsac

There are several minor districts producing red wines worth seeking because they represent excellent value when priced below four dollars, among the best buys in the world of wines. The white-wine districts are going through a transition, their wines once being sweet or half sweet; now they are being quickly vinified to make dry or flowery wines like those of the Loire; quantities may soon be enormous, for Bordeaux produces more white than red. The dry whites are most apt to be called Blanc de Blancs, although Pavillon Blanc is a popular name among some shippers. Brand names are beginning to appear; among the most interesting is a Graves in a pint bottle produced by Sichel and called Wan Fu, the "Wine of a Thousand Happinesses." Chinese restaurants are notorious for ignoring wine, which is a pity because so many taste so good with Chinese food. Sichel has bottled what the firm considers the best wine for Oriental cuisine. Until other fanciful brand names appear, the following district names should identify dry wines at low prices, under three dollars a bottle, maybe less.

>Entre-Deux-Mers
>Côtes de Bordeaux-Saint Macaire
>Graves de Vayres
>*Premières Côtes de Blaye

A list of red wines from the great vineyards of Bordeaux, arranged by district and township, is included in the appendix, although the wines are invariably too expensive to be considered here. Those of Saint Émilion call for special attention, not only because there are so many of them, but because the vineyard owners have resisted any sensible official classification. All of them want to be permitted to use the word *Grand* on their labels, because the word helps sell the wine. After much struggle, a rating was finally accepted. A dozen vineyards are permitted to call themselves (First Great Growth) Premier Grand Cru. Sixty-two others are entitled to be called Grand Cru, and when their wines come on the market, none of them should cost over five dollars a bottle. As well, there are almost a thousand other recognized vineyards entitled to add Saint Émilion to their names. They should not cost more than four dollars when they come on the market.

All these lesser growths, and even many of those entitled to be called Grand Cru, are lumped together by the trade as *petits châteaux*. The phrase is used for the minor vineyards of all the Bordeaux districts. Wines from many of them can be remarkable and deserve some special attention.

* Wine simply called Blayais gets to Paris in October, practically in the form of fermenting grape juice, to be the first wine of the vintage in the cafes. Most of it is less than ordinary, but may improve as the market grows. Similar improvements may widen the market for the sweet wines of Premières-Côtes-de-Bordeaux and its noted town of Cadillac; Loupiac; Sainte-Foy-Bordeaux; Sainte-Croix-du-Mont; and Cérons.

PETITS CHATEAUX

This little section has two groups of districts of the Dordogne around Saint Émilion and Pomerol producing red wines. A casual reader might skip over them lightly, just a couple of lists in a book that's full of them. They include a baker's dozen of names. They stand for several million bottles of wine that are some of the best buys among all the reds of the world. They should cost less than thirty dollars a case, although the trade seems to be trying to peg them at around four dollars a bottle; even then, they can be bargains. They are wines I buy by the case whenever I can find them, and if I find the first bottle tasted to be good, I drop everything, reach for the phone, and order another case. Many of them come on the market in small lots and are almost instantly discovered by wine buffs, so decisive action is called for. They are wines not to be missed, a corny old phrase of the trade that takes on meaning when you pull the first cork.

Saint-Georges-Saint-Émilion
Montagne-Saint-Émilion
Puisseguin-Saint-Émilion

Lussac-Saint-Émilion
Parsac-Saint-Émilion
Sable-Saint-Émilion

These wines are softer and faster maturing than those of Graves and the Médoc, because Merlot and Cabernet Franc (called Bouchet in Saint Émilion) predominate in the vineyards. The wines are often ready to drink four or five years after the vintage, although they may improve for a decade. The big shippers are beginning to offer a few of these wines, but most of them are bought by buyers representing importers, wholesalers, even retailers, who import them directly. The trick is to keep on the lookout for them, particularly when they are priced at around three dollars and change. There are a couple of hundred vineyards to choose from, but only tasting will tell if you've hit on a good one.

Pomerol's twin district is Lalande-de-Pomerol, particularly worth looking for. Lumped with these are Bordeaux-Côtes de Castillon and Bordeaux-Côtes de Francs, their vineyards being in the neighborhood and their best wines becoming Bordeaux Supérieur; a few may become château-bottlings, but the wines are not apt to approach the quality of Pomerol and Lalande-de-Pomerol.

Much more interesting are wines of Le Fronsadais, particularly those called Côtes-Canon-Fronsac. These are the wines the people of Bordeaux drink when they can find them, excellent and low in price because they are almost unknown. The district is small. Côtes-Canon-Fronsac can be good buys at three dollars, and are worth looking for. Its neighbor is Côtes de Fronsac, the wines not so highly regarded but good buys when the price is around two dollars. For quick reference, here is a list of these little-known districts:

Lalande-de-Pomerol
Côtes-Canon-Fronsac
Côtes-de-Fronsac
Premières Côtes de Blaye
Bourg, Côtes de Bourg, Bourgeais
Côtes-de-Castillon
Côtes-de-Francs

All these vineyards lie on the slopes above the north bank of the Dordogne, clustering around the heights of Saint Émilion and Pomerol, with a separate block across the Dordogne estuary from the Médoc composed of the slopes of Bourg and Blaye. Take note that the best of the latter is marketed as Premières Côtes de Blaye, while the reds of the former are known indiscriminately as Bourg, Bourgeais, or Côtes de Bourg.

NOTE ON BUYING PETITS CHATEAUX

Just below the vineyard name on the label appears the Appellation Contrôlée to which the château is entitled. This rating is what to look for. The lowest classification is Bordeaux, then comes Bordeaux Supérieur, followed by those with district names. Many of the wines equal those entitled to be called Great Growths. Most of the small vineyards and practically all of the lesser wines make up the blends of the shippers, but many of the better wines are marketed as vineyard wine with château names. Often enough to make it interesting, wine masters of the great châteaux will supervise the little-known vineyards, so that quality is often high. All these little-château wines are always worth trying when the price is under three dollars; if the wine tastes bitter or sharp, chances are it is simply too young, the time for drinking beginning about four years after the vintage.

Co-operatives are everywhere in Bordeaux—there are about sixty of them—handling the vintages of many small growers, providing them with technical advice and equipment. Their wines are often extraordinary, the Bordeaux and Bordeaux Supérieur blends often excellent. They are beginning to be marketed here.

The Loire

The smile of France, as the vale of the country's longest river is called, has vineyards all along its westward course, with dry whites at both ends and all the other types in the middle. Districts on the Upper Loire are planted in the Sauvignon Blanc of the Bordeaux vineyards (where it's called Blanc Fumé), producing the following:

UPPER LOIRE

Pouilly-Fumé   Sancerre   Quincy   Reuilly

NOTE: The neighboring district of Pouilly-sur-Loire produces wine made from the less distinctive Chasselas grape.

MUSCADET

Near the mouth of the river, surrounding Nantes, are the vineyards of Muscadet, those south of the river called the "Région de Sèvre-et-Maine," those north of the river called "Côteaux de la Loire." The first is supposed to be better, producing dry little wines made from the Melon grape, which does less well in its original home of Burgundy. To build up body, the wine is often left on the dregs during fermentation ("sur lie"); many prefer the fuller wine.

VOUVRAY AND THE TOURAINE

The Chenin Blanc comes into its own in the Middle Loire, where it's also called Pineau de la Loire, and where it produces the famous Vouvray. A wine that can be dry and fruity, it is most often made into a rich and golden sweet wine that can live for decades and into a fruity sparkling wine that ranks second only to Champagne. Similar wines come from its companion district, Montlouis.

Most of the wines of the Touraine are drunk in France, but some reds from the districts around Chinon get out. It is the birthplace of Rabelais, and the wines of Chinon may have been those he had in mind when Gargantua burst forth shouting, "Trinc!" Like their neighbors, Bourgueil and Saint-Nicolas-de-Bourgueil, they are made from the Cabernet Franc of Bordeaux, the grape that is used for the best rosés of the Loire.

SAUMUR AND THE ANJOU

The best wines of the Anjou are the sweet ones from Saumur: Côteaux du Layon, of which the best is Quarts de Chaume; and Côteaux de la Loire, of which the best is Savennières. The grape is Chenin Blanc, also used to make dry and sparkling versions, including the dry and fruity Jasnières from the district called Côteaux du Loir. The best red wine is Champigny, made from the Cabernet Franc, which is also responsible for the best rosés.

The Anjou is best known for rosé, the most familiar being simply Anjou Rosé, a common wine with an orange cast made from a grape called Groslot.

The wines of the Loire, all meant to be drunk young with the exception of the sweet white wines, are mostly drunk in France and are generally the best of what has come to be called *vins du pays*. The dry wines vary widely in quality, but the best of them are worth seeking out and should never cost over four dollars a bottle. When fame does not exaggerate price, the best wines should be less than three dollars, the ordinary run not much above two. For quick reference, the best wines of the Loire are summarized below:

Reds	Dry Whites	Sweet Whites
Champigny	Pouilly-Fumé	Vouvray
Saint Nicolas	Sancerre	Montlouis
Bourgueil	Quincy	Saumur
Chinon	Reuilly	Quarts de Chaume
	Muscadet	Savennières
	Jasnières	

Alsace

The Sylvaner is the favorite white wine of France, cheap, pleasantly fresh, no odd tastes—just good white wine that's light and flowery, exactly what the old joke referred to as unassuming wine, without pretension. And its popularity clouds the delight that is Alsace: a range of sprightly wines from German grapes done in the French manner. One can scarcely ask for more, and yet there is, and that's the Traminer.

The Traminer may have come from the Italian Tyrol, from the once-Austrian district of Tramin, now called Termino, and the grape may be an offshoot from vineyards farther east, but now its home is Alsace. The wine is fruity, flowery, especially delicious. And there is an especially spicy version from a special strain; it's Gewürztraminer, with an exaggerated flowery taste, not so appealing when a Traminer can be had.

The two wines became typically Alsatian because of the border shuffle between France and Germany over the centuries. Whenever the province was German, Alsatian vineyards were planted in lesser grapes so their wines would not compete with the Rieslings, from farther down the Rhine, only to be replanted in Rieslings when Alsace was returned to France. The Riesling makes the best wine of Alsace, no doubt about that, marvelously soft and full and balanced, but without the masterly elegance of those from the Rheingau and Moselle. But there's enough great Riesling in the world from the more northern Rhineland vineyards. Wise vintners long ago found delights could come from Traminer and Sylvaner—and much larger quantities of wine—so they decided to make a point of them by letting the grapes name the wine. They did the same with the Pinot Gris, which they chose to call the Tokay d'Alsace, and a pink wine called Pinot Rosé; a paler version they called *vin gris*. There are other grapes making fair wines rarely exported, but all those using the grape name must be made entirely from the variety on the label, and superior grades bear phrases such as Grand Vin, Grand Cru, or Grande Réserve; some of these are made from late-picked grapes or selected bunches, in the German fashion, but this is not always spelled out on the labels. Some vineyard names are used now and then, but most of them are actually brand names. Inexpensive blends are produced —mostly under brand names—the wine generally called Zwicker, with the best grades denominated Edelzwicker.

The best vineyards lie north of Colmar and extend for fifty miles—almost to Strasbourg—around such picturesque towns as Riquewihr and Ribeauvillé, Kaisersberg and Kientzheim, all of them tourist centers in the summer. Flower boxes festoon the windows, there are fountains in the squares, vineyards press close to the town walls, and everywhere are taverns for tasting.

The food is wonderful, a perfect foil for the wines, everything from choucroûte garnie to fowl and game birds stuffed with truffles, delicious stews, sausages fragrant and spicy, veal prepared elegantly or robustly—a splendid blend of Bavarian and the simple French cooking of the mountains. And to end the meal, the waiter will wheel up a cart of *alcools blancs,* distillates white as water made from berries and fruits and nuts. There's Kirsch from cherries, of course, and Mirabelle from yellow plums, and occasionally the rare Fraise from wild strawberries and Framboise from raspberries, and others from walnuts or hazelnuts. There's a strong family taste in these distillates aged in crocks—a taste of leather, some say, and mostly appealing to men—but their strength and vigor can grow on anyone, especially with cups of dark coffee.

There are some thirty thousand acres of vineland, but America drinks only about that number of cases each year, leaving the rest for France and its neighbors. The light wines from Sylvaner, Chasselas, and Pinot Blanc (here called Klevner) come from Haut-Rhin, the southern district, near Colmar, whose main town in Thann. Rieslings, Traminers, and Muscats come from vineyards farther north, above Colmar—Bas-Rhin—whose production center is Riquewihr. Some 14,000,000 gallons of wine are produced in the average year, nearly one bottle in five coming from a union of co-operatives that has more than 3,000 members.

Hugel et Fils
Half a dozen of the major Alsatian firms and many small ones were founded in the seventeenth century, Hugel being among the most prestigious. Established in Riquewihr, the walled town bright with flower boxes that is the most picturesque in Alsace, the

twelfth generation in the firm ships wines to some sixty countries. Bands of English students arrive each vintage to help with the pressing, a reason why the wines of Hugel are so popular on the English market, particularly an inexpensive blend called "Flambeau d'Alsace." The torch of Alsace is also held high by Hugel Rieslings and Muscats, produced in a fine, dry style; its Traminer is particularly distinguished.

IMPORTER: Dreyfus, Ashby, New York (a branch of Schenley)

Dopff & Irion

An outgrowth of a firm founded four centuries ago, Dopff & Irion is owner of the domain of the château of Riquewihr, but obtains most of the grapes for its wines from some 600 growers under long-term contracts with the firm. Its most popular blends are Crystal d'Alsace and Sylvaner Domaine Voltaire. The firm estate-bottles the wines of its Château de Riquewihr vineyards—Les Murailles-Riesling, Les Sorcières-Gewürztraminer, and Les Amandiers-Muscat—a practice rare in Alsace, where wines are generally identified by grape variety.

IMPORTERS: Dennis & Huppert, New York
Venge & Co., Los Angeles

Dopff

Stemming from the firm founded in 1574, Dopff is one of the largest vineyard owners in Alsace, and like its separate but sister company, estate-bottles many of its wines. Two of its most popular blends are Carte Grise and Charmant; its Riesling Schoenenburg and Gewürztraminer Eichberg are famous.

IMPORTER: Carillon Importers, New York

F. E. Trimbach

The first Trimbach appears in the annals of wine in Riquewihr in the early part of the seventeenth century. The firm expanded to Hunawihr a hundred years ago and finally to Ribeauvillé, where it is now managed by two brothers who are descendants of the founder. Their grandfather was one of the founders of the association of growers and shippers, and assembled the vineyard of Clos Sainte Hune in Hunawihr, which produces one of the best-known of Alsatian Rieslings. The collection of old vintages in the family cellar dates back to 1834; old bottles from the library are occasionally opened for comparison with present vintages and to honor visitors or celebrate great events. Among the most interesting of these is Gewürztraminer made from late-picked grapes; these Spätlesen are rich and fruity, with a distinctive spicy quality that's delicious with rich foods such as foie gras, but the wines have so much taste that they are usually served by themselves or at the end of a meal.

IMPORTER: Austin Nichols, New York (Liggett & Myers Division)

Louis Sipp
The third generation now manages the firm with the largest vineyard holdings in Ribeauvillé, specializing in wines from a township that produces some of the best in Alsace. The firm offers a line of specially reserved wines along with their regular bottlings, a growing general trend in Alsace, as well as wines from several varieties of Pinot, the grape of Burgundy. Planting of Pinot is being gradually extended in Alsace; the wines are generally lighter and less subtle than those of Burgundy, well worth trying when prices are reasonable.

IMPORTER: Crosse & Blackwell, New York (a division of Nestlé)

Kuehn
Another of the firms founded in the seventeenth century, Kuehn is one of the most distinguished in Ammerschwihr, a town almost completely rebuilt after being reduced to rubble. The new village won first prize as garden town of the year during the sixties. Kuehn wines are the pets of restaurateurs, and the firm has been zealous in courting favor with French chefs, mostly young, that concentrate on foods superlatively cooked as simply as possible and served with light sauces of great subtlety—what's called *la grande cuisine simple,* from the tradition begun by Fernand Point of La Pyramide. Many such dishes call for simple wines direct in taste; extremely subtle dishes may call for delicate wines of a matching finesse. Kuehn endeavors to supply both. As a result, many of the firm's wines are reserved for French restaurants. Distribution in the United States is limited.

IMPORTERS: Maison Seggermann, San Francisco
　　　　　　Seggermann Slocum, New York
　　　　　　Van Munching, New York

Preiss-Henny and **Caves Alsaciennes**

The Preiss family established itself in Mittelwihr early in the sixteenth century, producing wine from some one hundred acres of its own vineyards in the surrounding townships and marketing most of them under the family name; wines from grapes purchased under contract are marketed under Caves Alsaciennes. Their most famous wines are the Gewürztraminers produced on a mount that was once an almond orchard, Mandelberg. The firm offers an extensive line, including Pinot Gris and Pinot Noir.

IMPORTERS: Austin Nichols, New York (for Preiss-Henny)
House of Burgundy, New York (for Caves Alsaciennes)
Excelsior Wines & Spirits, New York (for Caves Alsaciennes)

A. Willm

Founded before the turn of the century by a winegrower of local repute, the third generation has extended the firm's reputation overseas. Exceptional wines are marketed as Grand Reserve, most notable being an estate-bottled Gewürztraminer, Clos Gaensbroennel, while good blends are sold as Cordon d'Alsace. Light, dry Alsatian blends are excellent with seafood and shellfish; Alsatians have begun marketing these with special labels showing oysters and lobsters and such to encourage the French to try the flowery wines instead of those from Burgundy or the Loire. Willm's version is called "Fruits de Mer—Escargots—Spécial." The trend is a good one, and such wines with pictorial labels and special designations are beginning to appear on our market, simplifying choice for buyers, suggesting ways of serving, encouraging them to try a wider range. Willm does this particularly well, so that their special reserves and estate bottlings will not be confused with their simpler wines, which are made for casual meals.

IMPORTER: Julius Wile, New York (Standard Brands)

Côtes de Provence

The favorite wine of the Riviera is the light, fresh rosé from the vineyards of Provence, from such seacoast towns as Cassis,

Bellet, and Bandol, and from others back in the hills. The wine glints beautifully on the shaded terraces of the resort towns overlooking the beaches, and tastes marvelous with the grilled fish, the bouillabaisse, the cold salads with olives and anchovies, the Frenchified versions of Italian dishes. Most of the wines come under VDQS, although those from the towns mentioned are rated as Appellation Contrôlée. There are some reds and whites, particularly the whites of Cassis, but rosés are the most popular.

The wines are best when bottled during the spring after the vintage or by the following fall at the latest, and should be drunk soon after, for freshness is their virtue. They are becoming fashionable here, although they are sometimes high in price, often as much as the superior Tavels.

Arbois and Côtes du Jura

In the foothills of the Jura, east of Burgundy and near the Swiss border, is a fifty-mile stretch of vineyard that produces excellent rosés and reds of the Arbois in the north, and a range of good whites to the south. There are special wines from dried grapes such as *vin de paille* and *vin jaune,* a sherrylike Château Chalon, and the sparkling wine of l'Etoile. All come under Appellation Contrôlée, and until recently only a little rosé and the novelty wines from dried grapes left the region. For the past couple of decades, however, an enthusiastic producer who markets seven out of the ten bottles made each year in the Jura, whose domain amounts to nearly 700 acres (the largest holding of vineyards coming under Appellation Contrôlée), and whose firm was founded by his ancestors in the seventeenth century, decided to change matters. His name is Henri Maire, his wines today go to a hundred countries, and many French producers think he promotes too much. His advertising claims sound as if they originated in California, but the wines are well made, many from grapes little known in the United States, and prices are reasonable. One blend, which he decided to call Vin Fou (crazy wine), sparkles a little and "has an efficacious action, well known to awaken sentiment and love." There's also a booklet that has a recipe for baked apples requiring an "injection de VIN FOU" every five minutes. Henry Maire could do equally well in the automobile business, or in cigarettes or soap. The difference is that he has something good to work with: healthy grapes and extensive vineyards in a lovely countryside, with every modern technique at his command to produce pleasant wines. His eventual success in this country (his importer, Banfi, began by bringing in only two of his wines) should open the door for the rest of the wines of the Appellation Contrôlée not yet imported, and more of those under VDQS.

Savoie

A small district between the south shore of Lake Geneva and the Italian border produces one of France's best sparkling wines, Seyssel, worth trying whenever it is found on the market. The neighboring township of Crépy produces some whites like those of Switzerland, made from the Chasselas.

The Midi and the Southwest

The Midi, north of the Spanish border and lying back from the Mediterranean, produces an enormous amount of ordinary wine from vineyards that extend all the way to Bordeaux. Whites under Appellation Contrôlée include Bergerac, Gaillac, Monbazillac, Montravel, and Côtes de Duras, the last three often being sweet. Reds include Bergerac and Fitou, the last being a small district producing some hundred thousand cases of a full red wine that has found a small market here.

Wines of the Midi coming under VDQS laws come from Costières du Gard, Minervois, and Corbières, are usually red, and should always be cheap. Perhaps the best of the VDQS wines is Cahors, made from the Malbec from vineyards near Toulouse, a wine that is dark and full and may take a decade to mature.

The Southwest embraces the ancient province of Languedoc, extending from Arles, in the Rhône Valley, to the Spanish border. It contains several districts of the Midi in the departments of Hérault, Aude, and Gard—particularly the sweet-wine districts of Frontignan (famous for the best of the Muscats), Rousillon, and Blanquette de Limoux (which sparkles). These come under Appellation Contrôlée, and several others come under VDQS.

FRANCE

The wines are simply ones to try when you come upon them. The reds and whites can be quite drinkable and even better than that. For a standard of comparison, look for Côteaux du Languedoc in a 67-ounce bottle, shipped by Georges Bonfils and imported by Austin Nichols.

Reds	White	Rosé
Cahors	Bergerac*	Cotes du Lubéron
Corbières Supérieur		
Corbières du Rousillon		
Minervois		
Fitou		

* Bergerac makes a lot of wine, some two million gallons, mostly white; the best of the reds—a scant fifteen thousand cases—come from Pécharmant.

NORTH AFRICA

Algeria produces more than a quarter billion gallons of wine, and when that country was a part of France, the best areas were underrated as VDQS. There are some 800,000 acres of vineyards, most of it producing ordinary wine that goes to France and Eastern Europe, the prices being low enough to make a cheap carafe wine that anybody can afford. The best are also cheap, but rarely reach major markets under their own names, because they would undercut other low-priced wines that have made a name for themselves. The best wines come from and are called Côteaux de Mascara, followed by Côteaux de Tlemçen.

Morocco has nearly 200,000 vineyard acres and produces some sixty-five million gallons of ordinary wine, the best being the light reds from around Meknes.

Tunisia has more than 100,000 vineyard acres, producing some forty million gallons of wine, the best being reds from around Tunis and Carthage. A classification called *Vin Supérieur de Tunisie* has been established to indicate wines that have been tasted by a committee of experts; the bottles of each lot of such wines are numbered. A separate committee has been established for wines from Muscat grapes.

GERMANY

―◄◆►―

Mosel-Saar-Ruwer

Nahe

Rheingau

Rheinhessen

Rheinpfalz

Franconia

Baden

Fine wines of the Rhineland are always white and mostly from the Riesling grape, although some excellent Sylvaners are made and some good blends from the Müller-Thurgau, which is a cross between the two. All this, and more, was once spelled out on German wine labels, often including the particular cask the wine came from, as well as the vineyard and the grower. More than anybody needed to know, many people said, and when the Common Market made it necessary for regulations of Italy, France, and Germany to dovetail, Rhineland designations were changed, causing an uproar. It's all a matter of sugar.

Grapes produce best when grown at the extremity of their range, the struggle to develop sugar also forcing the development of secondary characteristics that make for better wines. Some years, there isn't enough sun, so sugar is added to the fermenting juice to raise the resulting alcoholic content high enough to make a palatable wine that will last more than a few months. The practice is called chaptalization, after its developer, and is customary in Burgundy and Bordeaux, as well as along the Rhine. Wines containing 10 or 11% alcohol from natural sugar are pleasingly fresh but subject to changes and were once considered too light to ship. How wonderful to discover, then, a way to raise the alcohol to 12% or so without unbalancing the wines too much, giving them longer life and strength enough to travel. Markets distant from vineyard areas came to accept the heavier wines as normal; few people ever got a chance to taste the extraordinary lightness of natural wines. All the sugar added was converted to alcohol, of course, so the wines were still dry, but lesser wine makers took to adding more and more sugar to mask any flaws under the alcohol that was converted from the sugar. Modern methods eliminate the need for heavy chaptalization, but the practice is slow to die. Rhinelanders have always avoided the practice for their best wines, labeling them *naturwein,* unsugared wine, and have now made further distinctions that appear on the labels, at the same time simplifying the rest of the nomenclature. The uproar came because some wines have been downgraded.

Simple table wine—*Deutscher Tafelwein*—is ordinary wine bearing a regional or a town name, raised to minimum alcoholic content with sugar. Most of it is drunk in Germany.

Quality wine—*Deutscher Qualitätswein*—must have a larger proportion of natural sugar and may bear a vineyard name. Many of these low-priced wines are exported.

Special wines—*Qualitätswein mit Prädikat*—are natural wines without additions. There are several categories, which will make up most of the wines exported:

Kabinett wines are the equivalent of *naturwein,* from a now-limited number of vineyards.

Spätlesen are made from grapes picked late, producing wines that are more fruity than flowery.

Auslesen are made from selected bunches of grapes that have begun to dry up, resulting in rich and fruity wines. Overripe grapes from these bunches are gathered to make luscious *Beerenauslesen;* dried grapes from these bunches are separated and pressed to make the extra-sweet *Trockenbeerenauslesen.* Wines from selected bunches and grapes can be expensive, twenty dollars a bottle and more.

Nobody objected much to the division of Rhineland wines into sugared Quality Wines and unsugared Kabinett wines or the more specific categories. The uproar came from the number of vineyard names—of which there were 25,000—and many of them were consolidated into simple generic names (*Grosslagen*).

Thousand of names are to become hundreds, a region such as the Moselle being divided into districts (the German word is *Bereich*) like the one for the Mittel-Mosel that takes the name of the town of Bernkastel. Specific vineyards of good size (*Einzellagen*) will continue to be marketed, and an owner doing his own bottling will identify the wine as *Erzeugerabfüllung* or *Aus Eigenem Lesegut* (from his own harvest). But most wines will be marketed as Grosslagen, the collective vineyard names, by shippers. Buyers of the best grades will no longer look for *Original Abfüllung* (original bottling) on the label to identify estate-bottlings. They will continue to watch for the seal of the VDNV, *Verband Deutscher Naturwein Verstiegerer,* the group of vineyard owners who identify their wines with a funny-looking eagle whose body is a bunch of grapes. It appears on the left side of the label and is a guarantee of an authentic, unsugared wine.

The following lists of the principal towns in the six main regions contain the most important of the Grosslagen.

Mosel-Saar-Ruwer*

The look of the Mosel is changing because of the new laws. A couple of generations ago it was one of the most romantic places in Europe. You could take what was called the Drunkard's Railroad up the river from Koblenz, stopping at the wine villages along the way. And then, at Trier, you could float down the winding stream, stopping at the villages again, camping on the banks, sipping wine cooled in the river while you looked at the steeply terraced vineyards, where some pockets of vines were no larger than a country kitchen. The automobile changed all that, as highways were built along the banks. Then some of the vintners decided to simplify their holdings, building switchback roads up the slopes and putting in slabs of concrete as retaining walls where the land was really too steep for vines. The great gray faces look terrible from a distance, slashes and scars on the hills, but the vines can be tended easily from roads above and below. Now the old stone walls are coming out, more switchbacks are going in, and concrete seems to be taking over the slopes. The growers get vertical strips of the newly "rationalized" vineyards, and tending is much easier. Vines are being allowed to grow over the concrete scars, but not too many, because they rob the earth of moisture and of nutrients. The wines may be even better. The countryside is not.

* Wines from the two tributaries of the Moselle are included, to make up a single region. The French spelling of the winding river that starts in the Jura and borders Luxembourg, where the vineyards begin, is generally accepted, although the wine world prefers to call it *die Mosel*—dee MO zull—because the best wines come from the German vineyards.

Mosel

Bernkasteler Kurfürstlay
Piesporter Michelsberg
Graacher Münzlay

Wehlener Münzlay
Zeltinger Münzlay

NOTE: Other Grosslagen include Schwarzlay, Beerenlay, Nacktarsch, and Schwarze Katz for other towns, roughly in that order, of excellence. As in New Yorker, *er* is added to the town name to indicate possession.

Saar-Ruwer

Wiltinger Scharzberg

Oberemmeler Scharzberg
Trierer Römerlay

Nahe

The Nahe is perhaps the least known of German districts producing superior wines, the river that names it flowing into the Rhine at Bingen, across from the Rheingau. There are some four thousand acres of vines, producing a couple of million gallons a year, the wines low in price because they are not well known. At less than three dollars a bottle, they warrant tasting whenever they can be found.

Kreuznacher Kronenberg
Schloss Böckelheimer Burgweg

NOTE: Other Grosslagen include Schlosskapelle, Paradeisgarten, and Rosengarten, for various towns.

Rheingau

The Rheingau produces the most elegant of German wines, the greatest ones priced well above four dollars, although many good ones can be found for around three. Some of the greatest vineyards, such as Steinberger and Schloss Vollrads and Schloss Johannisberger, carry no names other than their own. When in doubt, Rheingauers are the wines to buy, for they are unmatched for their fine balance of fruitiness and dryness. The sweet wines from late-picked grapes are unequaled, and many of them may take ten years to develop. Kabinett wines from normally harvested grapes may take three years to develop in a good year, while lesser ones are ready as soon as they are bottled.

Hochheimer Daubhaus
Eltviller Steinmächer
Rauenthaler Steinmächer
Kiedrich Heilegenstock
Erbacher Deutelsberg
Hattenheimer Deutelsberg

Winkler Honigberg
Hallgartener Mehrhölzchen
Oestricher Gottesthal
Johannisberger Erntebringer
Rudesheimer Burgweg

Rheinhessen

Revolutionary mercenaries came from this region we call Hessia, which produces only a little less wine than its neighbor to the south, the Rheinpfalz. Here the Sylvaner reigns supreme, although the best wines are Rieslings. It is the original home of Liebfraumilch, which now comes from everywhere, but was first named after a little vineyard near the cathedral of Worms. The district today lies north of that city, extending to Mainz and around the bend of the Rhine all the way to Bingen. The Scharlachberg is a great hill of reddish soil that produces a big, soft wine, Bingen's most famous.

Oppenheimer Güldenmorgen or Krötenbrunnen
Niersteiner Auflangen or Spiegelberg
Nackenheimer Rehbach
Binger Sankt Rochuspelle

Rheinpfalz

This district on the border of France is also known as the Palatinate. The wines from its 35,000 acres were the best known of the Holy Roman Empire, and come from a stretch of hills called the Haardt. Several secondary grapes are planted, but wines from Riesling grapes planted in the best townships are the best. Lesser wines have an earthy taste, the German for which is *Bodengeschmack,* whose very sound is properly derogatory. Good ones are full-bodied and seem to taste their best with German dishes.

Ruppertsberger Hofstück
Deidesheimer Mariengarten

Forster Mariengarten
Wachenheimer Schenkenböhl

Franconia

Frankenwein comes from the district east of the Rhine, up in the valleys of the Main. The center of production lies around Würzburg, and most of the wine comes from the Sylvaner. The wines are traditionally shipped in the squat, round *Bocksbeutel,* which has been adapted for Portuguese rosés and for Chilean wines, among others. The wines are often called Steinwein, which is the name of a Würzburg vineyard that has been loosely adopted for the whole region. The wines are often remarkable, but not particularly known, and may offer good bargains.

Würzburger Himmelspforte
Randersacker Ewig Leben

Iphofener Burgweg
Escherndorfer Kirchberg

Baden

Much wine comes from vineyards across the Rhine from Alsace, from along the foothills of the Black Forest, and from the Swiss border near Lake Constance (the Bodensee). They are best drunk young and on the spot. Some is occasionally shipped abroad and curiosity may lead you to taste Mauerweine, Seeweine, or those from Markgräflerland or the Kaiserstuhl or the Ortenau. It's carafe wine, *Schoppenwein,* the most interesting thing about it usually being its names. Here are some of the Grosslagen for the various regions, which are usually preceded by the name of a town:

Bodensee—Sonnenufer
Markgräflerland—Vogetl Rötteln or Burg Neuenfels or Lorettoberg
Kaiserstuhl—Attilafelsen or Vulkanfelsen
Ortenau—Fursteneck or Schloss Rodeck

SWITZERLAND AUSTRIA, AND MIDDLE EUROPE

SWITZERLAND

Swiss wines are mostly white: from the shores of Lake Geneva; from vineyards around Lake Neuchâtel to the north; and from the Valais, which is the upper valley of the Rhône, as the river flows west into Lake Geneva. The commonest grape is the Fendant, which is really the Chasselas of the Loire, where it is considered the best of table grapes. Riesling, Pinot Noir, and Gamay are planted, particularly in the western end of the Valais around Dôle. The best white wine, Johannisberg, is a blend of Riesling and Sylvaner. Both grape and town names get on bottles, but not much wine gets out; the Swiss drink twice what they produce.

The Valais offers wines from such marvelously named towns as Sierre and Sion and Visperterminen. The last is the highest wine town in Europe and sensibly allows its wine to be called Visp. The Fendants are most widely planted, making just the wine for fondue. The wines are good but high in price because so rare, often costing four dollars a bottle. They are country wines, their number increased by many others from the many valleys, particularly those in the Italian-speaking region of Tessin.

Neuchâtel, the smallest of the three main regions, is the most popular, the wines being bottled quickly so that the secondary fermentation causes some bubbles to form in the wine. The slight sparkle is called "the star" and deposits tiny bubbles on the inside of the glass. Such "pétillant" wines make the tongue tingle.

The canton of the Vaud encompasses the vineyard areas along the north shore of Lake Geneva. The district of La Côte is west of Lausanne, wines coming from such towns as Mont-Sur-Rolle, Féchy, Bougy, and Vinzelle. Better and more plentiful wines come from the district of Lavaux to the east, from towns such as Dézaley and Saint Saphorin. Still more good bottlings come from the Chablais district, at the mouth of the Rhône as it empties into the lake, from towns such as Aigle and Yvorne.

Good wines all, many of them excellent, but so few in number that they should perhaps be left in the countryside where they are made, to be enjoyed there.

AUSTRIA

Vienna is full of good wines—from the surrounding countryside and neighboring countries: *Tischwein* from Czechoslovakian vineyards on the north; hearty reds and whites from vineyards east and south in Hungary and Yugoslavia; more from former provinces to the southwest in the Italian Tyrol—a bewildering collection mostly unknown in the United States, where French and Italian vintages dominate the market. The motley range goes with the goulashes and cutlets and chicken dishes of the trans-European cuisine that is first Viennese even when the sources were Russian, French, or German, but the favorite wine is as native as the bread and rolls and sausages that make of Austria a nation of snackers.

The wine is *heurige,* fresh and white, served by the carafe with what we think of as delicatessen or picnic fare, in Grinzing, a suburb of Vienna full of outdoor terraces, wine gardens, and music that may be gypsy violins and Strauss waltzes but is mostly concertina and guitar called Schrammel. Viennese love to talk of the folk-tune-love-song ring of sound that goes with the wine from little towns of which Grinzing, is only one, others being, Nussdorf, Kahlenbergerdorf, Heiligenstadt, Unterdoebling, Sievering, Neustift am Walde, Dornbach, Ottakring, Mauer, Oberlaa, Gross-Jedlersdorf, Strebersdorf, and Stammersdorf.

The taverns hang a bush above the door to show when the new wine's ready, the papers list them daily so you can get there promptly, and all of it is as old Bohemia as ever was. The grapes are mostly German, but there are a dozen varieties at least, and every pitcher in every place is different. The wine is light. You might drink pitchers of it with the sausages and the potato salad and the cold chicken, but you have to go there to do it.

The wines we get must be able to live in the bottle so that they keep their sprightly taste. The best come from up the Danube in the district called Wachau, particularly around Krems and Loiben. But there's also Gumpoldskirchener, from south of Vienna, and the wines of Rust from way down by the Neuseidlersee. Maybe you can find a record of Schrammel music somewhere—finding the delicatessen is easy—and wines from one of the many co-operatives or from Lenz Moser in Krems or Retz in Rust. Or maybe you will have to settle for Strauss and Gumpoldskirchener and goulash and be more Viennese than Bohemian, but there are worse ways to spend an evening than eating and drinking the way they do in middle Europe.

MIDDLE EUROPE

HUNGARY

Hungarian vineyards lie mostly in the West, around the lake of Balaton, with its district of Badacsony; in nearby Somló; and in Sopron, over toward the Austrian border. Near Budapest is the district of Neszmely, producing Rieslings and sweet whites from the Ezerjó grape, and farther north are more sweet wines from Eger. Eger also produces reds, the best known being the Bikavér, which means "bull's blood." The name of the grape usually appears after the place name on a label, but Egri Bikavér is made mostly from the Kadarka, which also is used in the districts of Szekszárd, where Vörös and various French grapes are planted. The place name is made to end in an "i" to indicate possession, the way "er" is added to New York. The great wine is the sweet and expensive Tokay, from the volcanic region of the Tokaj, in the far Northeast.

A single export group, Monimpex, markets all the wine for the state, which is imported by International Vintage Wines, the Heublein subsidiary. Much wine is made, more than in the United States, but the whites, which are on the sweet side, and the generally heavy reds have never found much of a market. At three dollars, they face the competition of Mediterranean producers.

YUGOSLAVIA

The fifth largest producer in the world, Yugoslavia markets all its wines through three export associations: the northern Slovenian vineyards, along the Danube, come in with white and gold *Slovin* labels; those from the Belgrade area, in the East, Serbia, come in gold and black labels as *Navip;* and those from the western provinces, along the Adriatic, are in full color and called *Adriatica*. The wines overlap, a Cabernet from Istria coming in under Adriatica and Slovin labels, for instance, but the wines differ. Never mind. All the famous grapes are grown, and native varieties such as Prokupac, which makes the Serbian Beaujolais; and Plavac, which is a wine mighty like a Rhône. The importer is Munson Shaw, a branch of National Distillers, and the wines are good value when under three dollars.

Reds

ADRIATICA

Plavac from Bol
Prokupac from Yovac
Refosk from Istria
Rizvanac from Slavonia

NAVIP

Gamay from Vencac
Prokupac from Vranjè

SLOVIN

Cabernet from Istria

Whites

Sauvigno from Fruska Gora

Rizling from Karlovci

Traminec of Jeruzalem

BULGARIA

Vineyards have flourished for centuries on the southern foothills of the Balkans and above the shores of the Black Sea, mostly producing red wines from native grapes and whites from varieties of the Muscat. All three hundred thousand or so acres come under the state monopoly, Vinprom, which has established regional wineries and planted many French and German varieties, raising production to 100,000,000 gallons in a good year, on a par with Hungary and Greece. A few are beginning to come into the States, at not much more than two dollars a bottle, priced low, like those of other countries whose wines are little known here, to attract a market.

The common red wine of Bulgaria is made from the Pamid grape, but the dark, full wine from the Melnik is preferred; the Cabernet is exported, because the name is familiar and the wine is appealing. The Dimyat is a grape producing fresh, aromatic dry whites, particularly those from Varna, the district called the pearl of the Black Sea; a light blend called Evxinograd is also made there. Two other whites exported are the Tamianka and the Rikat. All are worth trying when they appear on the market.

ROMANIA

The Greeks found wines in Romania when they set up their Black Sea colonies in the seventh century B.C. While many wines are still made from native grapes above the seacoast and along the rivers and in the Carpathian foothills, those coming to the West are mostly from French and German varieties. The most highly prized red is Babeasca Nicoresti, but there are also Pinot Noir and Cabernet, while a blend of red is marketed as Cabinet. A wide range of whites is made, those preferred by Romanians being sweet: the golden, raisiny Cotnari; earthy Murfatlar, with a taste of figs; light and fruity Muscat Ottonel. A drier wine is a soft blend famous for centuries as Perla de Tarnave, but called Dacia here so the name won't be confused with the carbonated German *Perlwein*. Also famous is a fruity wine named after the grape, Feteasca.

All of the production is controlled by the state monopoly, Fructexport, in Budapest. Production is something over 150,000,-000 gallons. Importers have been hesitant about bringing in wines from state monopolies and co-operatives, dreading the red tape of bureaucracy, but when good wines can be offered at around three dollars a bottle, some begin to find the will to overcome the difficulties. There is a lot of wine to draw on for an expanding market. Only a few local distributors have the wines.

CZECHOSLOVAKIA

Rhineland grapes are planted in Bohemia and Moravia, the provinces lying north of Austria; still more are planted in eastern Slovakia on the foothills of the Carpathians and the Tatra mountains, while the Furmint grape, which makes Tokay, is planted north of the Hungarian border. The country imports much more wine than it makes, but some of the whites are exported.

SPAIN and PORTUGAL

SPAIN

Spain has been making wines for more than three thousand years; it has about four million acres of vineyards—more than any other country—and produces about two thirds of a billion gallons of wine in a good year. But only in the past decade or so have good reds and whites come to this country, thanks largely to the encouragement of a few astute importers. What we drink from Spain is a credit to our wine trade, with assists from England and France.

War and desolation racked the vineyards until the arrival in the last decades of the past century of French vignerons seeking lands not devastated by the Phylloxera. They introduced Bordeaux methods in the Rioja, a region near the Basque country in the western uplands of the Pyrenees, below the French border. Spanish grapes in the high vineyards produced light, dry reds that were aged five years and longer in wood, in the ancient Bordeaux style, but recent decades have seen a shortening of this time—and better wines. Fairly rigorous controls gradually came into being, slowly spreading to other districts, so that now wines can be shipped from the Rioja by some two score producers who have substantial storing facilities. The best wines come from the district of Rioja Alta, with slightly fuller ones coming from Rioja Alavesa; Rioja Baja produces ordinary wines. The youngest wines are labeled *Cosecha,* meaning vintage, while those longer in cask are labeled *Reserva* and *Reserva Especial,* the last even now sometimes being kept too long in wood. All these reds are graded, too, by color from *rosado* through *clarete* to *tinto,* the last being dark-red wines often of considerable finesse, particularly when not too long in wood but with a few years in the bottle. Blending is customary, but occasional wines will carry the word *viña,* which indicates a particular vineyard, sometimes an indication of superior quality. The whites, called blanco, are not usually distinctive, the Spanish preference for old white wines generally holding sway.

The English, who had a liking for and made a trade of the fortified wines of Jerez, were early markets for the improved wines of the Rioja, and when French wine prices rose, American importers took to seeking out the wines first of the Rioja and then of other districts. There was no problem selecting the major shippers, among whom were:

C.V.N.E. (Compañía Vinícola del Norte de España) or CUNE	Bodegas Bilbainas
Marqués de Riscal	Bodegas Franco-Españolas
Marqués de Murrieta	Bodegas Riojanas
Federico Paternina	Vizconde de Ayala
	La Rioja Alta

And there were others to choose from. Britain, Belgium, and the rest of northern Europe have a long tradition of falling back on Spain when the wines elsewhere are high or scarce. Barcelona and the warm beaches and countryside of Catalonia are favorites for chilly northerners. Visitors to the Costa Brava became familiar with the wines—the whites of Alella, north of Barcelona; and from Panadés, to the south; the dry reds of Priorato, from the highlands behind Tarragona; the sweet reds and whites from Tarragona and Sitges; and pink wines from everywhere, usually called *rosado* or *clarete,* depending on color.

Control laws guarding the place names, *Denominación de Origen,* have come into being, but the long tradition of blending wines and the Spanish preference for old whites or dessert wines made a confusion of what was available.

As in so many countries where quantities of wine are made, producers large and small ask what sort of wine is wanted, blending to specification, not concentrating on what the soil and vines can do best. Something called Tarragona Port was marketed for decades, imitating the Portuguese wonders, but the wines were cheaper and much less good; many other wines were imitated, and there is still a tendency to use borrowed names. American importers seeking light, dry wines could find them anywhere, made from Spanish grapes, varieties of the Grenache (called Garnacha), and others. Consequently, a red, a white, a rosé, and a Sangria come from producers in Tarragona, Panadés, and the other regions.

Down the Mediterranean coast are the wines of Valencia, principally the red Benicarlos and rosés. Alicante is farther south and noted for its upland reds, now collectively called Montaña.

South of Madrid is the Don Quixote country, producing light red Valdepeñas; from over by the Portuguese border come the red wines of Toro. It is still the tradition for wealthy fathers to take their sons for a tour of Valdepeñas or the other regions to taste the various wines and make selections of casks of wines to drink during the coming year.

In general, the red wines are best, those from the highlands being lightest and most appealing, but it is sensible to try any new ones that come on the market, because exceptional wines— not just great values—can be found. Summing up, the regions to look for are the following, beginning with Rioja:

Rioja	Tarragona
Valdepeñas	Montaña
Panadés	Toro

There are several to try, and many more to come, but the following should be sought out:

Rene Barbier, Panadés—Imported by Frederick Wildman, New York
Bertran, Tarragona—Imported by Monarch, New York
Marqués de Olivar, Valencia—Imported by Monsieur Henri, New York
Yago, Rioja—Imported by Monsieur Henri, New York
Paternina, Rioja—Imported by Julius Wile, New York
Cruzares, Valdepeñas—Imported by Frank Schoonmaker, New York
Age, Barcelona—Imported by Schenley, New York

The great wines of Spain, however, are the Sherries of Jerez— dry Finos, nutty Amontillados, and the sweet Oloroso and Cream sherries that first became popular in England. The Finos are drunk as apéritifs in Spain, along with a particularly dry version called Manzanilla. These wines are stabilized and strengthened by the addition of brandy, although the dry ones are brought to only about 17% alcohol. Equally intense and dry wines, not fortified but best drunk as apéritifs, are those from Montilla and Los Moriles. Served cool or chilled, they are marvelous with shellfish, oysters and clams, and dishes like *paella.* They are perfect wines with *tapas,* bits of food served with drinks that include slices of mountain ham (*serrano*), almonds, shrimp, cheese, and practically any dish served with a cold mayonnaise as a main course or part of a buffet.

The sweet wines of Spain are famous but unfashionable—the Malagas and various Muscats, and the Malvasia of Sitges. The yellow wine of the Canary Islands—the islands also named the bird—was popular in Elizabethan England, but is no longer. Nor are the many sweet red wines of Alicante, called Tent, or those of Valencia and Tarragona. The unquenchable thirst for Sangria, lightly sweetened red wine given a little zest with lemon and orange slices, may encourage people to try these other wines, chilled or with ice added to them. But they are hard to find.

PORTUGAL

Portugal produces a lot of wine, some four hundred million gallons from nearly eight hundred thousand acres, most of it ordinary, to quench the national thirst, which approaches that of France and Italy and accounts for nearly thirty gallons per person a year. Tourists find them delicious—fresh whites with the many fish, fruity reds with the many stews—yet only a few wines, whose origin and production are controlled, warrant exporting. These are worth seeking.

The most unusual come from the Colares vineyards near Lisbon; trenches are dug in sand dunes, where the Ramisco grape is planted. Wines from this sandy soil take a long time to round out, and have an odd, tannic taste that is popular with the English, but the dune wines are usually blended with others grown in loam, the wines varying widely depending on the blending. All the wines are aged in big vats in a co-operative, and individual owners draw off their wines as they see fit, generally blending one year with another. The Portuguese custom is to label *Reserva* or *Garrafeira* wines kept for several years in bottle, those labeled *Vindima* being sold at once; holding the wines in bottle to round out before sale makes sense, but the holding adds to the cost. From near Lisbon also come sweet whites called Bucelas and Moscatel de Setúbal, and a dry white called Alcobaça, not often seen abroad.

Mostly red wines come from Dão, a mountainous region above the university city of Coimbra and below the Porto country of the Douro. Some white wine is made, much of which goes to lighten the red, made from the grapes used for Porto and from a variety such as the Pinot Noir of Burgundy. The red is full, like a Rhône, and is the Beaujolais or Chianti of Portugal.

The lightest, freshest wines of Portugal, are the *vinhos verdes,* from the north—red, white, and pink—called green wines because they are meant to be drunk young. Most of the wines are bottled before the spring following the vintage so that some secondary fermentation takes place in the bottle. The wine has a little sparkle that is lightly prickling on the tongue. Many of the rosés are carbonated to make them crackling, or slightly more bubbly—but not enough so that they would have to pay the customary high tax for completely sparkling wine.

Vinhos verdes are light in alcohol, not usually more than 10%, and several districts are recognized as producing typical wines in the land between the rivers Douro and Minho, which slopes down from the mountains to the coast. Going north are Panafiel, Amarante, Braga, and Lima; vineyards of Monçao, near the Spanish border, make fuller, fruitier white wines than are considered typical. Vines are everywhere, mostly trained on trees and trellises. There are some fifty thousand growers tending small plots, but a few large companies—Fonseca, Mateus, Lancer's—export most of the wines and focus attention on the pink ones. This is changing somewhat, California experts actively advising on the wine making and looking to a future when the whites and reds will become as popular as the rosés.

The great wine of Portugal is Porto, red wine from the steep valley of the Douro, whose fermentation is stopped by the addition of brandy. There is a white Porto made in the same way from white grapes, but drier, an effort being made to popularize it as an apéritif. It was called Port for centuries and England was the principal market, but the wine was so extensively imitated that it was decided to name the wine Porto to distinguish the genuine, which is shipped from Oporto. "Ruby" is the youngest of the range, fading with age to become "Tawny." In exceptional years Vintage Porto is made, to be drunk thirty years or longer after the vintage—after dinner, with walnuts. Great years to seek are '34 and '35, '42 and '45, '47 and '48, '50 and '55; 1960 is coming along nicely. They are bottled when about two years old, usually in London; they develop a heavy sediment and need careful decanting and are usually sold young, so that they can mature in cellars of houses where they are to be drunk and no jolting journey will dislodge the deposit. Blends of different years are also bottled early and handled the same way, but these "Crusted" Portos rarely have the distinction of the vintage wines.

Off the Atlantic bulge of Africa lies Madeira, where the fermented wine is stabilized with brandy, then stored in hot rooms called *estufas*, where the wines practically bake. These were the wines sent out on sailing ships, the sea change and the rocking giving the wine an extra something. They are named after the white grapes from which they are made, the driest being Sercial, which is drunk as an apéritif, like Fino Sherry. Almost as dry is Verdelho, then comes golden Boal, or Bual, which can be drunk with dessert, and finally, Malmsey. A light, clarified kind is called Rainwater. All of them are blended and none of them are fashionable, although Madeira is used often in cooking—or rather, low-priced imitations are.

So many Portuguese wines are being imported these days, especially rosés, all blended wines, that there is little point in specifying shippers. Generally the wines are well made, with few distinguishing characteristics, but look for the following at less than three dollars:

Vinho Verde   Dão   Colares

THE EASTERN MEDITERRANEAN

GREECE

Greece produces a hundred million gallons of wine a year. Most of it is flavored with *retsina,* resin, which makes the wine taste like turpentine, and what isn't resinized is usually sweet. Things aren't all that bad, because large companies and large co-operatives are finding overseas markets for something like ten million gallons in northern Europe and the United States, there's an Institute of Tasters that checks on the wines the way the *Consorzi* do in Italy, and you even get to like the white retsinas with souvlaki and the marvelous, lemony Greek stews; after a time you almost convince yourself that there's nothing better with lamb.

The big peninsula of the Peloponnesos, west and south of Athens, produces a quarter of the wines, one of the main producers of dry whites of Santa Laura and Santa Helena being the big co-operative of Patras. Reds include unctuous Mantinea and dark Nemea, but main production is in the sweet, rich, and costly Mavrodaphne. Dry, white Hymettus comes from Attica, south of Athens; passable reds come from the North, in Macedonia; but the legendary wines come from the islands.

Crete produces some dry reds. Rhodes has a dry white called Lindos. Samos produces mostly sweet wines, some fortified, from Muscats. The wine of Santorin is often dry; the sweet wine from that island is usually called Vino Santo. There are others, from Lesbos, Naxos, Lemnos. Some of them may begin to appear here, but the wines with brand names are the ones to expect, from such firms as Cambas, Achaia-Clauss, and the Société Hellénique—and from the co-operatives.

CYPRUS

One of the earliest wines known was that from the island of Aphrodite, a sweet wine made for festivals honoring the goddess of love. It came to be called Commandaria by the Knights Templar, who were given the island by Richard the Lion-Hearted in the twelfth century. The grapes used are the red Mavron, which makes a dark rosé called Kokkinéli; two reds, called Affames and Othello; and the white grape Xynister, from which come the dry wines Aphrodite and Arsinoe. Blended together, they make the sweet dessert wine and a large variety of fortified wines akin to the Sherries of Spain. The wines are said to be those introduced into Madeira, into Hungary's Tokay region, and into Sicily to make Marsala. There are some 100,000 acres of vineyards, untouched by the Phylloxera; there is extensive development along modern lines, with the planting of French varieties. Keo is the principal shipper; imported by Charles Morgenstern, New York.

ISRAEL

Vineyards in Israel were reconstituted before the turn of the century by the Rothschild family, and with independence were turned over to various co-operatives. Traditional sweet wines of middle Europe are made, but recent efforts have concentrated on dry wines from the best French and Rhineland grapes, with marked success. The wines are remarkably low in price and well distributed, but largely ignored because the popular idea of kosher wines is that they are sweet. Dietary laws require only that the wine be pure and unadulterated, which makes one hope that someday all wines will be kosher. Rishon-el-Zion is the principal co-operative, but at least a score of others produce wines, the one named being the most regularly imported—through its own agency, Carmel Wines, New York.

THE WESTERN HEMISPHERE

―――◆◆◆―――

California

New York and the East

Latin America

CALIFORNIA

Three bottles of wine out of every four we drink come from California, the best of them coming from vineyards near San Francisco. The North Coast counties of Napa, Sonoma, and Mendocino form a region above San Francisco Bay, while another, below the suburban sprawl, can be lumped together to include the South Bay counties of Monterey, San Benito, Santa Clara, and Alameda. Some of the vineyards are older than a century, but the best of them have been planted in the great European varieties by the last couple of generations. As in Alsace, the best wines are marketed by grape names.

The climate is almost Mediterranean, too hot in summer and scarcely cold enough in winter to give the grapes a necessary dormant period, although on certain exposures the climates of Bordeaux and Burgundy and the Rhineland can be approached. Whatever is lacking in soil or exposure is made up for by techniques that have been developed for grape selection, vineyard care, and controlled vinification—improvements that are revolutionizing wine making all over the world. Some experts claim that shy-bearing grapes such as the Cabernets and Pinots produce wines too small to warrant the great effort they demand, and too little wine.

The experts point out that attention should be paid to varieties bearing substantial quantities, that Chenin Blanc and Folle Blanche, Sylvaner and Traminer produce wines often superior to their European counterparts from along the Rhine or the Loire; Nebbiolo and Barbera do better than in Italy. Merlot and Malbec have not been planted enough. Pink wines from the Grenache Rosé equal those made anywhere. Zinfandel and Petit Syrah produce wines extraordinary and unique; Gamay Beaujolais is excellent; Napa Gamay is delightful.

True this may be, but Cabernet Sauvignon and Pinot Noir produce the best of the reds. Pinot Blanc and Chardonnay, Sauvignon Blanc and Johannisberg Riesling produce the best of the whites.

There is a shortage of all these varieties, although planting has doubled in the past decade. The law states that only a majority of the wine must be from a specific variety in order to so label it for the market. While the best growers believe that at least 75% of a wine should be from a particular grape if it is to carry the name of the variety, many are hard-pressed to meet that standard. Many of the large companies are, like their counterparts in Bordeaux, big shippers who buy grapes or wines, blending and tending them to maturity.

There is also confusion about the names. Years ago, the Sylvaner was called "Riesling" on wine labels, and the practice continues. The famous grape of the Rhine is called Johannisberg Riesling or White Riesling on labels. There are other examples.

Chenin Blanc is also called Blanc Fumé or Pineau de la Loire, names that are used in France. It's also marketed as White Pinot. The differing names are used in California to set one producer's wine apart from another, but it's confusing.

Authorities of the grape have decided that the Chardonnay is not a Pinot, but the wines are still called Pinot Chardonnay by most. Pinot Blanc is a different grape, quite good, and so labeled.

Then there are Gray Riesling and Emerald Riesling, hybrids that produce pleasant, ordinary wines.

Zinfandel is a grape not known in Europe, but probably related to the San Gioveto of Chianti. In North Coast and South Bay vineyards it produces excellent wines, but elsewhere it is mediocre.

Grape experts have decided that the Gamay Beaujolais is actually a mutation or a special strain of the Pinot Noir and that the Napa Gamay is the true Gamay of the Beaujolais district, in southern Burgundy. Both are pleasant wines, different in spite of the similarity of names.

When tasting, the confusion doesn't matter so long as the wine is good. There's great difference when you buy.

Suppose you'd like to compare a three-dollar Riesling from the Rhineland with its California counterpart; you'll have to make sure to buy a Johannisberg Riesling from a South Bay or North Coast producer. To compare a Sylvaner from Alsace with one from California, you'd have to buy a California Riesling. Don't confuse a White Pinot, which is Chenin Blanc, with Pinot Blanc, which is a Burgundy grape and is not in the same class with a Chardonnay.

For drinking, your best guide is the producer. Those located in the Central Valley produce enormous quantities of low-priced blends that should not be overlooked; many of them are pleasant to drink, particularly when chilled or served with ice, or mixed with soda or fruit juice.

NORTH COAST COUNTIES

The Christian Brothers

This teaching order of laymen who have taken religious vows supports some 175 schools and colleges, mostly through the sale of wines, which are marketed through a distributing subsidiary of Seagram's, Fromm & Sichel. They began making sacramental and fortified wines on a large scale after repeal, sending them to market under somber labels that discouraged all but the most thirsty. They changed the labels a decade ago, just as they changed the emphasis to table wines, particularly varietals, under the aegis of Brother Timothy. A master wine maker, Brother Tim was among the first to raise the quality of blends produced in volume. These generic wines, traditionally masquerading under European names, are now being marketed under brand names, so-called proprietary labels. Such kinds as "Chablis" and "Burgundy" will disappear from the market as soon as consumers become familiar with the new names.

The Christian Brothers have greatly extended their vineyards of varieties such as Pinot Noir and Chardonnay, but buy many additional grapes from independent growers on long-term contract with the order. Some of their wines are nothing less than astonishing, at prices among the most reasonable in California. The generic blends are generally light but good. For no good reason, their popularity in the market is much less than the wines warrant. Maybe it's because of those old labels, although the ones they use today aren't bad at all. There's even a back label, carefully and accurately describing what's in the bottle.

Reds	Whites
about $2	*around $3*
Claret	Chenin Blanc
Napa Rosé	Sauvignon Blanc
	Johannisberg Riesling
around $3	
Zinfandel	*over $3*
Gamay Noir	Pinot Chardonnay
Pinot Noir	Pineau de la Loire
Cabernet Sauvignon	Sylvaner Riesling

Robert Mondavi Winery

Robert Mondavi grew up in the family winery of Charles Krug, named after the man who was supposed to have planted the first grape in the Napa Valley. Mondavi managed the family firm until the early sixties, when the producers of Rainier beer agreed to go into partnership with him, putting up the money for a completely modern winery and almost a thousand acres of vineyard. Few wine makers are as daring, as inventive, or as straightforward as Robert Mondavi, and his wines express that spirit. The best grapes and the best techniques produce the best wines, and his are equaled by few.

Reds	Whites
under $4	*under $4*
Gamay	Chenin Blanc
	Riesling
	Fumé Blanc
around $4	*around $4*
Pinot Noir	Johannisberg
Cabernet Sauvignon	Chardonnay

Inglenook

Now a part of Heublein, Inglenook was one of the earliest producers of varietal wines in the Napa Valley. The company has more than a thousand acres of vineyards. Heublein acts as marketing arm for them and for Allied Grape Growers, which consists of some 1800 vineyard owners. Portions of the wines from Allied are made into a group of generic wines sold under the Inglenook name as North Coast County and Navalle.

Reds	Whites
around $3	*around $3*
Napa Valley Zinfandel	White Pinot
Gamay	Sylvaner Riesling
Napa Valley Gamay Beaujolais	Traminer

Beaulieu Vineyards

BV is also owned by Heublein, the vineyards adjoining those of Inglenook, numbering about a thousand acres. The wines are mostly varietals of high quality, with a Founders Line of varietals carrying house names such as Beaumont.

Reds	Whites
around $4	*under $4*
Cabernet Sauvignon	Château Beaulieu (Sauvignon Blanc)
Beaumont (Pinot Noir)	Riesling Sylvaner

Louis M. Martini

Louis P. Martini produces some of the most reasonably priced fine wines available in the world, being satisfied with a modest profit because he wants lots of people to be able to enjoy what he puts in bottle. His father, Louis M., was the same way. This unenlightened attitude is constantly being attacked by those in the trade who think he is taking advantage of his ability to produce good wines at low prices, casting invidious reflection on his competition. Perhaps more people have discovered good California wines through the Martini bottlings than through those of any other. The family firm owns well over a thousand acres of vineyard, many back in the hills that flank the Napa Valley, and the firm buys many grapes from other growers. The classic varietals are the mainstay of the line, but the company honors its Italian heritage by producing an outstanding Mountain Barbera, some generics, and a Moscato Amabile so light it is available only at the winery.

Reds	Whites
around $2	*around $2*
Mountain Red	Mountain Sylvaner
Mountain Claret	Mountain Folle Blanche
Mountain Gamay Rosé	Mountain Dry Chenin Blanc
	Mountain Riesling

Reds	Whites
around $3	*around $3*
Mountain Barbera	Johannisberg Riesling
Mountain Zinfandel	Mountain Gewürztraminer
Mountain Pinot Noir	Pinot Chardonnay
Cabernet Sauvignon	

Charles Krug

The original Krug came from Germany and went to work for Agoston Haraszthy, the father of California wine, finally setting up in the Napa Valley and training the next generation of wine makers in local techniques, including Beringer and Wente. The Mondavi family took over the winery a generation ago, the young sons of the founder growing up in the winery. They were among the first to determine that dry white wines could be made in Napa, given special methods of preserving acid in the grapes and of keeping the pressed juice cool during fermentation. What was developed has become standard practice in California and elsewhere, their pioneering encouraging further research. The firm believes in reasonably priced wines and markets a low-priced line of generic wines as CK.

Reds	Whites
around $3	*around $3*
Gamay Beaujolais	Dry Semillon
Mountain Zinfandel	Sylvaner
	Traminer

Beringer Brothers

The Beringer brothers came from the Rhineland over a century ago and proceeded to make popular blends that were the pets of Californians for generations. The firm was recently purchased by Nestlé, the vineyards being extended so that Nestlé would have a line of California wines to market along with those of its import branch, Crosse & Blackwell. Some of the old names have been preserved in a line called Cellarmasters Cuvée, the most distinctive being Barenblut and Grignolino. For the most part, concentration is now on a line of varietals.

Reds	Whites
around $3	*around $3*
Zinfandel	Gray Riesling
under $4	*around $4*
Pinot Noir	Pinot Chardonnay
Cabernet Sauvignon	Fumé Blanc

Sebastiani

For more than a generation the Sebastiani family sold wines to other producers for bottling, a practice that ended a little over a decade ago, making available directly some of the best wines made in the Sonoma Valley. Customarily the Sebastianis bought grapes from their neighbors, but by the end of the decade the family will own almost a thousand acres planted in certified vines. Distribution is limited to major markets.

Reds

around $3
Barbera
Zinfandel

Korbel

Major producers of sparkling wines, Korbel has become increasingly interested in table wines. By the end of the decade the firm expects to have something close to two thousand acres in bearing. Many of their wines are generics, blends such as Mountain Red and Mountain White, but a few varietals are coming to market, with more to follow.

Reds	Whites
under $4	*under $2*
Pinot Noir	Gray Riesling
Cabernet Sauvignon	Chenin Blanc

Italian Swiss Colony

Nearly a century ago an Italian grocer turned banker decided to do something about the flood of Piedmontese who had left their vineyards in the wake of the Gold Rush to make their fortunes in California. He set up a co-operative scheme on some 1,500 acres near a town he decided to call Asti, and the outgrowth is Italian Swiss Colony, which markets the wines of more than 150 Sonoma grape growers. This is part of a larger group, the 1,800 members of Allied Grape Growers, which controls a third of California production. All the wines are marketed through United Vintners, a subsidiary of Heublein.

Most of the wines are inexpensive blends, the top line being called Private Reserve; a low-priced line is called Gold Medal; in between is Napa-Sonoma-Mendocino; and there are other lines, plus pop wines. There is talk about marketing varietals from selected vineyards, but there are already a confusing number of wines in the lines. Considering that Heublein now markets BV, Inglenook, and other brands of United Vintners, including Petri, Mission Bell, Gambarelli & Davitto, and Lejon, the need is to shorten lines and reduce the number of brands. As for Italian Swiss Colony, the most interesting wines are the Italian types and the pop wines.

Guild & Cresta Blanca

Some 500 members with ten thousand acres market wines through their co-operative, Guild Wine Company. The group is a leader in experimenting with new varieties, one pilot project being Cresta Blanca Vineyards. This is a co-operative within a co-operative, some fifty members owning about a thousand acres of vineyards in Mendocino County. Marketing of some unusual wines from this group has begun. Traditional varietals and others such as French Colombard, Sauvignon Vert, and Early Burgundy. More will follow, as Guild members develop new and unusual wines from experimental plots—for blends in the beginning, but perhaps as varietals before the decade ends.

SOUTH BAY COUNTIES

Wente Bros.

The Wente family started their vineyards in the Livermore Valley nearly a century ago, with cuttings of Sauvignon Blanc and Semillon from Château d'Yquem. Their Château Semillon, patterned after Yquem, established their reputation; dry wines from those grapes are still among the best they make on the square mile of home vineyard. New plantings in Monterey will increase acreage to 2,500 by the end of the decade and include selected strains of red varieties developed from individual clones, or buds. These certified vines, from their own nurseries, planted in fumigated soil, mark the change that is sweeping through the vineyards of the quality producers. The vines and their grapes are considered to be the best ever developed and are in demand all over the world. Availability is limited now to California growers but will begin to appear in European vineyards before the end of the decade, ushering in a new age of wines that are expected to surpass anything known today. You can taste the first of them from Wente and other producers who are planting the certified vines, which include most of the vineyards now being planted.

Reds

under $3
Gamay Beaujolais
Petite Sirah

Whites

under $3
Blanc de Blancs
Sauvignon Blanc

Concannon

Another of the wine families, like Wente and Martini, the Concannons have nurseries of vines certified to be free of disease. Specially heat-treated vines from the wine college at Davis are planted in what's called mother blocks, and cuttings from these go into foundation blocks. When these cuttings develop, they go into increase blocks, from which come the cuttings to be planted in the vineyards. Only the best strains from the best varieties are worth the effort. Even then, the vines have to be four years in the vineyard before you can make a little wine and get an inkling of what may be in store. The gamble costs about $2500 an acre, and all of it is based on the logic that selected strains of disease-free vines will produce the healthiest of grapes and make the best of wines. Concannon is a leading experimenter.

The family produces reds and whites from some 300 acres of vineyard, bottling a few as special selections. They are so popular in California that little effort has been made to obtain national distribution. They can be found in only a few of the major markets and should be snatched up whenever they appear. Look for their Livermore Dinner Red or White.

Red	White
around $3	*around $3*
Petite Sirah	Sauvignon Blanc

Almadén

More than a century old, Almadén was among the first firms to plant the great European varietals, and was also the first to make wide use of grape names on labels. Now a division of National Distillers, the company has gone into the largest expansion program of all, suburban development having forced it out of the home vineyards in Santa Clara. Four thousand acres have been developed in San Benito County, with some sections up in Livermore; this area will be doubled by mid-decade. The blends called Mountain Wines are something more than two dollars a bottle, with non-vintage varietals at about three, vintage varietals around four dollars. The company made large plantations of Grenache Rosé a couple of decades ago, which produced the first American wine to equal its European counterparts.

Reds	Whites
around $3	*around $3*
Gamay Beaujolais	Pinot Chardonnay
Pinot Noir	Johannisberg Riesling

Paul Masson

A prestigious firm with extensive wineries in Santa Clara, it is now expanding into the Salinas Valley of Monterey County, with three thousand acres in the Pinnacles district and in the area south of Soledad. The wines are marketed by a Seagram subsidiary, and many of them have been introduced into foreign markets, becoming the first to gain much acceptance abroad. There are lines of generics and varietals, but the most interesting are the proprietary wines, such as Baroque. These wines with brand names are a way to avoid generic names, those deceptive borrowings from European geographic districts. Also, the marks are not limited to vague "traditional" tastes of wines. Tastes, instead, come from the grapes and the skill of the wine makers.

Reds	Whites
under $3	*under $3*
Rubion	Rhine Castle
Baroque	Emerald Dry
around $3	*around $3*
Gamay Beaujolais	Sylvaner
Cabernet Sauvignon	Johannisberg Riesling

Mirassou

This is another family firm, which used to sell its production to bottlers but began marketing its own wines when the younger generation of five brothers began to take part in operations. The family manages a thousand vineyard acres, replacing the home vineyards in Santa Clara with certified vines in Monterey, to the south; these will be extended during the decade. Their low-priced generic wines are among the most popular in California, but the varietals are the ones to take note of in any comparative tasting.

Reds	Whites
under $4	*under $3*
Zinfandel	Sylvaner Riesling
Petite Sirah	Chenin Blanc

Gallo

Gallo is the largest of the California producers, marketing well over a third of the wines of the state. They buy the entire output of the two largest co-operatives in the Napa Valley, and much more from North Coast growers and those in the Central Valley. They sponsor many experimental plots as well, and maintain the most extensive laboratory in the business. Type for type, price for price, their wines compare favorably with those made anywhere. The company produces scores of wines, with new ones appearing each year. There are wines with generic names, "mellow" wines whose fermentation has been halted so that some of the natural sugar is retained, flavored pop wines, apple wines, and apple wines flavored with strawberries—the range is enormous. Most of the wines sell for a dollar and change, although some are less. Hearty Burgundy and Chablis Blanc are popular; the newest sensation is Boone's Farm Strawberry Hill.

NEW YORK and THE EAST

Canada

NEW YORK

For most Americans, tasting the wines of New York State is like tasting the wines of eastern Europe: they're good but not quite what you expect. Few of us are used to drinking wines made from the native grapes of Yugoslavia or Hungary; the native American grapes are stranger, while the new hybrids have been so scarce that most people don't even know they exist. Nothing could be better for the wine drinker, because the growers have inferiority complexes about their wines in comparison to those from Cabernets and Pinots, and sell them at low prices to introduce them to the market. Until recently, most of the grapes didn't even have names—only numbers.

Grape growers are forever trying to improve their varieties. Southern vineyards need grapes that develop fruit acids, northern vineyards need grapes that will develop sugar, and both need grapes that will resist disease, yield substantial crops, and ferment smoothly. Frenchmen named Baco, Seibel, Seyve-Villard, and Couderc executed thousands of crosses, each numbered, and the French have named a couple of dozen. Germans and Americans have named others.

One of the most successful, widely planted in the upper reaches of the Rhine and the Danube, is a cross between Riesling and Sylvaner, called Müller-Thurgau. One of the worst is Alicante-Bouchet, which produces a dark wine of little character that is used to color reds that are considered too pale. In between are dozens of others, just beginning to appear on the market.

The pioneer American experimenter with Franco-American hybrids has been Philip M. Wagner, whose Boordy Vineyards in Maryland and western New York State introduced some excellent wines. His cuttings have been extensively planted in the Finger Lakes region, particularly by the Pleasant Valley Wine Company, now part of Taylor's, and Gold Seal. Among the most successful, which are currently available at less than three dollars a bottle, are:

Baco Noir—Wine resembles a light Cabernet when at least four years old. Formerly called Baco No. 1.

Chelois—Planted in lesser Burgundy vineyards; in New York State it develops a light, fruity red wine. Formerly called Seibel 10878.

Baco Blanc—A pleasant ordinary white wine. Formerly called Baco 22A.

Ravat Blanc—Produces a white wine similar to that of Chardonnay; extensively planted in Mâcon. Formerly called Ravat 6.

Rayon d'Or—A fresh white wine with good acidity. Formerly called Seibel 4986.

Seyval—Makes a fresh, dry white wine resembling the Muscadet of the Loire. Formerly Seyve-Villard 5276.

The grapes were once planted pretty nearly exclusively in the Finger Lakes region, mostly around Lake Keuka. There are now new vineyards in the Franco-American hybrids and even some in hardy strains of Pinot Noir and Chardonnay, Riesling and Cabernet, along the Hudson (at High Tor, Benmarl, Hudson Valley Wine Company and at Brotherhood Winery), in Chautauqua County, on the south shore of Lake Erie (primarily at Boordy Vineyards, which is now owned by Seneca Winery). The wines are mostly available in the New York area, but a few get to such distant places as Chicago, Boston, and Washington, D.C.

Somewhat wider distribution is made for the wines from the major companies of the Finger Lakes. The most extensive is Canandaigua Industries, which has vineyards as far away as Georgia and is planning more to the west as far as Texas. The largest firm is Taylor, which owns sizable experimental and hybrid vineyards and buys grapes from many growers under long-term contracts. Its most interesting wines are under the Great Western brand of its subsidiary, Pleasant Valley. Gold Seal was originally the most experimental of the group, thanks to the efforts of a wine maker from Champagne, Charles Fournier, who was the first to plant hybrids from the Wagner cuttings and was most successful with European vines, through the grafting efforts of Konstantin Frank. Frank's family had been brought from Germany to southern Russia by the Czar, where techniques of grafting and crossing were developed. These proved useful when Frank came to the Finger Lakes after the Second World War.

Frank has established his own Vinifera Wine Cellars and offers a small group of exceptional and expensive wines that include Chardonnay and late-picked Johannisberg Riesling.

The strongest believer in native American grapes has been Widmer Wine Cellars, at the foot of neighboring Canandaigua Lake. Probably the best is the white wine from the grape called Delaware. People still like—or are at least curious about—the once-famous Catawba, which has a pronounced, distinctive taste. The company markets mostly blends using some of these grapes with hybrids, brands called Naples Valley, Lake Niagara, and Lake Roselle.

Great Western offers sweetish Dutchess and Diamond, as well as Delaware and a pink Catawba, but mostly blends called Pleasant Valley. Their hybrids are the most appealing, particularly a Baco Noir and a Chelois. There's a sweet white called Aurora, after the grape, which was originally called Seibel 5279. The wine is like those from late-picked grapes in Alsace, although the company calls it a Sauternes type.

Experiment's the thing in eastern vineyards. Wines from the hybrids and hardy strains of European varieties are few and not widely distributed. They are wines to try when you can find them. A selection, including those from small or little-known California wineries, is listed with "A Representative Cellar of American Wines."

Great Western and Taylor

Now a branch of Taylor Wine Company, Great Western specializes in wines from native grapes and hybrids, marketing them separately from the parent company, which concentrates on a long line of popular wines. Taylor manages a thousand acres of vineyard, but most of its grapes come from almost 300 growers in a fifty-mile radius. Pleasant Valley operates on a similar but smaller scale, but taps the more than two thousand acres of hybrids that each year supply Taylor.

Reds
around $2
Baco Noir
Chelois

Whites
around $2
Aurora
Delaware

Gold Seal

American wine districts have drawn people from all over the world, recent generations becoming cellar masters for those who came before. Among these was Charles Fournier, trained in France, who took over management of Gold Seal in the forties and immediately proceeded to revolutionize eastern wines. He began planting hybrids developed by Wagner outside Baltimore; he pressed grapes more quickly and gently than usual so the foxy character would not be picked up from the skins; and he tried to get vinifera to grow. This had been tried without success for three centuries, but a transplanted German from Russia had an idea that quick-ripening root stocks would give vinifera vines a growing season that was long enough to develop resistance to the cold winters. Dr. Konstantin Frank was right, if you were satisfied with small yields. Fournier was, and the new wines were used to improve his champagne blends, with some left over for table wines. Fournier has retired now, but the new generation of scientists are improving all the techniques and even looking for new places to put new vines. In the wines developed by Fournier you can taste tomorrow.

White
under $4
Pinot Chardonnay

Widmer

Originally a Swiss family who began selling kegs of wines to other Swiss along the eastern seaboard, Widmer's Wine Cellars eventually managed a square mile of native grapes scattered along the steep shores of Canandaigua Lake, buying twice as many grapes from growers under long-term contract. Nobody in the Finger Lakes made better wines from grapes like Elvira and Delaware, Vergenne's and Moore's Diamond, nor from the newer hybrids introduced in the fifties. Now owned by a Rochester corporation and by the makers of French's Mustard, the firm is developing five hundred acres in Mendocino, California, with more to follow, thus becoming the first firm to offer varietals from both coasts.

Red

around $2
Naples Valley Red

Whites

around $2
Moore's Diamond
Riesling

CANADA

Ontario vintners on the Niagara Peninsula have been trying for years, like New Yorkers, and with about the same success, but now the big and protected valleys of British Columbia are planting noble vines instead of fruit trees. There's not much chance for an extensive American market, though, the wines being like those of Oregon and Washington and scarcely enough to satisfy Canadian thirst. The wines are worth trying when you are there.

LATIN AMERICA

ARGENTINA

Things are turned around below the equator, so the best wines of the world's fourth largest producer are in cool Río Negro, which lies south of Mendoza. The vineyards lie along the flanks of the Andes, planted by Italians a couple of generations ago by tapping the snow fields with a system of canals. Mendoza itself produces half a billion gallons on half a million acres—as much as Portugal. If you add the coarse wines from the northern province of San Juan, Argentine production nearly equals that of Spain, three quarters of a billion gallons.

Argentines sensibly drink up all the wines of Río Negro, but imports are beginning to come in from Mendoza. The best reds are made from the Malbec of Bordeaux, although other French and Spanish grapes make interesting wines. The Spanish Criolla makes the rosés, European varieties most of the whites. The thing is that the wines are coming in at something under three dollars, when what's needed are wines around two dollars. Still, they are wines to watch for and try . . . when the price is right.

CHILE

With something less than 300,000 acres of vineyards, Chile produces quite a bit more than 125,000,000 gallons, mostly from French grapes planted by an influx of French wine makers over a century ago. The best vineyards lie south of Santiago, in the valley of the Maipo, although other wines come from northern valleys of the Aconcagua and the Maule. They back up to the Andes, protected from Phylloxera by a desert to the north and Pacific breezes that help keep the louse from coming over the mountains.

The first wine I ever tasted in a restaurant was Undurraga Riesling, which sold for a dollar in its bocksbeutel for decades, and now sells for two. The French grapes do better, producing some of the best wines around; if only they were around more.

Laws controlling wines are superb, the class called *Gran Vino* having to be six years old, *Reservado* four, *Special* at least two. They will be sensations on the market if the Chileans can solve export problems, with which they get little help from importers who have vested interests in European producers or from American producers who feel they have quite enough competition. A deal is pending between the 17 largest producers and Seagram. The wines should be tasted whenever they can be found.

MEXICO

There are lots of vineyards south of the border, around Ensenada, in Baja California; in Chihuahua and Coahuila; and farther south, around Aguascalientes and Querétaro. Even on the highlands the climate is like North Africa; consequently the reds tend to be heavy and the whites tend to be bland. They are worth trying when you are there, and continuing improvement in method may make some of them worth exporting. A few come into the Southwest from time to time.

The Wine Trade

SHIPPERS
IMPORTERS
OTHER ELEMENTS
OF THE TRADE

SHIPPERS

Shippers buy wines from growers for maturing, blending, and bottling, then ship them to importers around the world. In Bordeaux and other regions, shippers may buy the bottled wines from famous vineyards, merely acting as exporting and selling agents, but their main business is blending wines under their own labels, which are supposed to vary little from year to year.

Through the years, many shippers have acquired vineyards, either to stabilize their blends or to gain exclusive marketing rights of famous vineyards. Some shippers own so many grapes that they are almost growers who ship their own wines, for example the distinguished firms of Louis Latour in France and Antinori in Italy. Equally, some growers buy so many grapes that they are in reality shippers, for instance Paul Masson in California. Most shippers, however, buy wines and blend them, marketing them under firm and brand names.

Some shippers bottle separately small lots of exceptional wines when they have a discerning audience willing to pay the price. Others don't bother, being cynical about the sophistication of the consumer. The very process of blending, adding a little of this and a little of that—even water and flavoring or coloring matter—is called "sophistication" by the trade. For cheap wines, no harm is done. Many fine shippers take great pains with wines bearing their brand names or regional ones. Other shippers use such designations for dumping wines in markets where anything alcoholic is acceptable; more than half the wines on the market are such bottlings. Good wines, blended or not, are a small fraction of what is offered.

Shippers are noble members of the wine world nonetheless, preserving distinctions from vintage to vintage and place to place. There are hundreds of distinctive wines in every price range. Only cheese offers anything like such variety, and for every cheese there are a hundred wines.

The American market is a special problem to shippers. The long sea voyage demanded sturdy wines. Past generations found that high alcoholic content protected wines from the rigors of travel. Americans became accustomed to strong wines, because shippers and importers concentrated on those with 12% alcohol and more. Wines light in alcohol, those that didn't travel or changed character as a result of shipping, came to be reserved for European markets. As a consequence, the range of wines offered in America was narrow, and relatively few came to be known. This demand concentrated on a few wines that became famous—Chablis and Pommard from Burgundy, Médoc and St. Émilion from Bordeaux—and prices were inflated.

Improved wine-making techniques, developed over the past decade or so, have made possible the shipping of wines light in alcohol, but the fashion for strong wines remains. The old and classic taste of Burgundy is light and fruity, for example, but Americans think of Burgundy as full and hearty, so Burgundies are made to meet the style to which we have become accustomed.

At the same time, Americans are impatient to drink the wines they buy, unwilling to cellar wines for the decade or so required for instance by the great château-bottlings of Bordeaux. Cellaring a wine for a long time ties up capital, and the result is that many wines today are fermented quickly so that they will be drinkable within a year or two of purchase.

Shippers go along with such market pressures, even reinforcing them, tailoring wines to demand. More Beaujolais and Chianti are sold than these districts can produce, so shippers are busily trying to develop interest in other districts. In the past decade, Muscadet, from the Loire, has become popular; as have Pouilly-Fuissé and Mâcon Blanc, from Burgundy; and Portuguese Rosé. Wines from the Côtes-du-Rhône are beginning to find a market, as are those from Alsace.

To preserve distinctions and avoid bastardized names that have become overpopular, leading shippers have begun to develop brand names for wines that once carried geographic names that could be used by anyone. The distinguished Burgundy shipper Louis Latour, with several small vineyard parcels in the township of Aloxe-Corton, blends the wines to produce a brand called Corton Grancey, a wine better than many Cortons produced from a single vineyard. The excellent Burgundy shipper Joseph Drouhin offers Soleil Blanc and Soleil Noir, blends of wines from southern Burgundy superior to many a Mâcon Blanc or Mâcon Rouge. Such wines from good shippers should be searched for.

The American tendency to insist on wines only from famous vintage years has been responsible for much false labeling. Shippers have not been able to sell non-vintage wines—blends of different years—until recently. Vintages on low-priced wines are ridiculous pretension, a wine costing less than $3 generally being drinkable when marketed.

Many shippers, such as Louis Latour, also own vineyards. (See lists under "Shippers.") These wines are often separately bottled and are the prizes in the line; the shipper will be proud of his ownership and will announce it prominently on the label. Many shippers have exclusive contracts with vineyard owners, relationships that may have continued over generations, and such wines will be given special attention and care; this may or may not be noted on the label, may or may not mean an inflated price for the wine.

Many growers who sell directly to brokers and importers may become shippers by handling wines of other growers, blending such wines into their own or bottling them separately. They are shippers only incidentally. The French indicate this by requiring that such growers call themselves "Négociants-Propriétaires" on their labels when the wine is blended with production from others, a particularity of no importance when the wine is good. In effect, many of the best California producers are shippers in this sense, buying wines to augment their own stocks.

Everything depends on how well the shipper blends. Good shippers blend skillfully, vastly increasing the quantity of good wine available and taking a small profit for their trouble. Some are so consistent that all their wines have a family taste, which may or may not appeal. Others are careful to preserve distinctions in their line of wines. Some offer a few outstanding wines in a long line that may be generally mediocre. Those with the best reputations are listed here by region and district, offering wines that are fairly widely distributed in the United States.

BORDEAUX SHIPPERS

Perhaps the most distinguished group of shippers in the wine trade are those of Bordeaux, several firms being centuries old. Traditionally they buy through brokers called *courtiers,* who periodically offer the wines of the various châteaux. There are some brokers who specialize only in bottled wines, but the majority offer wines that are still maturing in cask, the selling unit being a *tonneau,* which eventually provides about 100 cases of twelve bottles each.

Shippers on a preferred list can buy the *Première Tranche,* the first slice or offering of a particular château. The figure is usually 10% below the announced opening price and becomes available to those who have bought the wine consistently. Most shippers start buying a château at the market price, eventually working themselves into a position to buy the first slice. For this reason, it is hard for outsiders to break into the market; the great châteaux have been tied up for decades.

There is always a large supply of secondary wine available in Bordeaux, and from this the shippers produce their blends. Each shipper has his own idea of what the various markets seek, and blends his wines to a "style" or taste that he considers best. Consequently, there will be marked differences in the regional wines from one shipper, who may be concentrating on the market for light wines in France; another, who may be focusing on fast-maturing wines for the American market; still a third, who may be making full, soft wines for the Scandinavian or the Swiss market; and another, who may be making wines that develop slowly for the English market. Some shippers make lines of wines for each market. The English dominated the Bordeaux trade for centuries, and many quite-French firms have English names. Alsatians and Germans entered the trade during the past century, those firms having German names. Americans have begun to enter the trade, but the names of such firms are carefully French. Members of the various shipping firms, like their wines, are at home in any country, and the largest firms conduct tours in half a dozen languages. Most of the firms were originally located along the Quai des Chartrons, near the docks of Bordeaux, but the trade is now so extensive that some of the largest firms have established cellars and offices elsewhere in the city and in the surrounding countryside.

Trade is orderly. *Courtiers* offer samples of wines from the various châteaux, price fixed by demand, amount depending on what the shipper has bought in preceding years. Nobody is allowed to corner the market of a reputed château. Even when the shipper is the owner, a large portion is offered to the trade so that the wines of the château will be assured a wide distribution.

Château Lafite commands the highest prices, perhaps 80 on a scale of 100 for a new vintage, closely followed by Mouton-Rothschild, which may command a price of 70 on the scale. Other great châteaux—Latour, Margaux, Haut-Brion, Pétrus, Cheval Blanc, and Ausone—will cluster around 50 or 60. After the first eight châteaux, prices drop quickly. Other top-rated classed growths, perhaps a dozen, will rate 40 on the scale, a score more may rate 25. Château-bottlings of the next hundred vineyards may rate about 15 on the scale, so they would cost one fifth or less than the leaders. The spread of prices is wider than the differences in the wines. The greater the wine, the longer it will take to mature, perhaps 20 years in the case of the best châteaux, only 10 in the case of wines from "petits châteaux." Demand for wines from the little châteaux is increasing, because few customers are able to keep wines for a couple of decades or want to pay the price or tie up capital.

Shippers contract for wines even before the vintage, when stocks are low or customers demanding, but most sales are made in the year following the vintage, while the wine is still in cask. Bottling takes place during the third year after the vintage, some of it then being shipped to those who want to mature the wines in their own cellars. Inevitably, much of this wine is drunk at once by the impatient, long before it has reached maturity. Shippers, and even château owners, hold back as much of a good vintage as they can afford, in order to preserve the wine and to take the great profits that are assured for mature bottles. This is risky, because a following great vintage may depress the prices for an older wine. The trade is carefully ordered to minimize this danger.

The big shippers rarely buy more than a fraction of a good vintage, the rest being sold through brokers directly to customers around the world: retail and hotel chains and wine wholesalers. But what the shippers buy helps establish the prices for the wines. Shippers take good care of the wines they buy, but the same wine bought through brokers may be mishandled, so that a château's wines may taste fine in London but terrible in New York, or even vary from shop to shop. The best way to judge a good shipper is to try the low-priced regional wines he offers, and then try his little châteaux. If these are good, chances are that even more attention has been paid to high-priced wines from classed growths. Listed below are selections from leading shippers in the Bordeaux trade.

Shippers	Inexpensive around $4	Moderate around $5	Reasonable over $5
B & G	Cantegrive	Médoc	Margaux
Calvet	Graves Monopole	Bordeaux Supérieur	Saint Julien
Chanson	Cordon de Bordeaux	Ch. Rausan-Ségla	Ch. La Garde
Cruse	Bordeaux Rouge	Cruse Monopole	Saint Julien
Ginestet	Graves Extra	Haut-Médoc	Ch. de Marbuzet
Harvey	Ch. La Rode	Ch. Pailhas	Ch. Plantey
De Luze	Club Claret	Saint Estèphe	Ch. Paveil de Luze
Moueix	Médoc	Ch. Taillefer	Ch. Fonplegade
Kressman	Thalrosé	Entre Deux Mers	Ch. La Tour Martillac
Nicolas	Bordeaux Blanc	Médoc	Saint Émilion
Eschenauer	Ch. St. Germain	Ch. Olivier	Ch. Voigny
Sichel & Fils	Cave Bel Air	Médoc "Ruban Rouge"	Saint Julien
Schröder & Schyler	Ch. Jacquet	Ch. Vieux Robin	Ch. Kirwan

Bordeaux was the first of the great regions to establish markets abroad, and for their overseas customers they also obtained wines from other regions. The leading firms eventually developed lines of wine from Burgundy, the Loire, Alsace, the Rhône, and elsewhere, establishing offices and other facilities in the other regions when necessary. Bordeaux shippers today handle a large share of wines from other regions, and these "foreign" bottlings are looked down on, the idea being that Burgundians know Burgundy best, and so on. This is scarcely true, for many Bordeaux shippers have been established in other regions for generations, Sichel or Calvet or Cruse being as knowing about Burgundy as many local firms.

With their substantial resources, the Bordeaux trade has recently been active in developing interest in other wines, to take the pressure off the scarce Classed Growths of Bordeaux and the Great Growths and First Growths of Burgundy. With oceans of good wine available—ten million cases of Côtes-du-Rhône, a million cases of Mâcon Blanc—they see the world market pioneered by French table wines slipping away to other countries. The wines they are now introducing—the Blanc de Blancs, Bordeaux Supérieurs, and regionals from other districts, even wines with brand names—are sound wines at reasonable prices. They are some of the best buys on the market, and should not be overlooked.

There are scores of shippers in Bordeaux, many of them focused on European markets, who supply regional wines and château-bottlings to this or that local importer or distributor, or directly to retailers and chains. Others are shippers with headquarters in other regions, with branches in Bordeaux to provide wines to complete the lines of importers they supply. Château owners have also set up shipping branches. Haut-Brion, for instance, established Granvins when it was purchased by the American banker Clarence Dillon, because the former owners had been at odds with the Bordeaux trade, which had refused to handle old stocks of the château wines. The Mouton-Rothschild interests have set up a firm they call La Bergerie, to handle experimental wines and those from young vines.

The leading firms are listed here, wines from all of them being available in the United States.

Barton & Guestier

B&G is one of the oldest Bordeaux firms, founded in 1725 by an Irish Protestant whom the Barton family still calls French Tom. His descendants married daughters of the Johnston family, a shipping firm that also had Irish connections. The men of the family have always been partly schooled in England, like so many of the children of the Bordeaux trade, and have married English girls. French Tom took for partner a member of an Huguenot family from Brittany named Guestier that settled in Bordeaux, and all these connections made it possible to weather the Revolution and Napoleon, wines being shipped to Ireland when they couldn't be sent to London.

The firm owns some splendid Classed Growths: Léoville-Barton and Langoa-Barton in Saint Julien, Grand Pontet in Saint Émilion, and others, including holdings in Beaujolais and the Rhône. Long-time ties with Seagram, which controls the shipping firm, have made the wines well known in the States. And not always well liked, because the prices for the regionals have always been high, as much as three dollars for the non-vintage Bordeaux blends Prince Noir and Prince Blanc and the similar Burgundies Prince Rouge and Prince d'Argent. That was at a time when château wines were comparatively underpriced; B&G regionals were widely distributed and advertised, introducing thousands to simple wines that were pleasant enough to encourage further exploration. In blind tastings, B&G regionals generally seem to be light and soft.

IMPORTER: San Francisco—Browne Vintners (Seagram subsidiary)

H. & O. Beyerman

Founded in 1620 and still in the same family, its principal wines are Château Cantemerle, one of the most underrated wines of the Médoc; a secondary wine from a dependent vineyard marketed as Royal Médoc; and perhaps the best of the unclassified vineyards, Château La Tour de Mons.

IMPORTER: Banfi Products Corp., New York.

Birkedal Hartmann & Co.

Founded in the eighteen nineties, this family firm does a large business in Scandinavia and Canada and ships wines to small importers around the country, including O. I. Groosman in San Francisco, Stacole and Co. in Chicago, and James Moroney Inc. in Philadelphia.

Calvet

Calvet has the largest stocks of wine in Bordeaux, maturing nearly three quarters of a million bottles of Classed Growths and two million bottles of regionals. Much wine is shipped in cask to various parts of Europe, but a zealous member of the firm has figured that if the sales for a year were all bottled, there would be ten million of them and they'd stretch to Stockholm, which is a major market. In the cellars there are 6,000 storage casks. The firm suffered a horrendous fire in 1967, but the underground cellars and its wines were unharmed.

The firm was founded on the Rhône at Tain-l'Hermitage, then established in Bordeaux in 1823, in Burgundy in 1890. Another of the family firms, the older generations continue to guide the younger ones, who spend much of their time visiting the 98 countries where Calvet is sold. Calvet has been unfortunate in its American importers, who have been giant distillers not primarily concerned with wines, but new affiliations may change this. Young members of the firm have been eager to experiment with the light, fresh blends, understandably being cautioned against change by their elders, who don't want to risk their vast market. The rebuilding after the fire preoccupied the firm for several years, but now some attention is being paid to the American market.

IMPORTER: New York—Carillon

Cordier

The Cordier family began buying Bordeaux vineyards at the end of the past century and now owns more than a square mile of them, the largest holding in Bordeaux. Most famous are the two Saint Julien châteaux of Gruaud-Larose and Talbot, and the reconstituted Saint Estèphe vineyard of Château Meyney; in Sauternes, there is Château Lafaurie-Peyraguey; in Saint Émilion, the Clos des Jacobins. The family gives all these holdings enthusiastic attention, which extends to three vineyards in the primarily white-wine district of Premières Côtes de Bordeaux, where they are experimenting with red-wine grapes. There are various regional bottlings. A pair of these last is named after a handsome 18th-century family residence, Labottière, while another pair is called Plaisir de France. The family also owns vineyards in the Loire district of Sancerre.

IMPORTER: New York—Leonard Kreusch

Cruse et Fils Frères

The fifth generation of the family is now running the firm founded in 1819. One of the largest and most prestigious in Bordeaux, Cruse still follows the old rule that six of its twelve directors must have tasted every wine selected by the company. Vineyards owned by the family include the Classed Growths of Château D'Issan and Pontet Canet, which is the largest rated vineyard of the Médoc, producing 20,000 cases; others include Taillan and the white wine of La Dame Blanche. The regionals are consistently excellent and include not only Bordeaux and Burgundy, but also Rhône and Loire, with a traditional label that shows a round engraving of a vineyard surrounded by a laurel wreath, overprinted in black.

The firm has had the same importer for ninety years.

IMPORTER: New York—The Joseph Garneau Company

A. de Luze & Fils

Baron Alfred de Luze arrived in New York from the Swiss wine district of Neuchâtel in 1818 and set up a wine-importing business down on William Street. Two years later, success indicating he ought to ship his own wines, he established quarters on the Quai des Chartrons. His descendants run the firm, which owns Château Cantenac Brown, a full, fine Classed Growth that produces some 7,000 cases; another Margaux, Paveil de Luze; and others. They hold a permanent stock of nearly half a million gallons in vats, 15,000 casks of wines, and an average of three million bottles.

IMPORTERS: Boston—S. S. Pierce
Miami—Shaw-Ross Importers

Louis Eschenauer

The market for French wines boomed after the Napoleonic debacle, and to satisfy it a young man from Alsace came to Bordeaux in the 1820s and bought into a little firm. After a succession of German and Russian partners, Louis Eschenauer and five generations of his descendants became sole owners, only to sell a majority to an English firm in 1960. The John Holt Group of Liverpool had acquired the superb Classed Growth of Rausan-Ségla, and this joined other Eschenauer holdings and exclusivities:
Ch. Smith Haut Lafitte, Graves
Ch. Olivier, Graves
Ch. La Garde, Graves
Ch. de Lamoureux, Margaux
Ch. Roc Saint Michel, Saint Émilion
Ch. Branaire Ducru, Saint Julien
Ch. Voigny, Sauternes

Eschenauer is the third-largest shipper of Bordeaux, but most of its regional wines, which are marketed under brand names, are sold in England. Such brands as Camponac for Bordeaux, Marquiset for Haut-Médoc, Saint Simiac for Saint Estèphe, and Lancillon for Saint Émilion may begin to appear here. So may the Alsatian wines of Jules Muller, a firm recently acquired by Eschenauer, and the Burgundies of Caves de la Reine Pédauque, one of the largest Burgundy shippers.

IMPORTERS: New York—Julius Wile & Sons (Standard Brands)
New York—Austin Nichols
San Francisco—Bercut Vandervoort

Ginestet

One of the leading Bordeaux shippers, Ginestet is the owner of seven vineyards: the great Château Margaux, the Classed Growth of Cos d'Estournel and the Bourgeois Supérieur of Marbuzet in Saint Estèphe, La Fleur-Pétrus and Petit-Figeac in Saint Émilion, Petit-Village in Pomerol, and Tastes in Sainte-Croix-du-Mont. More important, perhaps, is the active acquiring of exclusive rights of distribution for other châteaux carried on by the grandson of the founder, Bernard Ginestet. The young head of the firm now has more than sixty such exclusivities from various Bordeaux châteaux, all together a formidable marketing group that greatly simplifies shipping and can result in considerable savings to wine buyers. It's impossible for an individual to keep track of the names of the châteaux, but when the reputation of a great shipper stands behind a number of them, buying is made easier.

Ginestet is also interested in marketing non-vintage wines. Vintages are a matter of importance only in the greatest wines, which are those that can live a long time. A wine that takes a dozen years to mature may be drunk too soon if the vintage isn't on the label. For wines ready to drink when marketed, vintages scarcely matter. In good years, one or another characteristic may stand out, to make for variety in the tasting. In unbalanced years, blending a light vintage with a full one will result in a non-vintage wine better than either. The public has been slow to accept non-vintage wines, but will come to do so by the end of the decade, as more and more of them appear on the market. Some of the best will come from Ginestet, which prides itself on its regionals, but knows they can be better if vintages are put on wines only of exceptional years. The aim is to follow the practice of the Champagne producers, who may make vintage wines perhaps every other year, reserving stocks of exceptional vintages to improve those of lesser years. Meantime Ginestet concentrates on providing a range of château-bottlings; Classed Growths, Great Growths, and Bourgeois Supérieur from the famous districts; and sound wines from the little-known areas of Bordeaux.

IMPORTER: New York—Kobrand

France Vinipole

The Champagne firm of Saint Marceaux changed its name and entered the Bordeaux business when the Harvard-trained owner of the famous Pauillac-Château-Pichon-Longueville, Comtesse Lalande—was named chairman and director. He is W. A. Mialhe, who also owns Château Siran in Margaux, part of nearby Château Palmer, and others called Dauzac and Ile Margaux, all producing wines now shipped by the renamed firm.

IMPORTERS: New York—F. Wildman & Sons
New York—Austin Nichols
San Francisco—Bercut Vandervoort

Les Fils de Marcel Quancard

This family firm owns a number of minor vineyards—La Tour St. Joseph, Le Calvaire, Bordes—but the most interesting is the largest, 125 acres of Château de Terrefort, on a hill between the Côtes of Bourg and Fronsac. The vineyard was dynamited out of the limestone rock, and then earth was brought in. The Romans trenched in this manner at Saint Émilion, but not with explosives and not on such a large scale.

The firm supplies wines to many retailers and distributors.

IMPORTER: New York—Excelsior

Pierre Jean

Vineyard owners for generations in Saint Émilion, they set up the family shipping firm between the world wars to develop the market for two of their excellent vineyards, Lapelletrie and Trimoulet. Added to these are a Montagne-Saint-Émilion, Vieux Château Negrit, and a Bordeaux Supérieur, Château Beaulieu, as well as some full bodied regionals.

IMPORTER: New York—Dreyfus, Ashby (Schenley subsidiary).

Quien & Cie.

The fourth generation now runs this century-old firm, which did much of its original business in Asia. Wines go to thirty countries today; the United States is its fastest-growing market, import arrangements being made state by state.

IMPORTERS: Washington, D.C.—Kronheim
Jersey City, N.J.—Renfield
San Francisco—Chrissa
Boston—Sheridan & Fitzgerald
and several others.

Nathaniel Johnston & Fils

Founded by a Scot in 1734, the firm shipped its first wines to the United States in time to celebrate independence in 1776. Lafayette took charge of their promotion in 1808, calling them the best in France. His popularity assured that of the wines. The seventh, eighth, and ninth generations now direct the firm, which does a large business in Lafite, Latour, Margaux, Haut-Brion, Mouton, and other Classed Growths, especially the reconstituted Saint Julien vineyard of Ducru-Beaucaillou and the Saint Émilions of Figeac and L'Angélus.

Their regionals have unaccountably waned in popularity here, perhaps partly because the firm has concentrated on the English market. They were one of the first to market a non-vintage blend at a low price, Grand Chartrons Red and White, which is gradually being discovered as one of the best of the low-priced wines.

IMPORTER: New York—Austin Nichols

Ed. Kressman & Cie.

Founded a little over a century ago and presently managed by a namesake of the founder, the firm thought of calling their blends "Monopoles," a name that has so appealed to the trade that almost every shipper has his own versions. The company does an enormous business in these wines, selling to various regional importers in the United States through an agent.

The family owns Ch. La Tour Martillac and Kressman-La Tour in Graves, as well as vineyards in Alsace. Each year, the firm selects a Saint Émilion château and offers it under the name Les Palmes. The idea is to point up the selection by the firm, rather than the château itself, whose name also appears on the label. A Médoc is similarly marketed, under the name Le Lauréat. The present Édouard Kressman is an articulate spokesman for the minor châteaux of the lesser-known districts, such as the firm's Château La Pierrière from Côtes de Castillon, near Saint Émilion, and Château Grand Chambellan from Lalande de Pomerol. He thinks that the hundreds of millions of gallons of lesser Bordeaux can be vinified in the modern way to produce fresh young wines that will appeal to markets around the world. The white of La Tour Martillac, for instance, is aged in large oak casks like those used on the Rhine, reducing contact with the air and preserving a fruity, clean taste. The trade is watching the results of the Kressman experiment—and market response—if not like wolves watching sheep led to pasture, at least like a bunch of puppies lurking at the kitchen door at suppertime.

Various importers.

Schröder & Schyler

Sixth and seventh generations direct the firm that claims to be the oldest in Bordeaux, founded by two gentlemen from Hamburg in 1739. They are owners of Château Kirwan, a Classed Growth of Margaux that the firm chooses to bottle in their cellars on the Quai des Chartrons, in Bordeaux. This is a break with tradition that some people feel has a bad effect on the wine. The label carries the phrase "Mis en Bouteilles au Château."

The firm offers a good collection of reasonably priced châteaux, none of which are château bottled. Reds include Vieux Robin, a Médoc; Respide, a Graves; d'Arthus, a Saint Émilion; and Savoie, a Bordeaux Supérieur. The white Graves is Malleprat, a white Bordeaux Supérieur is called Jacquet, and a Sauternes from a vineyard near Yquem is called Bellevue.

As befits one of the few firms that survived the Revolution, it is conservative. The tradition of château-bottling, after all, came along nearly a century after the firm's founding. A curious vintage rating is published in one of the firm's booklets. Its highest rating is "Very Good," and only four vintages are so considered: 1928, 1945, 1953, and 1961. Rated "Good" are such vintages as '55 and '59, '62, '64, and '66. Only "Fair" are '60, '67, and '69, while considered "Mediocre" are '63, '65, and '68. It is the most conservative of ratings in this hyperbolic age.

IMPORTER: New York—Dreyfus, Ashby (Schenley subsidiary).

Sichel

The Sichel family became merchants of wine early in the past century, founding their first firm in Mainz in 1857 and others in Bordeaux, London, and New York before this century began. Each of the firms today is owned and managed by cousins, the fourth and fifth generations of descendants of the founder, with the sixth coming along. The children are schooled in France and England, with stints in Bordeaux and on the Rhine and further training in other parts of their vinous empire. Unlike the Buddenbrooks of Thomas Mann, whose rise they paralleled, the Sichels have flourished, perhaps because each firm operates independently but co-operates easily, seeming to have the odd notion that business can be as pleasant as the wines they sell, with good years and bad and a certain conviction that wines, at least, are getting better all the time.

Peter M. F. Sichel, best known to Americans because he is the traveling head of the North American firm, served in counter-intelligence during the war, along with Frank Schoonmaker and Gregory Thomas, the wine buff now head of Chanel. The Nazis had confiscated all the Sichel Rhineland holdings, and at the end of the war, the two Sichel friends worked mightily with nobody knows how many others to have the properties restored. They were. The Sichels seem to have a capacity for making friends, and for years an odd piece of furniture or a painting would be recognized by one or another U. S. Government official who had been entertained by the Sichels, who would then take steps to see that it was returned. Partly out of gratefulness for government efforts on his behalf, Peter served for several years, first in Washington, then as consul in Hong Kong. A further reason was that Peter was due to head the American firm and disagreed with the organization of the senior partners. When they were due to retire, Peter took charge, disbanded the complicated distribution system, and arranged with Schieffelin & Company to handle the wines in the various markets, leaving him free to choose the wines and be their ambassador across the country.

The Sichel organizations have always bought wines and blended them for the markets, their principal brand being Blue Nun, but there has always been a brisk trade in the estate-bottlings of the Rhine and the Moselle, and in the château-bottlings of Bordeaux. Through the years, Sichel has acquired interests in such Classed Growths as Château Palmer and Château d'Angludet, and exclusive contracts with others, such as the châteaux of La Croix de Millorit, Mont Célestin, and Pierredon. More significantly, they have been leaders in offering selections of affordable wines of little-known districts or types, and using simple brand names or grape names for regional wines. Perhaps the most unusual of these is the light, soft white wine from the Graves district called Wan Fu. Peter's years in Hong Kong made him a devotee of Chinese food, and he devised the wine of a thousand happinesses to go with it.

The Bordeaux branch run by Peter A. Sichel is pursuing still another route to good wines at low prices; not only selecting wines, but buying grapes and making wines from them at the family's new Cave Bel-Air—by a new process, *macération carbonique*.

Now there are only a couple of hundred châteaux—some say three hundred, others hold out for five hundred—whose vineyards are worthy of traditional Bordeaux techniques, which call for two years in wood and three or more in bottle before they begin to be ready to drink. Most of the 30,000 growers have vineyards that average five acres and make wines casually, traditionally—and often poorly. These are wines bought for shippers' blends. Peter A.'s argument is that Bordeaux shippers should do what those in Alsace, Champagne, the Rhône, and elsewhere do: buy the grapes and make wines by modern methods so that the wine is drinkable after less time in cask and bottle—say two years for whites and three for reds, maybe even less. What's more, they should be picked while there is plenty of fruit acid in the grape and only enough sugar to make wines that may not be even 12% alcohol. What's still more, some of the natural sugar could be left after fermentation (it's called residual sugar) so that the wine doesn't taste too sharp.

Well.

Well. Well. Well.

The old cry in Bordeaux was that shippers were ruining the wines by blending driblets of good wines with floods of poor stuff. Shippers cut off the peaks to fill the valleys to make *la grande cuisine,* an old wine maker once said, pandering to public taste, which is low, cashing in on the reputation of the few top châteaux, which is empyrean. Peter A. thinks it's possible to make the poor wine better. Bordeaux had better do so, as the Common Market becomes commoner and low-priced French wines are forced to compete with those from Italy and even Central Europe, Spain, and Portugal. Bordeaux, says Peter A., can make wine more easily than any other region, in more variety, by using *macération carbonique.* Essentially, this means letting grapes ferment for a few days without crushing them, then completing the fermentation away from stalks, seeds, and stems so that the wines have little tannin. If they don't have much color, as a result, then add some older wine made by traditional methods. Don't try to make silk purses out of sows' ears, my grandmother would have said, and Peter A. would have agreed with her. When he started to buy grapes, all his charm was needed to talk the first grower out of an acre's production. In 1972 they produced a hundred thousand gallons of Cave Bel-Air wines—Claret and Sauvignon Sec. Peter A.'s wines will be on this market when Peter M. F. thinks it's time; meanwhile, noting that Americans like the California pattern of naming wines after the varieties from which they are made, he is busily introducing Blanc de Blanc Sauvignon, Pinot Chardonnay, and Pinot Noir Gamay. There's also Corbières, one of the best districts of the Midi, where most of France's table wine comes from. And there will be more to come, as the prices for classic wines go higher. Sichel is a house to watch.

"With classified growths in Bordeaux going through the roof and Burgundies becoming out of reach we are all looking for other situations," says Peter M. F. "I think that you will find that Beaujolais with village names will find their rightful place here to replace some of the extremely expensive Burgundies and I think you will also find that people will be going into selling

Côtes-du-Rhône, possibly even some of the village wines there, as well as Corbières and all kinds of other things. There will be an evolution certainly in the next couple of years. I believe this will ultimately bring down the prices for highly rated Bordeaux and Burgundies, in a market more and more receptive to values for money in wine."

IMPORTER: New York—Schieffelin

BURGUNDY SHIPPERS

Unlike those of Bordeaux, the great vineyards of Burgundy are divided up. The shippers have great difficulty getting their hands on sizable stocks, because many owners sell their wine direct—to restaurateurs and hotel chains and buyers for distributors and retail stores.

A grower with a few hundred cases of wine from a Grand Cru or Premier Cru has no trouble selling his wines in good years. He is stuck in bad years, of course, so he must compensate by charging high prices for his good wines. Shippers use this predicament as pressure on a small grower, agreeing to take his wines in bad years for blending in exchange for his good vintages. Even so, the shippers get little of the good wine, so most of their business is done in regionals—wines that carry the name of the district or township.

Some idea of the problem can be grasped when you consider that the largest vineyard of the Côte d'Or, the Clos de Vougeot, has some sixty owners, each of whom makes wines in his own way. The vineyard is a scant 125 acres and produces scarcely 12,000 cases of wines in a plentiful year—a size and production topped by many a Bordeaux château.

What's more, the wines that have made Burgundy famous come from the single slope of the Côte d'Or, a scant thirty miles in length, and amount to hardly 12,000 acres of vinelands. The great vineyards are in a narrow band of soil where the flatland meets the hill, but the township lines cut across them at right angles, extending far out into the flatland, where only ordinary wines are made. By adding a great vineyard name to that of the town, even these flatland wines can masquerade as being like their distinguished neighbors. Such wines make up the bulk of what the shippers sell.

Since there is so little wine to work with, one might assume that there are few shippers in Burgundy, but the region probably has more per vineyard acre than any other in the world. Many of them are in Beaune, and there is page after page of listings in the Beaune phone book. A closer scrutiny will show that many firms have the same phone numbers, because a Burgundy shipper may use a different name for each country he supplies. A block in one of the towns has offices of several shippers on it, all with entrances to a common cellar underneath, all of it owned by a single firm. The owner has to be careful to show his overseas agents into the right office, so that a midwestern importer, for example, won't cotton to the fact that his major competitor is getting wines from the same source. Only the labels change.

Burgundy shippers were of greater interest to Americans a decade ago, when many of their wines were three dollars or so a bottle. Now even the regionals run above four dollars. For no good reason, the township of Pommard has become the most popular of all those in the southern half of the Golden Slope, the Côte de Beaune, and the prices now hover around ten dollars for a vineyard wine, nearly seven for a township wine. If a Pommard is offered for much less, there is probably something wrong with the wine, or the wine is a fake.

Most wine buyers have long since lost interest in paying six dollars for a Burgundy regional, even in those rare instances when a shipper offers a particularly good bottling with a town name. The wines have been priced out of the market.

Shippers have turned their attention to southern Burgundy's abundant supply for moderately priced wines, with Beaujolais taking the place of the now astronomically priced vineyard and township wines of the Côte d'Or. Lower appellations of Aligoté for whites and Passe-tous-Grains for reds (a blend of Pinot Noir and Gamay) are being offered, often for less than three dollars. When they are called Blanc de Blancs or Pinot Noir Gamay under a shipper's name or a brand name, they may cost slightly more, because better wines are used in the hope that a customer will be encouraged to try other wines in the line.

The smaller Burgundy houses concentrate on vineyard wines and perhaps blends of these, labeled Premier Cru and occasionally Grand Cru. A few township wines—popular Pommard or less-known Santenay for reds, Meursault or Chassagne-Montrachet for whites, southern Burgundies such as Beaujolais and Pouilly-Fuissé—may be added to complete a line.

To give some idea of low-priced wines still available from Burgundy, those from a few of the leading shippers are mentioned, to be used as standards of comparison. These wines might be tasted against similar bottlings from the large Bordeaux firms that maintain establishments in Burgundy, and for further exploration, a list of major Burgundy houses offering a line of Bordeaux regionals is included.

Bouchard Père & Fils

One of the many houses that have been established by the venerable Bouchard family, the firm offers a group of distinguished township wines and estate-bottlings, but few low-priced ones. A red and a white called Bouchard Monopole sells for a little more than three dollars, a Beaujolais Supérieur for a little less.

IMPORTER: Hartford, Conn—Vintage Wines (Heublein)

Louis Jadot

A shipper of outstanding reputation, the firm owns vineyards in Beaune, Corton, and Chevalier-Montrachet, but also markets estate-bottlings and vineyard and township wines from elsewhere in Burgundy. A good shipper like Jadot will see that only the best wines will be marketed under his own name, downgrading a vineyard wine to a township wine or even a regional when necessary. A vineyard may be so divided that owners may produce too little for marketing, so a good shipper may buy several such lots, combining them so that there will be at least a thousand cases or so to market, not as an estate-bottling but as a wine from the vineyard. Several lots from various First-Growth vineyards in a township may be combined and marketed as a Premier Cru of the town, while lots from various towns may be marketed

SHIPPERS 151

as Côtes-de-Beaune-Villages. Jadot does this with great skill, but the operation is expensive. The only wines now available from him that fall within the price ranges of this book are:

Beaujolais   Beaujolais Blanc   Mâcon Blanc

IMPORTER: New York—Kobrand

Joseph Drouhin

A highly regarded Burgundy shipper, Drouhin offers a distinguished range of Burgundies, but only Beaujolais and brands called Soleil Noir and Soleil Blanc are under $4.

IMPORTER: New York—Dreyfus, Ashby (Schenley subsidiary)

Mommessin

A large shipper, Mommessin has several regional distributors, offering mostly high-priced township wines, along with Beaujolais for less than $3.

Piat Père & Fils

One of the largest shippers of French wines, the firm was founded in Beaune in 1849, with other installations in Mâcon. It has always offered a long line of low-priced wines, but now only a few of the southern Burgundies are under four dollars. For a sampling, try Beaujolais Vallières and the white Mâcon Viré, each about three dollars.

IMPORTER: New York —Monsieur Henri (Pepsico subsidiary)

F. Chauvenet

A firm that developed an enormous market for its sparkling Burgundy, Red Cap Chauvenet, offers a well-made line of township wines and some estate-bottlings, only a few of the southern Burgundies being now offered for less than four dollars. For a sampling, try Chauvenet Rouge, Les Amandières, a non-vintage red; and Bourgogne Aligoté Grand Pavois, a dry white, each around three dollars.

IMPORTER: New York—Austin Nichols (Liggett and Myers subsidiary)

BURGUNDY/BORDEAUX SHIPPERS

Some of the large Burgundy shippers maintain installations in Bordeaux, and vice versa, mostly offering modestly priced regionals from both areas.

Burgandy shippers in Bordeaux:

Bichot
Bouchard Père et Fils
Chanson
Chauvenet
Jouvet
Mommessin

Bordeaux shippers in Burgundy

B&G
Calvet
Cruse
Lichine
De Luze
Sichel

RHINELAND SHIPPERS

Like Burgundy shippers, those in the Rhineland have to fight for the wines of hundreds of vineyards made by more hundreds of growers, who like to sell directly to the trade. German shippers are forced to concentrate on regionals, with high-priced estate-bottlings on the side.

Unlike Burgundy shippers, they have a lot of wine to call on, all of it white. The best of it is Riesling, from Rheingau and Moselle vineyards—which might be considered similar to Burgundy's supply from the Côte d'Or. Much of it is Sylvaner, from Rheinhessen, Rheinpfalz, and Franconia—which might be likened to the production of southern Burgundy.

Frankenwein, from Franconia vineyards around Würzburg (which is up the Main river from the Rhine) are light whites marketed in stubby flasks called bocksbeutels. Moselblümchen, Zeller Schwartze Katz, and Kröver Nacktarsch come from the Moselle and form a second group. With Liebfraumilch, they form a trio of regional wines. Shippers offer all of them, along with town wines from each district. For further explanation, including *Grosslagen,* see page 81 ff.

The German shippers do very well with all this, putting out neat lists of all the names, even preserving distinctions in the wines. But the real differences come from the flowery Kabinett wines and the progressively fruitier Spätlesen and Auslesen. They are nice to drink during the day, with smoked or salty snacks instead of meals, the wines getting progressively sweeter until you end up with fruit and the Spätlesen, capping the climax with a luscious Auslesen served by itself.

You can thus compare the different grades of wines from one shipper or taste a single grade from various shippers, most pleasure seeming to come from having several bottles in succession with several people, over a period of time. It's a nice way to while away an afternoon by the water, or to watch a sunset, or to pass a summer evening. The wines should change; after drinking them a few times, you'll discover the fascination of German wines, which is quite unlike the drinking of any other.

Much of the wine is bought at auction, and many of the large growers ship their wines themselves, so that importers have their own lines of German wines. One of the best of these is Madrigal, imported by Kobrand, and their line of regionals, which is priced around four dollars, is an excellent standard of comparison. Of the other brands, the best known is Blue Nun from Sichel, similarly priced. Once having selected a standard of comparison, the thing to do is to shop around.

Annheuser & Fehrs

Vineyard owner Annheuser joined with Fehrs to market his wines over a century ago, the Annheuser family becoming sole proprietors after the death of Fehrs. The grandson of the founder, in his thirties, received much of his training in business with the American branch of the family in St. Louis, where his uncle is a partner in the beer firm of Anheuser-Busch. The wine branch has always been close to the American market, largely concentrating on producing good regionals and offering estate-bottling from the family holdings. These include Kreuznacher Steinberg and Schloss Bockelheimer Königsberg, two of the best vineyards of the superior but little-known region of the Nahe.

IMPORTER: New York—The Joseph Garneau Company (Brown-Forman division)

Deinhard & Co.

Hanns Christoff Deinhard was engaged in the wine trade sometime in the seventeenth century, but it took several generations for the descendants to get around to keeping regular records, which begin on May Day of 1794. To make up for the lapse, the firm puts Hanns's picture on all its table wines. Offices are in the cathedral town of Koblenz, where the Mosel meets the Rhein, so that members of the firm can dart off south to get to their share of Bernkasteler Doktor or rush east to their holdings on the Rheingau; just in case, they have a branch office in the middle of the Rheingau vineyards, in Oestrich. Their regionals have been popular for a dozen generations, indicating a certain understanding of Rhine wines and the people who drink them.

IMPORTER: New York—Julius Wile, (Standard Brands subsidiary)

A. Steigenberger

Owners of a chain of hotels, including the Frankfurter Hof, the firm is the largest user of quality wines in Germany. They offer a line of regionals and vineyard wines from the stocks bought annually for the hotel chain.

IMPORTER: New York—Munson Shaw (National Distillers subsidiary)

IMPORTERS

Importers supply one bottle of wine out of every five drunk in this country, a figure that hasn't changed much for the past couple of generations. Importers who elected to stay in business during Prohibition sold a certain amount of sacramental and "tonic" wines. In the six hectic years between repeal and *Blitzkrieg,* they busied themselves getting back into legitimate trade and working up a little distribution. People who'd been to Europe or who'd come from there drank most of what was offered.

Chianti got a big play in spaghetti joints. Except for Champagne among sparkling wines, Vermouth among aromatic wines, Sherry among fortified wines, all of which sold themselves if at all, there wasn't call for much else. The generation of importers since World War II worried themselves about sating America's raging thirst for scotch. They offered lines of wines, but their distributors showed more interest in fast-moving forty-dollar cases of whiskey than in slow-moving twenty-dollar cases of Chablis (Shabliss, what's that?). A wine drinker's map of the United States looked like *The New Yorker*'s one showing Boston, Washington, and Florida as suburbs of New York, with splotches for Chicago, San Francisco, and Los Angeles, and some space in between.

History shapes importers, importers shape shippers:

The American consumer? He talks dry but drinks sweet. You couldn't sweeten up the Liebfraumilch a little, could you?

Only a thin upper crust drinks wine. How about calling that rouge of yours Château something?

Wine snobs drink labels and famous names. Why not put a couple of gold crowns on it and call it Château Lafite Brion?

You can't sell wines without vintages big on the label. Let's call your blend Cuvée 49. That's a great year and nobody'll notice it's just a vat number.

Importers had learned through bitter experience. A young, fresh wine meant to be drunk within months of bottling might languish on shelves for a year. Any vintage less than great had to be given away. A great château-bottling that would take two decades to mature would be drunk four years after the vintage. Wines of less than 12 per cent alcohol were called watery. It was almost impossible to get anybody to taste little-known wines, let alone buy them. Put a new spirit on the market and you could sell a few thousand cases the first year; a new wine might sell a few dozen.

Wine drinkers were almost a secret society until the sixties. It was a pity. Fine Bordeaux and Burgundies were selling for three dollars or so in 1965, wines that cost two to three times as much in the early seventies. They were golden days for a few. Tasting groups burgeoned in Boston and Washington, Chicago and Dallas, on the Coast and in New York. First with public-relations campaigns, then with a little advertising, the big regions and their importers began dipping into metropolitan markets.

Watching prices and sales, importers of the seventies began trying to have new thoughts about wines and those who drink them. The flood of Sangria from Spain and the pinks of Portugal and the pop wines of California appealed mostly to youngsters, and maybe mostly because of price. But all the traditional wines of France and Italy were selling as well, disappearing from the shelves in weeks instead of months. There simply wasn't enough Bordeaux or Burgundy to go around—not among the known wines, anyway—so the only thing to do was to raise prices and seek out new wines. But this was scarcely possible. Supplies were short.

In the five years around the decade's turn, only 1970 produced a large crop and many great wines, the best reds of which won't be drinkable before the end of the decade. The years before and since have produced small crops, to send prices soaring. Even unknown wines can be sold for three dollars a bottle when famous wines have risen to ten dollars or more, and particularly when customers don't trust wines under two dollars, figuring they can't possibly be any good. A good quantity of good '73 has helped to stabilize prices.

The new decade was a fine time to introduce new wines, particularly if they were fairly palatable, and in 1972 probably more new wines were introduced than in the preceding decade. Devaluation and higher shipping costs raised prices across the board, and all the new names confused buyers. No matter. People were drinking wines. The major importers were slow to move, adding carefully to their lists. Then suddenly everybody was getting into the wine business, big corporations and fly-by-nighters, willing to take small profits on large volume and to spend money on advertising. They were buying everything in sight—not just wines but wineries—and making contracts with new suppliers such as the state monopolies and co-operatives. Such groups presented difficulties but had large quantities of good ordinary wines. As the market widened, interest spread from high-priced, exceptional wines to low-priced, simple ones.

Even people with lots of money resisted paying four dollars a bottle. Postwar travel had introduced millions to fresh inexpensive, young wines. To find them, a scramble began. We are in the midst of it today.

Old-time importers familiar with world-wide business began to extend themselves. The wines they now bring in set a standard by which to judge the wines imported by newcomers to the business. Some familiarity with the traditional importers helps a wine drinker to find his way among all the new bottles on the market. The principal old-line importers are presented briefly to guide those seeking a few good bottles among the many.

Importers with national distribution are mostly concentrated in New York, the major port of entry. Many of them maintain offices on the West Coast and in other cities. Together they account for most of the wine entering the country. In numerous cases, however, their markets may be less than country-wide. Ports such as Boston, Baltimore, New Orleans, Houston, Chicago, and San Francisco developed a wine trade, with local importers supplying the surrounding areas; many of them have retained their franchises. While national importers are dealt with in this book, wines listed from them may be locally available under the name of another importer. The wines will be the same.

Austin, Nichols

Now a subsidiary of Liggett & Myers, Austin, Nichols was for years one of the old-timers among the distributors that grew after repeal. They had a focus on wines that began to sharpen with the fifties, as they gradually extended distribution along the East Coast, concentrating on wines at a time when other distributors were busy with liquors. When they headed west with their wines, they had a large selection of château-bottlings of Bordeaux and estate-bottlings of Burgundy and the Rhineland. Now in charge of sales is Abdalleh Simon, born in Baghdad, then schooled in England and Beirut, who is helped in buying as well as selling by a young English expert, Gerald Asher. They are a formidable combination, with warehouses in Bordeaux as well as New York, an extensive knowledge of wines and markets, and resources to invest when they think they should. Their listing of Bordeaux stocks occupies three pages in the telephone-book-like catalogue of importer offerings. As an example, here is a selection of their *petits châteaux:*

under $4	around $5
Bonnet, Bordeaux	Greysac, Médoc
Picque-Caillou, Graves	Loudenne, Médoc
Guiraud-Cheval Blanc, Côtes de Bourg	La Tour Pavillon, Médoc
Despagnet, St. Émilion	La Bécade, Haut-Médoc
	Haut-Corbin, St. Émilion
	Dassault, St. Émilion
	La Louvière, Graves

Banfi Products Corp.

Two brothers born in Connecticut were sent to the Italian branch of the family for schooling, eventually returning to set up an importing firm to bring in Italian wines. The firm is run today by the second generation of Marianis. No firm brings in such a variety of Italian wines. They represent a couple of dozen Italian houses, including the Barolo of Borgogno. Borgogno owns much of the hill of Canubbi, which is reputed to be the best in the district, but the wines cost between five and fifteen dollars a bottle. The firm's most popular Italian wines are the Sicilian wines of Segesta, the Frascatis of Marino, and the Lambrusco of Riunite, as well as Chiantis from five different houses, ranging from two to four dollars a bottle.

Banfi has long since branched out. Their Bordeaux shipper is Lalande for regional wines; they stock some forty château-bottlings. Their Rhineland shipper is Langguth, who provides them with an equal number of estate-bottlings along with the regionals. They have a representative collection of Burgundies and Rhônes, but, like many importers, they find the wines hard to come by. They are the largest importers of Swiss and Austrian wines.

REDS

under $3
Segesta Sicilian
Soderi Chianti Classico
Riunite Lambrusco

around $3
La Rioja Alta Reservo "904"
Borgogno Grignolino
Sartori Bardolino

around $4
Lalande Les Chartrons
Le Tuquet (Graves)
Château Royal (Haut Médoc)

WHITES

around $3
La Rioja Alta Blanco
Langguth Piesporter Riesling
Schwanberg Neuseidler Spätlese

around $4
Langguth Piesporter Goldtropfchen Spätlese
Chatenay Neuchâtel Goutte d'Or
Chatenay Johannisberg du Valais

Browne Vintners

The import arm of Seagram's, Browne Vintners distributes the French wines of Barton & Guestier, the Rhineland wines of Julius

Kayser, the Italian wines of Brolio, Ricasoli, and Bersano, as well as the California wines of Paul Masson and the world's best-known Champagne, Mumm. B&G have been the best-distributed of French regionals for decades, because of the immense quantities of spirits placed in trade channels each year by Seagram, just as Paul Masson is the most widely distributed of American producers; Seagram overseas business has also made it possible for Paul Masson to pursue world markets, introducing American wines in such places as Germany and Hong Kong.

B&G is so familiar as to be almost ignored by people who have become interested in wines; the prices for their regionals have always seemed to be slightly higher than many others available and even on a par with inexpensive château- and estate-bottlings, and while Americans seek out brands in most things, they tend to reject them when it comes to table wines, properly assuming that unadvertised bottlings will offer more value. In comparative blind tastings, however, B&G bottlings are generally among the most popular, the large volume of sales making it possible for the firm to acquire excellent stocks for their blends. Prince Noir and Prince Blanc are non-vintage Bordeaux blends, Prince Rouge and Prince Argent are their Burgundy peers, and at less than four dollars they are likely to be the most palatable of wines in places where selection may be limited. B&G Rhônes, Côtes-du-Rhône, and Domaine de la Meynarde are around three dollars, for example, and can be the best buys available, as are the various Beaujolais, particularly their Château de Pizay and their Château de Pizay-Morgon. The firm controls some particularly distinguished Bordeaux châteaux: the Saint Juliens of Léoville-Barton and Langoa-Barton, the Saint Émilion of Grand Pontet, La Tour Blanche in the Médoc, and Cantegrive of the Côtes de Castillon.

The Barone Ricasoli of a century ago developed the proportions of grape varieties to be planted in Chianti vineyards and even the vinification techniques used today. His Brolio and Ricasoli Chiantis are deservedly the most famous. The Bersano wines of the Piedmont have similar stature. The Rhine wines of Julius Kayser, of which about a dozen are usually marketed, sell for not much more than three dollars and merit consideration in any comparative tasting; the firm's headquarters are on the Moselle, and some tasters prefer their Moselles to their Rhine wines from the other regions.

IMPORTERS

Reds	Whites
under $4	*around $3.50*
B&G Médoc	B&G Blanc de Blancs
B&G Mâcon	B&G Muscadet
Brolio Chianti	Kayser Moselblümchen

A separate company called Bon-Sol has been set up under the Seagram banner to import low-priced blends from Europe and South America, in regular wine bottles, but also in a 50-ounce size, which is about the size of a magnum, or double bottle. The wines of Bon-Sol will be the first inexpensive imports to be widely distributed in the large size, and the idea is that it will compete with half-gallon jugs, the lesser quantity permitting the offering of a better wine at the price of the popular jugs. Bon-Sol thus hopes to attract a lot of jug-wine buyers.

Still another Seagram division has been set up to market the wines of the fourteen major producers of Chile, giving a wide-range national distribution. Many of the wines will sell for less than four dollars and should offer good value in an expanding market.

Carillon

Carillon Importers was started after World War II by a couple of businessmen familiar with the wine trade, the business growing with the interest in wines. The founding partners, now deceased, acquired a few lines over the years, and when Liggett & Myers was seeking areas of expansion, the small company was purchased and began growing at once. They have Alsatian wines from the large firm of Dopff, Greek wines from the major shipping firm of Achaia Clauss, the tremendous range of Bordeaux from the large firm of Calvet, and a line of German regionals from the highly regarded firm of Hallgarten. High prices of French and German wines have sent them searching among Italian shippers, and they now represent Fazi Battaglia of Verdicchio, Bertani of Verona, Giannozzi of Chianti, Alberini of Lambrusco, and Contratto of the Piedmont. As in Italian opera, a quintet is a good thing to start with, and gives a good idea of how quickly firms respond today to demands of the market place. A decade ago, a firm in the wine trade might have taken four or five years to open up a new area. Companies like Carillon now do it in so many months.

Reds	Whites
around $3.50	*around $3.50*
Bardolino Bertani	Soave Bertani
Achaia-Clauss Mavrodaphne	Fazi-Battaglia Verdicchio |//
Reds	Whites
Calvet St. Émilion	Dopff Gewürztraminer
Calvet Latour Montagne	Marnier Lapostolle Ch. de Sancerre

Crispin Wines

A Belgian who involved himself in the steel business in Houston became annoyed at the rapt attention paid to high-priced wines and decided the best thing to do about it was to concentrate on sound wines at low prices. He set up an importing company in 1971 to handle the wines of a large combine called Unifrance, which ships much wine in bulk, and under its banner he arranged for importing the bottled wines of various French co-operatives. Some forty such groups from regions all over France are now represented by Crispin. The wines vary widely, but they are worth trying when they can be found.

Crosse & Blackwell

America's surging interest in wine encouraged Nestlé to buy the venerable house of Crosse & Blackwell as the decade began, setting it up as a wine importer focusing on France, Italy, and Switzerland for openers. The list includes a rounded selection of regionals and estate- and château-bottlings from a dozen shippers, among them Moueix and Dubroca of Bordeaux, Jaffelin and De Villamont of Burgundy, Louis Sipp of Alsace, Visah of Spain's Valdepeñas, and Calissano of Italy's Piedmont. With emphasis on quality wines in a growing market, there is an opportunity to bring in unknown wines and find a market for them, a focus for the new firm that makes it worth watching.

Reds

under $4
Calissano Freisa d'Asti
Ch. Dillon (Haut-Médoc)
Jaffelin Bourgogne du Chapitre

Whites

around $3
Jaffelin Bourgogne du Chapitre
Sipp Riesling Grand Réserve
Castel Byria—Cortese

around $4
Gay Fendant La Guérite
Johannisberg La Floronde—Valais

Dennis & Huppert

Founded in 1950 by two partners familiar with the European wine trade, the firm quickly built up a New York trade which was gradually extended into the South and the West. The company was purchased by a New Orleans company, Sazerac, which bottles a famous local cocktail. Perhaps the most interesting wine in a list that changes with a certain frequency is that from the Argentinian producer Bodegas y Viñeros López, whose headquarters are in Mendoza. A line of full-bodied wines is called Estanciero, while a line of light wines is called Pampas. They retail for less than $3.

Dreyfus, Ashby

Between the wars, Michel Dreyfus sold scotch on the continent and Champagne in England before coming to New York in time to provide wines for the World's Fair of 1939. The various pavilions needed agents to clear their native wonders through customs and get them through the maze of docks and warehouses and red tape to the world of the future around the trylon and perisphere. Many of the restaurateurs knew Mike from Europe, and those caught here by the war or those who decided to stay and bring haute cuisine to a populace hungry for it continued to need Mike to get wines for them. By the late forties many of these men had fanned out through the country, and Mike sold his firm to Schenley to simplify distribution, remaining as head of the independent division. A polyglot group trained by Mike now runs the company.

Dreyfus has been called the last of the wine salesmen in the old tradition. Dapper as a boulevardier, gracious as an Edwardian prince, shrewd as a banker, he would enter a restaurant and stop for a drink at the bar, paying for his single drink with a five-dollar bill—a little something to encourage the bartender to pour what Mike was importing. Seated at his table, he would order a bottle of wine, even when alone. "When you're in the business, never order a half bottle," he'd tell his salesmen. "Not only does it show stinginess, but it implies that you can't even afford a bottle of wine. Restaurant people are great gossips, so never let them think that you are anything but prosperous. And never finish the wine; always leave some for the waiter. He's your salesman, and how can he learn to know your wines unless he tastes them?" Sometimes he'd order a competitor's import, and when the owner or wine steward would ask him what he thought of it, as invariably happened, he would say it was good, so graciously and in such a tone that the questioner would know that Mike really didn't think it was as good as one of his own wines. A master of the put-down-by-approval, he would at the first opportunity send over a bottle of his own wine, saying it was a new shipment or a new vintage and asking the restaurant people to tell him what they thought. He would always sign for his check, paying promptly when the bill came in, because restaurateurs are always short of cash. He would tip the waiters separately, and there was always a five-dollar bill for the steward and usually another for the captain. Tips for lunch —perhaps a chop and salad—might be twenty dollars; he'd build up his check by sending a bottle of his own wine to a party at a nearby table, on the flimsiest excuse. He'd notice they were ordering veal; he'd have the steward say, "And please try this bottle that's good with veal, with Mr. Dreyfus' compliments." "Even the clientele of a restaurant can be salesmen for you," he'd tell his staff, "and they need education, just like the waiters."

To spread the gospel of wines, he was instrumental in starting and supporting various tasting and dining groups, the Chevaliers de Tastevin and the Wine and Food Society; among others, and a charity or social affair could scarcely be held without wines from Dreyfus, Ashby. As a result, he "started" many wines in this country, introducing Pouilly-Fumé from the Loire, then Muscadet. When other importers began bringing in wines from those districts, he realized he'd made a mistake. What he needed to guard his market was exclusivity. The next wine he brought in—an unknown rosé from Portugal—was introduced with a brand name, Mateus, and in a few years it became one of the top sellers in the land. There are dozens of Portuguese pinks on the market, but few to match Matoose, as it's called by the hoi polloi, in the trade and out, or Mah-tay-oosh, as it's called by the particular.

Mike was one of a handful—Schoonmaker, Sichel, and Lichine were others—instrumental in developing the American palate for good wines during the postwar decades. His company—like Wildman & Sons, Munson Shaw, and Julius Wile—gave an English touch and a personal tone to a business that had once been dominated by beer and booze. The rest of the trade was always mystified as to how Mike sold wine where no wine was known before, but his secret was simple. He set quotas. In a drawer of his desk was a blue examination book, one of those that students write their finals in. Each page was devoted to a wine, states listed down the column, years listed across the page, a decade ahead. Let's say Mateus sold two cases in Montana last year. When the mood hit him, Mike would get out the blue booklet, think a moment, then jot down for Montana a quota of three cases for next year, five for the following year, ten for the year after that. Each state had to meet its quota. It was as simple as that. Salesmen were known to spend hundreds of dollars to sell a few cases, and there were rumors that they often bought up small quotas themselves. And there was always the fear on the part of distributors that failure to meet Mike's quotas could mean the loss of one of the popular Schenley whiskey brands. After all, what's a couple of cases of wine when you might lose the franchise for a thousand cases of scotch? In the trade, that's called clout. Mike's best weapon, however, was his way with his salesmen—restaurant people and diners—and his taste. Past fifty, a man begins to taste sweet, it's said, finding dryness even in wines full of fruit or those with residual sugar. Mike never did. Even when he retired in his seventies, he was discovering wines sharp with acidity and well balanced with tannin, so that young ones tasted fresh and full and sharp, and those with the potential for aging would round out into clean, silky, or velvety delights. Perhaps his greatest contribution to the American wine trade has been his championing of small and unknown clarets from the less-known vineyards of Bordeaux, his popularizing of them encouraging others to follow his example.

Dreyfus, Ashby Selections

Reds

around $3
Château Beaulieu
Ch. Savoie
Côtes-du-Rhône Red

around $4
Soleil Noir
Beaujolais-Villages
Hermitage Red

Whites

around $3
Soleil Blanc
Sylvaner
Ch. Jacquet

under $4
Traminer
Muscadet
Neuchâtel

Dulong Importers

In 1972, just in time to celebrate the hundredth anniversary of its sister firm in Bordeaux, Dulong Frères, a new company, was set up in New York to bring in simple French wines in half gallons. Dulong Importers introduced Écu Royal, a line of five wines; a dry red Claret and a soft Country Red, a dry Blanc de Blancs and a soft Country White, and a partly dry Grenache Rosé. They were sensations at four dollars, opening the market for other regional blends from other parts of France and from other regions of Europe. The line has quickly expanded to include a dozen Bordeaux châteaux- and estate-bottled Burgundies from such domains as those of Prince de Mérode, Bachelet, and Lignier. Bottlings in regular sizes, all with the Dulong brand, include the following:

Reds	Whites
around $3	*around $3*
Côtes-du-Rhône	Muscadet
Beaujolais	
Corbières	
around $4	*around $4*
Beaujolais Brouilly	St. Véran
Château de Carignan, Bordeaux	

Excelsior

When a retailer begins selling wines, he wants to bring them in direct, bypassing importers and their wholesalers and their markups. This was crucial before and after World War II, when importers were concerned with spirits, so two refugees from Europe set up a wine-importing firm in 1939. One of their tasks was to clear lots of wines for retailers—one hundred cases or a thousand—handling the details of registering brands and clearing shipments through customs. Such wines were good buys for customers, and many's the wine that became known through this channel. Other importers performed this service for favored retailers, if only to encourage them to stock their spirits, but Excelsior did the job particularly well.

The original partners died, and successors gradually developed a line of specialty wines—ones that were not produced in enough quantity to be sold generally, but only to stores that had built up a trade with customers who bought not names but unique bottlings. Many of the wines came from small Bordeaux châteaux or small producers in Burgundy or the Rhineland.

Excelsior was the first to bring in wines of the Argentine, which is the world's fourth-largest producer and whose wines are little known here. As everybody gets bigger, more and more specialty importers concentrating on finding new and exceptional wines are needed. A look at Excelsior will show them how to do it.

Reds	Whites
around $3	*around $3*
Ch. Trinité Valrose (Bord. Sup.)	Pinot Chardonnay Ninot
Beaujolais Ninot	Bernkasteler Riesling (Rudolf Müller)
Arrigoni Chianti	
*San Felipe Tinto (Argentina)	*San Felipe Blanco (Argentina)

around $4
Domaine de l'Olivette (Rhône)
Ch. Cheval Noir (St. Émilion)
Ch. des Tours (Beaujolais Brouilly)

Garneau

The Joseph Garneau Company was founded before the Civil War; the first great house it came to represent was Veuve Clicquot-Ponsardin. The new company was personally selected by The Widow, whose Champagne came to be called that, at least partly in tribute to one of the first international businesswomen. The fine Bordeaux firm of Cruse appointed Garneau as importers in the eighties. Shortly after the turn of the century the prestigious Rhineland firm of Annheuser joined the group, the founder of that vineyard-owning family having taken a liking to Garneau on one of his frequent visits to the American branch of the family, who had settled in St. Louis and begun making beer. In succeeding years Garneau involved themselves in the Italian wine trade and now represents Bolla, Cella, and Frescobaldi. The firm is now the import division of Brown-Forman Distillers.

* The first Argentine wine to be imported, brought in from a popular Mendoza shipper in 1967. Tinto is a Burgundy type, so called, but it is made from Cabernet Sauvignon. Blanco is a blend of Pinot Blanc and Riesling.

IMPORTERS

Reds	Whites
around $3.50	*around $3.50*
Cruse Gamay	Marqués del Lagar
Frescobaldi Chianti	Fratelli Cella Frascati
Bolla Valpolicella	Bolla Soave
around $4	*around $4*
Cruse Bordeaux Rouge	Cruse Blanc de Blancs
Cruse Merlot	Annheuser Laubenheimer

Heublein

The house that vodka built has headquarters in Connecticut, in the insurance city of Hartford, where a gentleman from Bavaria opened a restaurant in 1859. It got to be called Heub's, and when the sons took over the business, they began bottling wines for the extensive catering business that had grown up, also acting as wholesalers and importers for others. In 1892 they prepared a gallon of martinis and a gallon of manhattans for a picnic to be held by the Governor's Foot Guard, which was rained out. The jugs were refrigerated, but the outing was rained out the following week, so orders came through to throw the cocktails out. As is only natural, the man assigned the task could not resist tasting the cocktails. They tasted fine, and he said so. His name is lost, but the courage of his conviction led the brothers to taste them too, and they decided to bottle cocktails for clubs in the neighborhood. This was a time when each bartender had his own notions about cocktails, usually bizarre, and Heublein Club Cocktails, the first to be bottled, became popular. They needed a good gin, couldn't find what they liked, and made Milshire's, following the English potstill system.

Vodka came along right after repeal, the formula brought to America by the man who had supplied the raw materials to the Smirnoff family. Smirnoffs had begun making the vodka in 1818, and just before the First World War a million bottles a day were sold in Russia. Nothing like that happened in the United States, and Heublein bought the rights on the eve of World War II, when sales amounted to 6,000 cases a year. By the time peace came, Californians had discovered the Bloody Mary, followed by the

Moscow Mule, Screwdriver, and Bull Shot, to say nothing of the Vodka Martini. Sales began to leave Heublein breathless, and Heublein decided to share that idea. It's still nothing like the old days of the czars, but sales are up to a million bottles a week.

Heublein added Vintage Wines in 1965, with Lancer's Rosé from Portugal, soon to be followed by United Vintners, a wine-producing co-operative that includes Inglenook, Petri, and Italian Swiss Colony, among others. Along the way, it acquired Beaulieu Vineyards, one of the most prestigious of Napa Valley producers, and distribution of Harvey of Bristol, a firm that had done some expanding itself, going beyond Sherry and Port into a distinguished collection of table wines, notably Bordeaux. Heublein has the Rhônes of Paul Jaboulet Ainé, the Burgundies of Bouchard Père et Fils, the Italian wines of Bertani and Ancilli, and all the wines of Hungary, marketed by the state monopoly.

Through its expanded International Wines subsidiary, which handles the imports, an auction is held each year made up of wine assembled during the past twelvemonth, usually a few old bottles that sell for thousands of dollars and cases of new vintages that sell for hundreds. Nothing has done so much in recent years to interest Americans in wines; news emphasis is on price, but astonishment leads to talk, and talk leads to trying a bottle. The path is the same as the one that Heublein has followed to become one of the largest firms in the wine trade.

Reds	Whites
around $3.50	*around $3.50*
Bouchard/Beaujolais Sup.	Marconnay Vouvray
* Harvey's Grand Vin du Patron	Harvey's Wehlener
Harvey's Le Duc Gascon (Haut-Médoc)	Munzlay
Harvey's L'Abbé Benin (St. Émilion)	Badasconyi Keknelyu
Egri Bikavér (Hungary)	(Hungary)

* Harvey, which owns the great Château Latour and distribution rights to Château Saint Georges of Saint Georges-Saint Émilion, has a special way of handling its Bordeaux regionals. Brand names are given to wines from 'petits château"; in case they want to shift from one château to another, the name will remain the same, giving a certain market continuity.

IMPORTERS

The House of Burgundy

Right after repeal, a couple of Frenchmen set up The House of Burgundy to supply good vintages to countrymen running restaurants in Manhattan. For a third of a century the two Henris, Aymonier and Malval, brought in a bewildering collection of small lots from good French vintners, and when M. Malval retired at the beginning of the decade, a foreign correspondent came into the firm. He is Robert Fairchild, scion of the publishing company that reports on the fashion world through the pages of *Women's Wear Daily*. Fairchild's interest in wines began in Paris, but has now widened to include California, because the firm now distributes the excellent sparkling wines of Hanns Kornell and the distinguished table wines of Robert Mondavi, both Napa Valley producers.

The list of French wines is prestigious: Burgundies from Prosper Maufoux; Provence rosés and whites from Domaines Ott, whose Château de Selle Rosé was one of the first imported; Bordeaux wines of Alfred Schyler Fils; Alsatian wines of Château de Mittelwihr; Rhônes of Jean Pierre Brotte; and Salon Champagne. Only a few of the wines are under $4.

Reds

around $3
Côtes-du-Rhône Brotte
Schyler Bordeaux Rouge

Whites

around $3
Sylvaner, Preiss-Henny
Maufoux Mâcon Sup.

Kobrand

Kobrand is the house that gin built in little more than a quarter of a century into perhaps the most successful independent house in the trade. Founded in the forties by an executive involved since repeal with the buying of wines and spirits for Macy's, in association with another, whose family had been in the wine trade for generations, Kobrand was established to market Beefeater in the United States. The English gin came to the market at a time when there were shortages in scotch and other spirits and when large segments of the market were turning away from whiskies, but probably the main reason for its success was that the new firm concentrated on quality and ignored price. People have always been confused about what makes quality in drinkables, the way they resolve the puzzle being to buy the most expensive product on the market. When it comes to diamonds and furs and cars and houses, lots of money is involved. When it comes to spirits, the difference is a dollar or two—a small price to pay to feel like a millionaire. Kobrand has always seen to it that proper value is given for the price asked, that their wines and spirits are always among the best available, with no compromise. It's a simple formula, which smacks of mother love and rockbound coasts and old-time religion. It works like a charm in mass markets, where emphasis is on getting more for less.

The line has expanded slowly. Kobrand is the exclusive distributor for Château Margaux, the only one of the Great Growths of Bordeaux that is available from a single importer. Margaux is owned by Ginestet, a distinguished Bordeaux shipper owning several châteaux and producing an excellent line of regionals—all of them exclusive with Kobrand. The wines of Louis Jadot, recognized as one of the two or three outstanding shippers of Burgundy, are imported by Kobrand. Through Weinexport Hattenheim, a remarkably good collection of German regionals and a small group of excellent estate-bottlings is offered. The most highly regarded Tavel, Château d'Aquéria; a fine Chianti, Nozzole; some excellent Rhônes; and a few other wines extend the line. One could wish that some less expensive wines could be added to the line, but that's not the way the firm goes. At Kobrand, you get what you pay for.

Reds	Whites
under $5	*under $4*
Ginestet Médoc	Ginestet Graves Extra
Beaujolais Jadot	Barre Muscadet
Nozzole Chianti Classico Riserva	Madrigal Johannisberg Riesling
León Pinot Noir (Panadés)	

Monsieur Henri

For more than twenty years, Monsieur Henri was managed by three brothers, sons of the founder, who made it into the biggest-selling of all wine importers. Beginning early in the fifties, they decided that Americans wanted to drink inexpensive wines. Mostly devoted to supplying New Yorkers, they gradually expanded across the country. They were among the first to use radio commercials for wines, and then television. They introduced Yago Sant' Gria, the bottled version of the Spanish summer drink based on red wine with orange, lemon, and lime juices added, the first truly successful pop wine.

Among their suppliers are the largest of Burgundy shippers, Piat et Compagnie; the Italian house of Orfevi, and the German firm of Franz Weber. In the process, they acquired interests in Spanish wine-producing areas and bought an upstate-New York vineyard. They long ago went beyond the two-dollar-a-bottle market and hold large stocks of château-bottlings and estate-bottlings. The firm was purchased by Pepsico, the soda-pop company, in 1972, but the brothers still manage the firm, busier than ever. They offer literally hundreds of wines; as an example, from Spain's Rioja, they have the wines of Marqués de Murrieta and Marqués de Riscal, Condal Reserva, and Yago. They buy Burgundies from at least twenty growers and shippers, and regularly stock more than 100 Bordeaux châteaux and as many German estate-bottlings. They have grown in just the way the market has, pacing the American wine drinker every step of the way. As a sampling, here are a dozen low-priced offerings of Bordeaux châteaux, selling for under five dollars a bottle in New York. Or you can buy a nicely matured bottle of Château Lafite-Rothschild '55 for $175 a bottle.

Bordeaux Château Reds

under $5

Ch. de Liche (Graves)
Ch. Camargan
Ch. Mesthamas
Ch. Giron (Premières Côtes de Bordeaux)
Ch. Verdus (Médoc)
Ch. La Gouinière (St. Émilion)

Ch. La Croix (St. Émilion)
Ch. Haut Combes
Ch. Tabernottes
Ch. Colombier
Ch. du Grande Boussuet
Ch. de Taste (Médoc)

Charles Morgenstern & Co.

Founded as a food-importing firm shortly after the turn of the century, the firm came to be called Asche-Bandor, after the Danish fruit wines the firm began to bring in; the name was changed when the line broadened to include other wines and spirits, particularly cordials. Some of the most interesting of these are Merrydown wines, from England; well-made fruit wines, including currant, gooseberry, and elderberry—wines that most people have read about but never tasted. There are also ginger wine; mead, made from honey; and the importer particularly likes the orange wine. These are not pop wines in the generally accepted sense of the word but true wines carefully made from fruits; they are priced around two dollars a bottle. The most surprising is a wine from grapes, the first ever available from England, a Riesling Sylvaner. Some excellent wines come from Cyprus, from the giant firm of Keo, which supplies much wine to the eastern Mediterranean; to be noted is the Rosella, a light rosé, and the classic Cyprian dessert wine Commandaria. A rare and unusual wine from France is Pineau des Charentes, a lightly sweet wine that has grape juice added to it. The firm specializes in low-priced wines remarkably well selected.

Reds

under $3
Keo Othello
Torres Coronas (Spain)

Whites

under $3
C. da Silva Isabel Branco (Portugal)
Keo Aphrodite

Munson Shaw

Founded nearly a century ago, the firm is now the import subsidiary of National Distillers, bringing in Duff Gordon Sherries, Cockburn Ports, Cossart Madeiras, Laurent Perrier Champagnes and Bossière Vermouths, as well as Bordeaux bottlings from Dourthe Frères. Through T. Jouvet & Cie, both Bordeaux and Burgundy regionals are imported. Rhônes are imported from one of the most illustrious shippers, Chapoutier, a firm that has been in Hermitage for a century and a half. Much older is the shipper of Marquisat, Pasquier-Desvignes, a family that has been making Beaujolais for more than five hundred years. Rhineland wines come from Steigenberger, a shipper that operates a chain of German hotels; while Italian wines come from the well-known house of Bertolli. The least-known wines of the group are those from Yugoslavia, which are shipped by three co-operative marketing arms, each with a brand name. Navip is the brand for the wines of the province of Servia; Slovin covers wine of Slovenia, in the North and along the Danube; and Adriatica is the name for wines along the coast. Yugoslavia is the fifth-largest wine producer in the world, its vineyards planted in the traditional noble vines and also in native ones with strange names. Red varieties include Plavac from Adriatica, and Prokupac from Navip; whites include Sipon from both Slovin and Adriatica. At less than three dollars, they are among the best buys on the market.

Reds	Whites
under $3	*under $3*
Adriatica Cabernet (Istria)	Navip Smederevka (Semendria)
Adriatica Refosk (Istria)	Slovin Traminec (Jeruzalem)
Navip Gamay (Vençac)	Adriatica Traminec (Radgona)
around $4	*around $4*
Marquisat Beaujolais-Villages	Marquisat Beaujolais Blanc
Chapoutier Côtes-du-Rhône	Steigenberger Moselblümchen

Renfield

Importers are notorious for not blowing their own horns, to such a degree that a customer rarely knows the name of the company that brings in his favorite wines and spirits. One of the few exceptions is Renfield, which has long advertised its blue chips—Piper-Heidsieck, Martini & Rossi, Cointreau, Rémy Martin, Gordon's, Haig & Haig—but the company brings in few table wines. The most important of these are the Veronese wines of Lamberti, and Melini Chianti and Orvieto. Today, when new import firms are entering the trade each month, old firms are having trouble getting recognition. Perhaps the early wine importers received little attention because that was focused on famous brands of spirits, Champagnes, and Vermouths, table wines being secondary. Only a few concentrated on table wines—Wildman, Julius Wile, S. S. Pierce—leaving room for others to enter the field. Wine importers with many names from many places are only now establishing themselves the way Renfield has. Now, if only the company of blue chips would bring in more wines . . .

Reds	Whites
around $3	*around $3*
Lamberti Bardolino	Lamberti Soave
Lamberti Valpolicella	Orvieto Melini
Chianti Melini	Lacrima d'Arno Melini

Julius Wile Sons & Co.

Julius Wile and two brothers set up as shippers' agents in 1877, soon to be joined by Bernard Blum; their sons and grandsons have developed the firm into one of the most respected in the trade. Company officers spend long hours serving on importer committees that act as advisers to promotion campaigns for Champagne and cognac, Bordeaux and Sherry, Italian wines and German wines; they have been active in relations with government agencies involved with taxing and regulating the industry, in organizing importers to solve mutual problems. It's not exciting to read about, nor is it exciting to do, but without the decades of groundwork, importers would not be able to handle the enormous flood of wines beginning to pour into the country. The firm is now a subsidiary of Standard Brands.

The main business of the House of Wile (the name of the shipper when it comes to wines) has been the careful building of brands. In Burgundy it is Chanson Père et Fils, founded in 1750, some of whose cellars are in the ramparts of Beaune, the capital of the Cote d'Or; the firm owns portions of a dozen First Growths and several lesser parcels. Wile also brings in Bordeaux châteaux under the Chanson name. On the Rhine it is Deinhard, in business earlier but incorporated later. In Tuscany it is Antinori, who have been producing wines for four centuries but are Johnny-come-latelies to the export business, having shipped for only one. In Alsace it's Willm, whose Clos Gänsbrönnel, is one of the few vineyards in that area whose name appears on labels.

Wile's major Bordeaux supplier is Prats Frères, owners of the distinguished Classed Growth from Saint Estèphe Cos d'Estournel, whose vineyards neighbor those of Château Lafite. Others include Château Malbec and Château Falfas among the reds, the white Graves of Château Piron, the Barsac of Château de Laulan. For French country wines, the shipper is Jules Alby.

Reds	Whites
around $3.50	*around $3.50*
Antinori Bardolino	Antinori Est! Est! Est!
Chanson Ch. Malbec	Chanson Pinot Chardonnay
Chanson Cabernet Sauvignon	St. Vincent
	Deinhard Piesporter Forellenwein
around $4	
Villa Antinori Chianti	Ch. Olivier (Graves)
Chanson Pinot Noir St. Vincent	Hanns Christoff Deinhard Liebfraumilch

NOTE: Like other major importers, Julius Wile has various low-priced wines, usually a short list of regionals, imported for clubs, restaurants, and hinterland retailers without access to a variety of low-priced wines from noted shippers. They are not often carried by big-city retailers, but their existence can be discovered in a few minutes' discussion, and a retailer can order them by the case. One such brand from Wile is Marson & Natier, for regional Burgundy and Rhônes.

Frederick Wildman & Sons

No firm has so delighted wine lovers as Frederick Wildman. Originally, the founder directed the fine old firm of Bellows & Company, selling that to National Distillers in the forties but keeping the wines, because the big firm was not then interested in the wine business. His sons, nephews, and daughters' husbands came into the business, which concentrated only on the very best of wines. It is now a subsidiary of Hiram Walker.

They are importers of the Domaine de la Romanée-Conti, a group of the greatest Burgundies. They are importers of the wines of Louis Latour, the dean of Burgundy shippers. No less distinguished are the Burgundies of Domaine Ropiteau-Mignon. There are the Chambertins of Armand Rousseau et Fils. There are the white Burgundies of Domaine Leflaive. An outstanding shipper of Chablis is J. Moreau Fils, an outstanding shipper of the Loire is Ackerman-Laurance, an outstanding shipper of Rhônes is Domaines Chapoutier, and Wildman imports all three along with a host of smaller producers to fill out the line.

Rhineland wines imported by Wildman are those of Langenbach, a firm both venerable and venerated, particularly noted for the excellence of its German regionals. They have one range denominated Meister-Krone and a slightly higher-priced range called Crown of Crowns, in addition to their estate-bottlings.

A difficulty faced by any importer is the multiplicity of wine names. A famous shipper's name will identify a range of wines and serve as a brand name. An importer is faced with the problem of building up the name of a shipper and then losing the shipper to another importer, or of wanting only a single wine from a shipper, or of wishing to offer a group of regionals from various producers under a single name. Wildman chooses to do this under the name of Wildman et Fils for an extensive selection of French wines, which include Pouilly Blanc Fumé and Sancerre from the Loire, as examples. They are invariably wines to look for.

For some years the firm has published for consumers a quarterly newsletter written by Frederick Wildman, Jr., that does much more than extol the virtues of the firm's wines; it presents valuable information about regions and vineyards and vintages and all things vinous. The scion of the founder made his first vineyard tour at the age of six and more recently wrote a book about vineyard touring for anybody wanting to follow in his footsteps, *A Wine Tour of France,* published by Morrow.

The wines set a standard for the trade. They were never low in price, and when money was no object you could be sure of getting a fine bottle if you bought a Wildman selection. Suppose you wanted to serve a really good Chablis or Meursault or Montrachet —that's six or eight dollars—then have one of the Romanées or a Chambertin—ten or fifteen dollars. With drinks before and a little cognac after, a dinner for four would cost twenty dollars before you even thought of food. Most people—and most importers—settle for wines of less distinction and lower price. There weren't many such excellencies as those brought in by Wildman, scarcely enough to meet the demands of knowing and well-off wine lovers, but as prices increased, Wildman saw themselves serving a narrower and narrower segment of wine drinkers. More and more people began to look for young, fresh, simple wines. Many of them asked Wildman to put their skill at tasting and selection to work to find such wines. Their beginnings in this direction have been astonishing.

Just inland from Barcelona is the hilly Catalonian district of Panadés, where many Frenchmen settled toward the end of the past century, when Phylloxera devastated their home vineyards. One such family was René Barbier's. Wildman offers their fresh, light wines for about three dollars a bottle. Frenchmen also settled in the uplands of the Pyrenees, farther west, replanting many of the vineyards of the Rioja, the best of Spain's regions for table wines. One of the best and largest firms there is CUNE, Compañía Vinícola del Norte España, so called because the *V* in their monogram looks like a *U*. There are some old and expensive wines from the firm, but also two light reds and two dry whites for about three dollars. The Grand Duchy of Luxemburg has vineyards along the Moselle, just before it enters Germany, and Wildman offers three crisp light whites from there for less than $4. They have even found some similarly priced wines from Bordeaux, from the Rhône, from Alsace, from the Loire, and from Italy. Somewhat higher-priced wines are listed below. They disappear almost instantly from the shops, because they are probably consistently the best buys among inexpensive wines on the market. Wildman continues to set a standard for the trade.

Reds	Whites
under $4	*under $4*
Louis Latour Bourgogne Select	Louis Latour Pinot Chardonnay
Wildman St. Georges-St. Émilion	Lorentz Fils Sylvaner (Alsace)
Wildman Moulis (Médoc)	Wildman Pavillon Blanc du Rhône
Ch. La Dauphine (Côtes Fronsac)	Wildman Crozes-Hermitage
Ch. Latour de By (Médoc)	Wildman Sauvignon Blanc Touraine
Wildman Pavillon Rouge du Rhône	Wildman Muscadet Select
Clos des Champs, St. Joseph (Rhône)	Wildman Vouvray Langenbach Niersteiner
Santa Sofia Valpolicella	Meister-Krone
Guido Giri Dolcetto d'Alba	

Peartree Imports

In the past decade several small importing firms have come into being, usually headed by men with ideas of their own that they have not been able to carry out as executives of large importing firms. They usually know wines and markets well, preferring to concentrate on a few well-chosen wines rather than to sell long lines. Such a man is Leonard Birnbaum, who left Renfield after twenty years because he wanted to offer brands well known elsewhere but not in the United States—a few products that would fill up gaps on a retailer's shelves with unusual wines that would be noted. With a small firm, there is also the chance to try new ideas, not an easy thing with a company that is being successful with traditional methods. The best-selling sparkling wine in France, for example, is a sparkling white Burgundy called Kriter, much cheaper than Champagne but made in the same way. This was imported along with an excellent but unknown Champagne called Delbeck. As for wines, a greatly underrated Bordeaux château is Lafon-Rochet, whose vineyards have been reconstituted; the Bordeaux trade is always hesitant to help develop such a château, preferring to concentrate on old stand-bys, so here was a chance to offer a new wine to the curious. So that only exceptional wines of the château are offered, lesser vintages are marketed as a non-vintage wine under a different label, Château Vieille-Chapelle, at a reasonable price. To offer wines in the three-dollar range, a Cabernet Sauvignon and a Sauvignon Blanc de Blancs are being offered. From the Rhône come the wines of J. Vidal Fleury. A small firm with a few such lines can offer retailers brands with assurance of quality and supply that will be advertised and promoted—and not be available everywhere—so a retailer has some motivation to suggest them to his customers. Often enough, wines from such small importers are excellent values, their rarity adding to their interest.

Producers of wines in quantity often prefer to work with small firms because of the attention paid their products, and one such group is the shipper of Rusticano, a brand name for blends of Italian wines marketed in 68-ounce bottles. Peartree is introducing the wine, market by market, hoping that personal contact with retailers (who will suggest the wine to their customers) will make the wines known without heavy expenditure for advertising. Such an approach to the market makes it possible to offer good wines at reasonable prices, but depends on discerning customers willing to try new items. The bewildering number of new wines offered confuses retailers as well as customers, so wines like Rusticano may be lost in the shuffle as advertised brands struggle for prime positions on the shelves. The hope is that the market may be broad enough to absorb all good wines offered and that Rusticano will find its place. Rusticano retails for about $4 for 68 ounces.

Of particular interest is a group of small Bordeaux châteaux and regionals, priced under four dollars:

REDS

under $4
Cabernet Mau
Château Puyfromage (Bordeaux Supérieur)
Château Melin (Sables-Saint Émilion)
Château Canteloup (Premieres Côtes de Bordeaux)
Château La Tour St. Bonnet (Médoc)
Château La Tour Colombier (Lalande-de-Pomerol)

Wine Imports of America

Wineimports, as the once-small New Jersey importers like to call themselves since they went national in 1969, is run by the two Lemme brothers and is the largest independent importer of wines. The firm claims to bring in more than five hundred, something approaching one hundred of them being sold as selections by Lémé Frères. Patterned after the original operation of Monsieur Henri, which concentrated on large volume and low price, the firm now has a substantial collection of château- and estate-bottlings. Most of their business is done in regional wines, which vary more than they should, perhaps, but frequently represent good value.

Hudson's Bay Company

The oldest international company in the world, founded three centuries ago to develop the fur trade in North America, entered the wine trade in the United States in 1972. From beaver hats to *bons vins* in a dozen generations. Haste makes waste.

The company, now headquartered in Winnipeg, entered the American market with a cautious step, introducing three wines: Vinho Vida, a Portuguese rosé; Del Gamba, a Chianti; and Vinho Verde, a Portuguese white. Another trio followed, plus a Sangria, and now they are recovering from the shock, waiting to see the reaction. Reports so far indicate the continent is taking the whole thing calmly.

The venture, though, illustrates the enormous interest in the United States as a wine-drinking country. Banks have financed wine purchasing for decades, extending long lines of credit to importers and to winegrowers, at least in California. Much money has been invested in foreign vineyards and shipping companies by American firms, and most importers have been absorbed by giant corporations. Wine is one avenue by which American business has become internationalized and by which foreign capital enters the American market. What remains to be seen is what effect this investment will have on wine quality and price. Hudson's Bay is watching closely.

OTHER ELEMENTS OF THE TRADE

———◆◆◆———

Growers

Co-operatives and Monopolies

Agents and Buyers

Trade Listings:
Beverage Media
and Patterson's

Wholesalers and Distributors

Wine Selections

Growers

Owners who tend their own vines, then make and bottle their own wines, produce most of the great wines in the world. The method is called château-bottling in Bordeaux, and estate-bottling in Burgundy, along the Rhine, and elsewhere, and is a way of guaranteeing the authenticity of vintages from outstanding vineyards. Usually expensive, most of them are without the province of this book, but they set the standards of the regions from which they come.

Many growers sell their wines in cask for bottling by shippers; others sell their grape crops to shippers who make the wines. Brokers handle many of the transactions, and most wines come to market through shippers, although some of the best in Burgundy and along the Rhine are sold at auction.

A big grower with an established reputation may buy his neighbors' grapes and add them to his own, or even buy his neighbors' wines for blending with his own, a practice common in Burgundy, California, and many other places. These wines may go to shippers, but many are put on the market directly, through agents. By acting as his own shipper, a grower may make more, even offering better wines for less than those of the shippers, but in poor years he may be stuck with a lot of bad wines.

A grower may own several sections in different vineyards, all of them together forming a domain that might add up to a hundred acres or so and provide several thousand cases—enough to market directly to a retailer or a restaurateur, even an airline or a hotel chain. Many of these domain wines are bought up by distributors and importers for what's left of the carriage trade. Importers buy up or tie up more vineyard wines so that they can be presented on their lists. Essentially, however, a goodly share of the best vineyard wine gets to market from growers acting as their own shippers. The large Burgundy shippers compete with all these elements of the trade for the domain wines.

Co-operatives and Monopolies

Pity the poor winegrower with a few acres of not-so-glorious vines. In a bad year his wine is awful, and in a good year it may not be so good, because he can't afford the chemical analysis that tells him the exact vinification processes he should follow. Nor does he have the modern presses and other paraphernalia that would let him get the best from his grapes. He hasn't the wines or the connections to enter lucrative distant markets. There are many like him in every region, and thousands have banded together to form co-operatives. Where the state has taken over the land, vintages are handled in modern wineries, and marketing is handled by state monopolies. Both kinds of organizations produce some of the best bargains in the world of wines, sound blends in large quantities.

There's always the cry that the few good wines are lost in the vats to make poor wines drinkable, but the young graduates of the wine schools and the shrewd old vintners who run the centralized wineries aren't that dumb. Exceptional wines are made separately, to be offered at premium prices or to be drunk by the wine makers themselves. With substantial quantities to market, the groups can afford to rip up poor vines, operate tractors and other cultivating equipment, even hire marketing experts. Some develop brand names, like the co-operative in the Médoc that offers La Rose de Pauillac.

Co-operatives mostly provide wine for home markets, our importers generally preferring to work with private companies. As a consequence, the largest of Israel's score of co-operatives has set up its own export firm, Carmel Wine Company, to market its wines in the United States. Others, such as the enormous Provins in Switzerland's Valais, sell lots of wine to various distributors around the United States, a route followed by groups in Alsace, the Rhône, Austria, and elsewhere. Distributors like to buy wines direct, taking the import profit for themselves, but hesitate to bring in wines that may compete with those of an importer who provides them with a big-selling Scotch or English gin.

Importers show the same hesitancy when it comes to working with state monopolies, but Heublein, for example, handles

Hungarian wines from the state export board, Monimpex. Trade organizations of various Soviet republics and those of Algeria and Morocco have been eying the thirsty American consumer, but the complexities of trade and politics have blocked them from the market. As Americans begin to thirst for wines as they have for Scotch, these unknown wines begin to appear. The Algerian growers claim that they can lay down a case of good, hearty red wine in New York for under eight dollars, scaring importers who are having trouble laying down Bordeaux regionals for less than twelve. Perhaps what the Algerians have to do is raise their prices, in which case they'd still be able to offer wines that would sell for about two dollars a bottle. There are lots of changes on the way. One of the most promising to watch out for is the introduction of wines of co-operatives and state monopolies.

A list of co-operatives isn't very helpful. There are some sixty of them in Bordeaux, for instance, hundreds of others around France, more hundreds elsewhere. Most of them are concerned with local markets, although many are now venturing into the European Community, now that uniform regulations simplify the distribution problems among the countries of the Common Market. Importers and buyers have sought out several of them.

In general, a wine from a co-operative is worth trying. It should be low in price, well under $4.

Agents and Buyers

Some of the best buys available can be direct imports from growers, called DI's by the trade, which hates them. Agents may represent several growers in a region, selling their wines directly to wholesalers and retailers, by-passing both shipper and importer. This makes for friction in the trade.

DI's sound great. A shipper may add 25% profit to a wine, an importer a like amount. A wholesaler may do the same. A retailer buying direct can eliminate all these profits, and if he's big enough to buy from the grower, he wipes out the agent's 10%. This saving is not always passed on to the customer.

DI's are usually sold in 100-case lots, the production of perhaps an acre of vineyard in a good district. Agents can approach growers with tiny holdings, therefore, but there are risks because the wines may vary widely from year to year. DI's and all their different labels are confusing to the customer, who has enough trouble keeping track of what comes from shippers in the different regions. There must be a hundred Chiantis on the market, as many Liebfraumilchs, even more Beaujolais.

Still, agents offer many good wines from small vineyards that would ordinarily be lost to the shippers' blends. DI's are a constant pressure on shippers and importers to keep prices down. Agents frequently perform a service for importers, who may represent shippers in important regions like Burgundy or Bordeaux but may need a few wines from elsewhere to fill out a line.

Buyers operate much like agents, roving the districts to find wines not only for shippers and importers, but for anybody else who uses lots of wines. The list is long today: airlines, hotels, retail chains. Some buyers concentrate on finding wines for restaurants and clubs, even tying up stocks for investors. A growing amount of good wine is diverted from regular trade channels for these special markets.

Independent buyers opened up the market for fine wines in America. Men such as Frank Schoonmaker and Alexis Lichine visited the vineyard country three and four times a year, tasting scores of wines a day, buying a cask here, a few dozen cases there. When Schoonmaker began buying, in the thirties, demand was pretty well satisfied by the few wines from famous vineyards brought in by importers like S. S. Pierce in Boston and Frederick Wildman in New York. Writing to satisfy an editor's curiosity, Schoonmaker found that there were dozens of fine wines not offered on the American market. When growers asked him to see if anybody was interested, Schoonmaker inquired for them at hotels such as the St. Regis and of retailers such as Sam Aaron of Sherry Wine & Spirits. By the end of the thirties, Schoonmaker was making selling trips all over the country, and Lichine was his sales manager. After the war, Lichine began buying on his own. Between them, they offered top wines from small producers to interested stores and restaurants. As consumer interest grew, men such as George Sumner, who owned one of the best small wineshops on New York's East Side, began buying. Scarcely a great wine from a famous region went unbid for as American buyers competed with those from England and Belgium, Scandinavia and Switzerland, even with the Germans and the French. Americans had the edge when the dollar was strong, and for a time New York was a better place to buy wines than London or Paris. As prosperity returned to Europe, bargains began to disappear. The world-wide craze for wines is sending buyers scurrying into new districts, seeking new wines.

To distinguish his wines from those of the big shippers and their importers, Schoonmaker devised a neck label that identified each bottle bought from him as a "Frank Schoonmaker Selection." Others followed suit; many importers began identifying their own selections, and one firm even paid a royalty to a lady with a certain social standing so they could put her name on the bottles as the selector. It got so that retailers began demanding neck labels describing wines as their "Special Selections." Canny buyers quickly learned to ignore this ploy, to their loss, because men like Schoonmaker and Lichine continued to bring in superior wines, while a retailer's "selection" was usually put on a wine bought directly at a low price and often indicated a bargain. A list of some of the leading selections appears at the end of this chapter. If one of them turns out to be good, others are worth trying.

Trade Listings: Beverage Media and Patterson's

A monthly catalogue, thick as a phone book, lists for the trade in every region of the United States every wine and every spirit available for sale through licensed importers and distributors. Any store will carry one bottle out of one hundred, or fewer, usually name brands that will turn over quickly. In addition to brands supported by advertising and promotion, major importers have lines of unpromoted low-priced wines offered as a service to clubs, restaurants, and retailers who don't have access to a large variety of inexpensive wines whose quality is backed by a reputable importer. Importers don't like to sell them, particularly, because they undercut their market for their promoted brands and do not return much of a profit. There they are, however, to be ordered by the case by anybody with access to the trade catalogues.

A customer can find out about such wines during a brief discussion with a retailer, who can look up in his price lists the secondary lines offered by any of the importers. He will invariably be willing to order a case for you, case buyers still being a rarity.

The situation is much like that of a bookseller who stocks the current best sellers but has to order from the publisher most books more than a few months old.

Wholesalers and Distributors

Wholesalers put shipments from importers in big warehouses and then send salesmen around to bars and restaurants and clubs to take orders for the goods. Distributors do the same thing, and nobody seems to know the difference between the two.

Sales managers don't trust salesmen, so they hold sales meetings every Friday afternoon to tell them what to push the following week. Push merchandise (PM's to the salesmen) are items that move slowly, and if you sell some, maybe you get a bonus. Many wines are PM's, even today.

Salesmen don't trust retailers who buy from various distributors. A salesman is usually convinced that a retailer is buying all his stuff from somebody else. To encourage the retailer, there are special prices on certain items each month. They are called post-offs, at a few dollars less than usual—if you buy five cases, or ten, or two. Some retailers take advantage. When you press them for an order, they break down and say OK, give me a mixed case of wines—two Burgundies, two Bordeaux, four each of Chianti and Liebfraumilch. No Beaujolais; the guy down the street is selling Beaujolais below my cost; did you make him a special deal?

Salesmen sometimes wax enthusiastic and ask to be put on nothing but wines. They go around to the stores and help arrange the bottles. They put up little signs that say THIS IS GOOD WITH FISH, TRY THIS WITH YOUR NEXT PICNIC, HAMBURGERS TASTE BETTER WITH WINE, things like that. Whiskey salesmen think wine salesmen are crazy.

And that may be more than you need to know about wholesalers and distributors. But watch out for PM's and post-offs. They may be great buys.

Wine Selections

FRANK SCHOONMAKER SELECTIONS

Shortly after leaving college, Frank Schoonmaker began writing travel pieces for *The New Yorker,* and when repeal was in the offing, he wrote a series of articles about wines for that magazine and others. Simon & Schuster asked him to expand them into a book, and with the help of a fellow journalist, Tom Marvel, *The Complete Wine Book* was published in 1934. One thing led to another.

People wanted to drink wines, not read about them, and many of the ones he mentioned couldn't be found in American shops. Hardest to find of all were Burgundies from the great vineyards, divided as they were among several owners so that few of the growers could make more than a few casks of wine—not enough to supply the national market that the big importers of spirits were organized to serve. About all the Burgundies that could be found on the New York market were Monopoles of the shippers and blends of wines bearing township names such as Pommard and Gevrey-Chambertin. Schoonmaker had met dozens of growers with fabulous wines, eager to serve what was left of the American carriage trade. Schoonmaker began providing Madison Avenue shops with Burgundies, Rhônes, Rhines. How logical it all seemed!

But every label had to be registered—in Washington and with the New York State control board. There were problems with corks and bottles. Many of the reds threw a sediment; the wines changed in bottle. Customers drank wines before they had aged enough in bottle and didn't like them. Even the dozen or so top wine shops, including the odd one in Boston or Washington or Chicago, couldn't handle a hundred cases of a particular wine, and there weren't enough restaurant and hotel wine lists to absorb any cases left over. Smaller shipments weren't economical. Lots of people talked wine, but few knew enough to tell good from great, having become accustomed to shippers' blends. Clerks were ignorant. Schoonmaker had an educational job to do and a selling job. He couldn't be everywhere, tasting in Europe and overseeing shipments, so he found a few interested people to help, among them Alexis Lichine, who became his sales manager. The New York World's Fair brought many knowing Europeans to its pavilions to run cafes and restaurants, many of whom decided to stay and open restaurants in Manhattan. They began buying Schoonmaker's wines, but war brought an end to everything.

The same problems persisted into the fifties. Those times were hell for small importers, but they were heaven for anybody who knew the slightest thing about wines. French place-name control laws came into extensive use, and while they spelled out the Great Growths of Burgundy, they were skimpy on the First Growths. Most people were happy with Chablis, passing up Pouilly-Fuissé. Most people were happy with the Chambertins and Vougeots and Romanées, passing up Nuits-Saint-Georges and Musignys and Fixins. Everybody knew about Pommard and Montrachet, but there were also Volnay and Monthélie. Many First Growths went for less than three dollars a bottle. The story was the same in Bordeaux, along the Rhine, and elsewhere.

The market widened during the fifties, helped along by the growing number of restaurants and shops whose owners knew what they had on their shelves, and Schoonmaker began introducing his wines in many of the major cities. This paving of the way for wines didn't help him too much, because others began bringing wines in, distributors began to sell enough to buy direct, and the major importers began expanding their lines. As the market expanded still more during the sixties, Schoonmaker was content with the business he had, employing the minimum number of people, handling an ever more selective group of suppliers. People he'd trained began entering the business, and sometimes at big tastings in New York, it seemed that everybody was one of his customers, or somebody who had accompanied him on tasting trips, or somebody whose first bottle of wine had been a Schoonmaker Selection. If America is becoming a wine-drinking continent, much of it is due to the efforts of Frank Schoonmaker. The firm is now a subsidiary of Pillsbury.

ALEXIS LICHINE SELECTIONS

Lichine came of age shortly after repeal, promptly fell in love with wines, and began finding happy homes for them as manager for Frank Schoonmaker. He continued laboring on their behalf during the war as an American liaison officer with French forces in North Africa. One of his duties was to set up staff headquarters as the armies landed on the southern coast of France and moved up the Rhône Valley, and he took as his responsibility the job of finding wines for the generals' tables and seeing to it that the American officers knew enough about what was in the bottles to win respect from the French. He roved all over Burgundy seeking hidden stores among the small growers, so successfully that he determined to continue the process with the coming of peace. The love affair has lasted forty years now, and the wine world will never be the same.

American owners of Château Haut Brion, the family of banker Clarence Dillon, had set up Granvins to market wines, and Lichine went into partnership with the company, buying and selling. "I have to fight to buy the wines and then I have to fight to sell them," said Lichine, describing his activities in the fifties. Small Burgundy growers, who might have a few hundred bottles of wine from their holdings in the great vineyards, often had generations-old ties with restaurant owners and merchants in Switzerland, England, and northern Europe, and while wines sold in America earned dollars, they seemed to disappear; there was no stream of letters praising the wines, enthusiastic visitors were few, and it meant little to see a wine list from the Waldorf or 21 with their names on it, for such places were unknown in Burgundy.

And the wines were unknown on this side of the Atlantic. Place-name control laws were now vigorously in force, but no American book listed them or did much of a job delineating the wines. This reporter accompanied Lichine on an extended buying trip of France and the Rhine, writing accounts of each district in the light of the laws, of what the wine makers said, and of what was tasted in the cellars and on the tables of the grower, Lichine guiding the neophyte every step of the way. A chapter written back in Paris would then require a second visit to the district for checking. After five months, a manuscript was finished, and following a year's editing, *Wines of France* was published by Knopf in 1951. It proved so successful that Lichine began working on an encyclopedia, principally with William Fifield, which was eventually published in 1967.

With a group of millionaires who had waxed enthusiastic about wines at his urging, Lichine bought Château Lascombes and what was promptly renamed Prieuré-Lichine, in Bordeaux, and began reconstituting the vineyards, eventually extending the holdings to Burgundy. He instituted an annual art show at Lascombes devoted to "Wine and the Vine," established an award, the Tasse d'Or, for the best Burgundies each year, and was named a member of the Académie des Vins de Bordeaux, the only American in the group of forty. This was an acknowledgment of his efforts to revamp the outdated 1855 classification of Bordeaux, which had concentrated on wines of the Médoc and Sauternes, ignoring Saint Émilion and Pomerol and all the wines of Graves except Château Haut Brion. The old classification categorized some fifty vineyards, a few of them no longer in existence, while the suggested new one includes vineyards in all the main districts, nearly one hundred fifty of those that produce outstanding reds and whites.

So successful were his efforts that Lichine was approached toward the end of the sixties by representatives of the large English brewing combine Bass Charrington. The group wanted to extend its wine business, and eventually Lichine sold his export and import companies but maintained an interest in the wines to be bought and sold. Few people in this century have been so zealous in their love of wines, with such good effect.

WARREN B. STRAUSS SELECTIONS

Warren Strauss was trained in the hotel business in Switzerland and served in the Quartermaster Corps during the war, then gravitated to the wine trade, establishing himself as an agent for a group of European wine firms in 1958. Wine was a familiar creature in New York and only a few other metropolitan markets in those days, and shops away from these main channels of distribution had trouble getting wines they could have exclusively—a necessity in developing a clientele. Strauss concentrated on merchants in suburbs and small cities who wanted to increase their wine business, offering them wines that would be available nowhere else in the neighborhood—on a basis of direct import so that the markups of the importer and the distributor were eliminated. A merchant might have to buy fifty cases of wine, then a large order, but he could sell the wines at a price below those of the large importers. Many cheap wines thus come into the market through agents, but Strauss chose to focus on quality wines from European houses that had no major importer to provide national distribution.

A self-effacing man, Strauss has never chosen to identify wines as his personal selection, usually identifying his bottles with a strip label that merely indicates the wine was imported by the Warren B. Strauss Company. Selection, after all, is made by the wine merchant from the hundreds that are offered to him, and he deserves the credit—and approval by his customers—when the wine is good. Strauss looks on his role as one of seeing to it that the offerings are the best available at the price, spending much of his time seeking out new wines to intrigue the growing market. It is through agents like Strauss that some of the most interesting wines on the market can be obtained.

Reds

under $4
Château Beau Rivage
  (Bordeaux Supérieur)
Beaujolais-Villages, Louis Tête
Côtes-du-Rhône, Domaine de
  l'Enclos

Whites

around $3
Bernkasteler Riesling,
  Rudolf Müller
Vinho Verde, Moura Basto
Rousette de Seyssel, Fichard

GEORGE SUMNER SELECTIONS

During the thirties and forties you could buy more good wine in New York than you could anywhere else in the world, most of it sold to the carriage trade, through East Side wine shops. Outlanders from New England, the South and the Southwest, the Midwest and the Rockies, ordered wines regularly from stores like Sherry Wine & Spirits and M. Lehmann. Madison Avenue was Wine Alley, with stores like Vendôme and Charles, M. Luria and Surrey's, Colony and Ambassador.

Among these was the shop of George Sumner, who became so interested in wines that he sold his shop and moved to Europe to buy them. He acted as a broker, buying lots of château-bottlings on the Bordeaux market, representing small growers in Burgundy and along the Rhine who could supply a hundred cases or so of estate-bottlings, seeking out good vignerons along the Loire and the Rhône. Distributors in smaller cities began buying from his list, importing direct to bypass the markups of the big importers, promoting George C. Sumner Selections. Retailers would ask him to find wines they could offer exclusively, and from a mimeographed list of a couple of pages, his selections grew to a bound catalogue offering hundreds of wines. It was a personal business, varying widely from year to year, as importers began tying up more and more producers, but scores of small growers have developed markets through his efforts, and Sumner Selections can be found all over the country.

MACY'S TASTER SELECTIONS

Macy's has shown a strong interest in wines ever since repeal, but their tasters have generally been anonymous. The custom has been to buy lots of wines and spirits, then market them under the store labels, large volume ensuring excellent quality for the money. The wines are generally typical of the regions from which they come and are good standards to use for comparative tastings.

HARVEY SELECTIONS

Harvey's of Bristol made a reputation with their Sherries, which they bought in Jerez and blended in Bristol. Success led them to buy lots of other wines, particularly in Bordeaux and Burgundy, bottling them under their own labels. In the fifties they bought their own vineyards and storage facilities in the Jerez district to ensure a regular supply, and when the firm was taken over by the large Gilbey complex, various wine contracts and holdings came to be marketed under that name. The regionals of Burgundy, the Rhine, and the Moselle are generally reasonable in price and well selected, and they offer a worthy group of small châteaux, including among the reds Château La Rode, Pailhas, and Platey, which cost around three dollars; similarly priced whites, less interesting, include Château du Pick, Jean Jervais, and Mayras.

TYTELL EUROPA WINES

Several importers have developed company or brand names to distinguish their wines on the market or have set up a buying office in the various regions, through which they will clear lots of wines and whose name they will use on the labels as an umbrella. Among these are the wines marketed as Tytell Europe Wines, variously spelled Teitel for German wines and Henri Tytell & Fils for French wines and others. The name is a trademark of Monarch Wine, which developed the market for sweet kosher wines made from Concord grapes under the brand name of Manischewitz. The regionals are meant to be competitively priced, the trade phrase for cheap wines, and many of them are excellent, although varying from shipment to shipment. The lots and shippers change, but the name remains constant, a simplification that benefits the buyer when he finds a good lot. Many of the regionals are the lowest-priced on the market, and they are always worth trying in comparative tastings.

LEONARD KREUSCH SELECTIONS

Another line of low-priced wines, the name was originally used as a trademark for Rhine wines and today represents the largest volume of imports of German wines. The line now includes many excellent estate-bottlings from the Rheingau and the Moselle, the good wines of Bordeaux and the Loire shipped by Domaine Cordier, and some Burgundies from Domaine Grivelet, a Burgundy shipper. A long line of Rhônes and Burgundies is imported under the Leonard Kreusch trademark, and there are lines from Italy, Spain, and Portugal as well; good regionals can be found in the lines, such as a Pinot Noir Saint Victor and a Gigondas marketed as Domaine de Sainte Anne. Especially to be noted are the Bordeaux blends from Domaine Cordier under the brand name Plaisir de France, which cost about two dollars a bottle.

Appendix

WINE TASTINGS

TOP BORDEAUX CHÂTEAUX

STOCKING A SMALL CELLAR

THE COUNTRY WINES
OF FRANCE

VDQS

SWEET WINES

EXPANDED LIST
OF SHIPPERS

WINE TASTINGS

Wine tastings are confusing, no matter how they are set up. There are too many wines, two or three to a table, the tables ranged around the room, the crowd moving from one to another. To reduce the milling, some tastings seat a few people at a table with the wines in the center and a commentator at a microphone to tell about the wines as they are drunk. One group in New York worked out a combination of the two, people sitting at long tables to taste the first three wines while a commentator describes them, then getting up to taste other wines set out on tables around the room.

After a few such tastings, people find that they don't learn much, so they band together and decide to hold tastings of their own, with no more than a dozen people and a dozen wines. Each person or couple brings a dish for a buffet, a committee picks the wines, and the cost of them is split. This makes a nice sort of party, not too much work or too much expense for anybody, and everyone gets a chance to taste several wines with a variety of foods.

Experts don't think tastings are successful, because the affairs quickly turn into parties. Tasting gets lost in the shuffle. They are quite right, of course. A professional taster visiting a grower or shipper goes at the matter quite differently. A dozen wines from a single vintage or a vineyard will be lined up on a table, the wines poured into glasses before each bottle. He looks at all the wines, mentally eliminating any that are cloudy, then smells them all, noting which are best. Then he confirms what he has smelt by tasting, selecting the three or four that he prefers. The whole business might take five minutes. Then he will taste another batch. Every tasting should follow a similar pattern. At home, only three or four wines might be chosen for tasting, the wines to be served later at dinner. Choosing the wines is the problem.

Ideally, they should be close together—the same type or price, or from the same vintage. Any one of the three elements can change, but not all the variables. Recently a consumer magazine decided to try to do just that, concentrating on wines costing under $4 a bottle. The results were inconclusive.

They selected fifty reds and fifty whites and a score of pink wines, limiting choice to wines in national distribution. This meant passing up many good wines, for local distributors constantly provide their markets with wines produced in quantities too small for general offerings.

A panel of experts was selected, and the wines were tasted in groups of five, three groups to a session. Each expert rated each wine against the others in the group, and the consensus was published. The panel met each week for several months, tasting each wine at least twice. The groups of five were set up randomly, except that Burgundies were tasted against other Burgundies, Bordeaux against Bordeaux, and so on.

Was a two-dollar Liebfraumilch as good as a three-dollar one? Was a Bordeaux regional better than a California claret? Was a California varietal from Pinot Noir, the great Burgundy grape, in the same league with a Burgundy from Burgundy?

Experts call this confusing apples with oranges. Wines vary too much, from blend to blend, from year to year, from place to place, to make meaningful comparisons. Four California wines marketed as Chablis, for example, were tasted against a Burgundy regional costing twice as much. This was a possible comparison, but tossed in with them were two California varietals (a Pinot Blanc and a Chardonnay), a shipper's Chablis, a Chablis Grand Cru, and a Pouilly-Fuissé. The tasters were confused. The results were more so.

You might like to try the various Liebfraumilchs on the market. The four tasted by the panel of experts are listed below, their number to be augmented by whatever others you can find locally. They are arranged in ascending order of price, from $3 up.

>Langenbach Liebfraumilch Meister-Krone
>Julius Kayser Liebfraumilch Glockenspiel
>Hanns Christoff Deinhard Liebfraumilch
>Liebfraumilch Blue Nun

So it goes, region by region, and you can taste regularly for months, comparing wine after wine, for your own amazement.

Some of the low-priced wines you will like, some of the high-priced ones you will dislike. Tasting blind, you will find that a wine you hated one time you will like another, simply because tastes change from day to day—yours or the taste of the wine. After a few tastings, though, you will find the sort of wine you like. For me, young wines that are fresh and fruity seem to have the most appeal. For convenience, on the following pages I have arranged in groups the wines tasted by the panel of experts, so that you can make your own comparisons.

I have left out some of the wines. A Château Lafite-Rothschild '64 was included with the Bordeaux, which is a wine not yet ready to drink; a ten-year-old, ten-dollar bottle from a Gevrey-Chambertin vineyard was included, but it was not mature either. A single red from Portugal and one from Spain were tossed in, but only confused the tasters.

GROUPS OF WINES FOR COMPARATIVE TASTING

Select a few bottles marketed as California Chablis. In the blind tasting by the panel of experts were the first four wines listed. Only one of these do I like, so I have added a few others. You will have no trouble picking the one I like, and you will find at least two others that you like, each costing less than two dollars, or about that.

>   Italian Swiss Colony Gold Medal Reserve Chablis
>   Gallo Chablis Blanc
>   Almadén Mountain White Chablis
>   The Christian Brothers Chablis
>   Charles Krug Chablis
>   Mirassou Chablis
>   Paul Masson Chablis
>   Inglenook Chablis

You will have to shop around for these, for not every store will have them all, and you will find several others you might add to the group. The name only identifies a white-wine blend in

California, more or less dry, so you could also taste in the same group blends that are simply called Mountain White.

There is no point, though, in comparing these wines with French ones labeled Petit Chablis, Chablis, Chablis Premier Cru, or Chablis Grand Cru; such wines will simply be different.

*

Lavergne Pavillon Rouge de Bordeaux
Barton & Guestier Médoc
Sichel Médoc Ruban Rouge
Cruse Médoc La Dame Rouge
Ginestet Margaux
Chanson Château La Garde

Sichel Saint Émilion
Cruse Saint Émilion La Garderie
Barton & Guestier Saint Émilion

The Christian Brothers Napa Cabernet Sauvignon
Paul Masson Cabernet Sauvignon
Louis M. Martini Cabernet Sauvignon
Beaulieu Vineyard BV Cabernet Sauvignon

NOTE: Low-priced château-bottlings from the Médoc, and wines called Bordeaux Supérieur, might be added to the first group. There are many inexpensive Saint Émilions that could augment the second, while almost every major California producer markets a Cabernet Sauvignon, to augment those lists. There is not much point, however, tasting the wines of one group against those of another.

*

Gallo Chianti
Italian Swiss Colony Chianti
Guild Vino da Tavola Red
Famiglia Cribari Vino Rosso da Pranza
Paul Masson Rubion

NOTE: There are many wines called Chianti from California, and many with Italianate names, all of which can be included in this group for comparison. Villa Armando, Franzia Brothers, and Louis M. Martini, among others, deserve inclusion.

❉

    Widmer Naples Valley Red
    Taylor Lake Country Red
    Boordy Vineyards Red Wine
    Great Western Pleasant Valley Red Wine
    Great Western Baco Noir Burgundy

NOTE: New York State red wines can be tasted against those from Ohio and Missouri and New Jersey, all having a family taste.

❉

    Gallo Paisano
    Roma Burgundy
    Gallo Hearty Burgundy
    The Christian Brothers Burgundy
    Mirassou Santa Clara Burgundy

NOTE: Any California wine labeled "Burgundy" is simply a blend of red wines, so any others might be added to the list. Only one Pinot Noir varietal from California was included in the tasting, but several can be found in most shops, all worth comparing against each other.

❉

    Latour Beaujolais Supérieur
    Cruse Beaujolais
    Jadot Beaujolais
    Chanson Beaujolais Saint Vincent

NOTE: Beaujolais and Beaujolais Supérieur can be tasted against each other without too much confusion, but Beaujolais-Villages and those bearing township names are in a different class, so comparison is not too helpful. In California, Napa Gamay and Gamay Beaujolais are different grapes, so comparison is not particularly revealing.

❉

    Soderi Chianti Classico
    Melini Chianti Classico
    Brolio Chianti Classico
    Ruffino Chianti
    Villa Antinori Chianti Classico
    Ruffino Riserva Ducale Chianti Classico

❉

TOP BORDEAUX CHÂTEAUX

Médoc Châteaux by Commune

MARGAUX and NEIGHBORS

Margaux
Brane-Cantenac
Cantenac Brown
Cantemerle
Durfort
Giscours
Lascombes
Malescot Saint-Exupéry
Palmer
Prieuré-Lichine
Rausan-Ségla
Rauzan-Gassies

PAUILLAC

Lafite Rothschild
Latour
Mouton Rothschild
Lynch-Bages
Pichon-Longueville (Baron)
Pichon-Longueville (Comtesse)
Duhart-Milon
Pontet Canet
Mouton Baron Philippe
Grand-Puy-Lacoste
Batailley
Haut-Batailley

SAINT JULIEN

Beychevelle
Branaire-Ducru
Ducru Beaucaillou
Gruaud-Larose
Gloria
Léoville Barton
Léoville Las Cases
Léoville Poyferré
Langoa Barton
Talbot
Saint Pierre
Lagrange

SAINT ESTÈPHE

Calon-Ségur
Cos d'Estournel
Montrose
Cos Labory
Capbern
Les Ormes de Pez
De Pez
Phélan Ségur
Meyney
Marbuzet
Tronquoy-Lalande
Lafon-Rochet

Lesser-known Médoc Châteaux

MARGAUX

Ferrière
D'Issan
Kirwan
La Tour de Mons
Marquis d'Alesme Becker
Marquis de Terme
Angludet
Bel-Air-Marquis d'Aligre
Boyd-Cantenac
Paveil
Siran

PAUILLAC

Grand-Puy-Ducasse
Clerc-Milon-Mondon
Croizet-Bages
Haut-Bages Libéral
Lynch-Moussas

OTHERS

Chasse-Spleen
Dutruch-Lambert
Gressier Grand Poujeaux
Poujeaux-Theil
Fourcas-Dupré
Fourcas-Hostein

La Lagune
Belgrave
Bel Orme
Parempuyre
Paveil
Ville George

Top Bordeaux Châteaux from Various Districts

GRAVES	SAINT ÉMILION	POMEROL
Haut-Brion	Cheval Blanc	Pétrus
La Mission Haut Brion	Ausone	L'Évangile
Pape Clément	Belair	La Conseillante
Domaine de Chevalier	Canon	Vieux Château Certan
Haut Bailly	Figeac	Gazin
Carbonnieux	La Gaffelière	Lafleur
Malartic-Lagravière	Pavie	La Fleur-Pétrus
Fieuzal	Clos-Fourtet	Petit-Village
La Tour Haut Brion	Magdelaine	Trotanoy
La Tour-Martillac	L'Angelus	Certan-de-May
Smith Haut Lafitte	Beauséjour-Duffau-Lagarosse	Certan Giraud
Bouscaut	Beauséjour-Fagouet	Beauregard

※ ※ ※

Olivier	Canon-la-Gaffelière	Clos l'Église
Laville-Haut-Brion	Croque Michotte	Clos l'Église Clinet
Couchins	Curé Bon La Madeleine	Lagrange
Larrivet-Haut-Brion	Larcis Ducasse	Nenin
La Louvière	Trotte Vieille	Latour à Pomerol
La Tour Léognan	Ripeau	La Pointe
La Garde	Villemaurine	La Croix
Pique-Caillou	Corbin	Mazeyres
Cabannieux	La Dominique	Rouget
Gazin	Fonroque	De Sales

NOTE: The first dozen châteaux in the above lists are generally rated higher by the trade than the others listed.

STOCKING A SMALL CELLAR

Those of us who drink a bottle of wine or two a week and have friends in for dinner now and then can manage well enough by keeping a few bottles on a shelf and by making frequent trips to the neighborhood wine shop. Consumption might average a case a month. The choice on hand for any particular meal is limited, though, and since one of the pleasures of wine is variety, a small cellar is a modest luxury.

The cellar can be two or three cases of ready-to-drink wines—a three-month supply, say, with bottles regularly replaced during the quarterly sales. Or the cellar can be five or six cases kept in a closet, sixty or seventy bottles on hand at any one time, that would be drunk up in a year or less. Closets are likely to be 70° or so, varying as much as 10° from day to night and season to season, temperatures that age wines quickly. To store wines longer than a year calls for steadier and lower temperatures, the ideal being in the low fifties.

As for the wines, most of them should be red, because reds taste better with more dishes than do whites. The proportion should be two to one, with perhaps a dozen different reds to choose from. Mixed cases of twelve different wines provide a wide choice, but six pairs of wines per case offer the chance to try a wine a second time. Any favorites can be bought by the dozen.

Wines most consistently available are those from American vineyards and from the big European shippers and their importers. Best buys will be found in the various lists, but a good starting list of imported bottlings might include the following:

Reds

1 case Bordeaux "petits châteaux"
1 case Rhônes
1 case Beaujolais
1 case Spanish or Italian
1 case Yugoslavian, Hungarian, and Greek
1 case Portuguese, Chilean, and Argentinian

Whites

1 case Alsatian or Mâcon
1 case Rhine or Moselle
1 case Loire or Italian

For unusual wines, try getting mixed cases from individual importers, or any new wines that come on the market. But probably the greatest variety of low-priced wines comes from American vineyards; a wine cellar can be composed of these alone.

A Representative Cellar of American Wines

Listed here is a 25-bottle cellar that offers a fair cross-section of California wines, plus an additional 25-bottle cellar that includes some New York State bottlings. The cost for all 50 of these wines might come to $150, particularly if some special bottlings are included. If excellence is desired no matter the cost, then there are the expensive bottlings from small producers such as Mayacamas and Stony Hill and Freemark Abbey, all noted for their Chardonnays; there are the Cabernets of Heitz and Chappellet, the Pinot Noirs of Hanzell and Parducci. A single mixed case of these might cost $100. Occasionally to be found are the bottlings of Souverain Cellars, Spring Mountain Vineyards, the Beringer Brothers, or Ficklin. Other vineyards whose wines can be found occasionally are listed under "A Special Case," along with those from some eastern vineyards.

25-BOTTLE CELLAR

6 *Cabernet Sauvignon,* from The Christian Brothers, Almadén, Paul Masson, Beaulieu Vineyard, Louis Martini, Mirassou
4 *Pinot Noir,* from Louis Martini, Beaulieu Vineyard, Inglenook, Robert Mondavi
4 *Zinfandel,* from Charles Krug, Louis Martini, Buena Vista, Parducci

4 *Chardonnay* or *Pinot Chardonnay,* from Wente Brothers, The Christian Brothers, Charles Krug, Robert Mondavi
3 *Johannisberg Riesling,* from Louis Martini, Charles Krug, Paul Masson
3 *Sauvignon Blanc,* from Wente Brothers, Mirassou, Concannon
1 *Schramsberg Brut* Sparkling Wine.

50-BOTTLE CELLAR

25 bottles as listed above

3 *Gamay Beaujolais* or *Napa Gamay,* from Weibel, Mirassou, Almadén, Charles Krug, Louis Martini, or Robert Mondavi
2 *Petite Sirah,* from Concannon and Parducci
2 *Barbera,* from Luis Martini and Sebastiani
2 *Baco Noir* or *Chelois,* from Great Western or Bully Hill

3 *Grenache Rosé* from Almadén, or *Gamay Rosé* from Inglenook or Louis Martini, or *Cabernet Rosé* from Beaulieu Vineyard (Beaurosé) or Buena Vista

2 *Semillon,* from Wente Brothers, Concannon, or Mirassou
2 *Pinot Blanc,* from Wente Brothers and Mirassou
2 *Chenin Blanc,* from The Christian Brothers, Charles Krug, Robert Mondavi, or Louis Martini
3 *Sylvaner,* from Louis Martini, Buena Vista, Mirassou
2 New York State whites, from Widmer's Wine Cellars, Gold Seal, Great Western
2 sparkling wines, from Gold Seal, Hanns Kornell, Korbel, Almadén

A SPECIAL CASE

From New York State, get wines from Vinifera Wine Cellars,

STOCKING A SMALL CELLAR 211

run by Dr. Konstantin Frank; Widmer's Wine Cellars; Bully Hill; and the High Tor, on the Hudson.

There's also Boordy Vineyard, outside of Baltimore, in Riderwood, Maryland; and a newer Boordy Vineyards in Westfield, New York. In Marlboro, New York, are the tiny experimental vineyards of Benmarl.

When traveling—through New England, the Middle Atlantic States, and in the South—be on the lookout for local wines, most of which are available only in local shops and/or at the vineyards themselves. South-facing slopes of the White Mountains, the Green Mountains, the Alleghenies, and the Blue Ridge Mountains have been planted with small experimental plots, and you never know when you'll make a new and interesting discovery.

John Canepa, whose own White Mountain Vineyards, in Laconia, New Hampshire, now offers wines on the market, is president of that state's Grape Growers Association, and he may be able to tell you of some new ones. In the towns of Birchrunville and North East, in Pennsylvania, there are other small vineyards to look for; in New Jersey, Renault makes some interesting wines at Egg Harbor, near Atlantic City. In New York State, investigate Canadaigua Industries, in Canadaigua; and the Hammondsport Wine Co. (also owned by Canadaigua), in Hammondsport.

Probably the greatest potential area for quality vineyards is the heights of the Blue Ridge Mountains. But only a keen eye and local gossiping will lead you to any of them. Also check out Richard's Wine Cellars, in Petersburg, Virginia; the company, by the way, is experimenting with plantations in the Carolinas and contemplating plots as far west as Texas, some in hybrids. Most of the southern vineyards are currently planted in Scuppernong, a variety of the Muscadine, which is probably this country's oldest cultivated native grape. The sweet wine is worth trying—and stocking, if you like its wild taste.

In Ohio, you can find Meiers Wine Cellars at Silverton, near Cincinnati, and other vineyards on islands in Lake Erie and near Sandusky. You may or may not find the wines interesting.

Travelers to Washington and Oregon will find vineyards in the Yakima Valley and the Snake River Valley. On the way, stop in Idaho—at the town of Troy, near Moscow—and try to sample the Zinfandel. No matter where you travel in foothill and valley country, chances are you are never more than an hour or so from a new vineyard. These wines aren't for your cellar, perhaps, but worth tasting for the future.

Definitely for your cellar, however, are wines from the small California producers, many of them available only when you are taking a trip to the Coast. Even then, you may have to go to the wineries themselves. Here is a list of varietal producers whose wines you may want to stock in addition to those already mentioned:

Bear Mountain Winery	Novitiate of Los Gatos
Bertero Winery	Oakville Vineyards
Bisceglia Brothers	Opici Winery
Brookside Vineyard Company	Pedroncelli Winery
David Bruce	Ridge Vineyards
Chappellet Winery	San Martín Vineyards
Filippi Vintage Company	Simi Winery
Freemark Abbey	Souverein Cellars
Heitz Winery	Sterling Vineyards
Llords & Elwood Winery	Villa Armando Winery
Mayacamas Vineyard	Windsor Vineyards
Château Montelena	Wooden Valley Winery

THE COUNTRY WINES OF FRANCE

France has something like 3½ million acres of vineyards, less than a fifth of which produce wines coming under Appellation Contrôlée. Production approaches two billion gallons in a good year, but only about a tenth can be marketed as Appellation Contrôlée. Americans know mostly Burgundy and Bordeaux, the best known of them now high in price, and a few of the less expensive wines of the Rhône, the Loire, and Alsace. To correct this, the French have begun promoting other wines produced in volume and coming under Appellation Contrôlée regulations, including a group being marketed as "country wines," which sell for around three dollars a bottle. Nine wines are initially included:

Côtes-du-Rhône—fruity reds
Corbières—full reds from the Midi
Bordeaux Rouge—light, often-pleasant, low-priced reds
Entre-Deux-Mers—dry, often-soft whites from a large Bordeaux district
Mâcon Blanc—dry whites from southern Burgundy
Alsace—flowery whites
Muscadet—dry whites from the Loire
Rosé d'Anjou—soft, light, pink wines from the Loire
Côtes de Provence Rosé—fresh, light, pink wines from the Riviera

This is a remarkable selection, representing every major wine-producing district, each of the wines being produced in large volume. These are excellent wines to use for comparative tastings, when you want to see how wines from Eastern Europe or South America, say, stack up against their French counterparts. When conducting such tastings, though, be sure the prices are about equal, a four-dollar bottle being generally superior to one that costs three.

All the wines should be drunk young, within a couple of years of the vintage, for they are past their peaks when much over three years old. Importers have been bringing in most of these wines for years, but the campaign serves to focus attention on them, paving the way for other unfamiliar bottlings, particularly those from along the Loire and the Rhône.

"Country wines" referred once to those wines typical of a district, *vins du pays,* which were rarely shipped out of the country or even out of the countryside. Better grapes in the vineyards and better wine-making practices—to say nothing of wider interests, which mean the wines are bought as soon as they appear on distant markets—make wines promptly available in good condition and still fresh and sprightly. When less than three dollars a bottle, they are excellent buys.

VDQS

A complete list of *Vins Délimités de Qualité Supérieure* presents an uneven group of wines, some worth being listed as Appellation Contrôlée, such as Cahors or Corbières, and others that are overrated, such as those of the Auvergne or of Orléan or of Lyon. A list of those from the Midi is useful, because lesser wines frequently come in from that vast region, and those from the Rhône and Provence should be noted if only to distinguish them from others, entitled to Appellations Contrôlées. Before the North African departments became independent, their wines were listed, and need inclusion if only for future reference. Here is a selection of these:

Midi

Cabrières
Côteaux de Saint-Christol
Côteaux de Verargues
La Clape
Corbières Supérieurs
Corbières du Roussillon
Costières du Gard
Faugères
Minervois

Picpoul de Pinet
Pic-Saint-Loup
Quatourze
Rousillon des Aspres
Saint-Chinian
Saint-Drézéry
Saint-Georges-d'Orques
Saint-Saturnin

Southwest

Cahors
Côtes de Buzet
Côtes du Marmandais
Côtes de Fronton
Béarn
Villaudric
Lavilledieu
Irouléguy
Tursan

Rhône and Provence

Côteaux du Luberon
Côteaux d'Aix
Côtes du Ventoux
Haut-Comtat
Vin de Châtillon en Diois

Côtes de Provence
Côteaux de Pierrevert

Algiers

Ain Bessem Bouria
Côtes du Zaccar (Milliana)
Haut-Dahra
Médéa

Oran

Ain-el-Hadjar
Côteaux de Mascara
Côteaux de Tlemçen
Mascara
Monts du Tessalah
Mostaganem & Section Kenenda

SWEET WINES

France produces a goodly number of sweet wines: sherry-like straw wines or *vins de paille* (those that have been left to dry on straw mats): and fortified wines, mostly from Muscat, Grenache, and Malvoisie grapes. These can be drunk chilled—as apéritifs—or as a dessert, or with one. Not fashionable, a list of those coming under Appellation Contrôlée can be helpful to an explorer. They should cost less than $3 a bottle.

Banyuls
Côtes d'Agly
Côtes de Haut-Rousillon

Grand Rousillon
Frontignan
Maury

Muscats:

Beaumes de Venise
Frontignan
Lunel
Rivesaltes
Saint Jean de Minervois
Pineau des Charentes
Pineau Charentais
Rasteau
Rivesaltes

EXPANDED LIST OF SHIPPERS

Burgundy

A. Bichot & Co.	Dreyfus, Ashby, New York
Bouchard Père & Fils	Vintage Wines (Heublein), New York
Champy Père & Cie.	Briones & Co., New York
Chanson Père & Fils	Julius Wile & Sons, New York
F. Chauvenet	Austin Nichols, New York
Joseph Drouhin	Dreyfus, Ashby, New York
Dufoulour Frères	Dreyfus, Ashby, New York
Drouhin Laroze	Kobrand, New York
Louis Jadot	Kobrand, New York
Geisweiler & Fils	House of Wines, Washington, D.C.
Jaboulet-Vercherre	Regional distributors
Louis Latour	Frederick Wildman, New York
Liger Belair	Dreyfus, Ashby, New York
Lupe Cholet	A. Fantozzi, Chicago
	Imported Brands Inc., New York
Moillard Grivot	Frank Schoonmaker, New York
Patriarche Père & Fils	Casanove-Opici, New York
Piat & Cie.	Monsieur Henri, New York
Charles Vienot	Monsieur Henri, New York
Pasquier Desvignes	Munson Shaw, New York
La Reine Pédauque	
Remoissenet Père & Fils	Bonsal Seggermann, San Francisco
	Excelsior, New York
	House of Wines, Washington, D.C.
Ropiteau Frères	MGM Imports, Los Angeles
	Frederick Wildman, New York
Les Vignerons des Côtes Mâconnais	Eric Lambert, New York
Union des Co-operatives Vinicoles de Bourgogne	Frank Schoonmaker, New York

EXPANDED LIST OF SHIPPERS

Rhône

Père Anselme, Châteauneuf
Brotte, Châteauneuf
Chapoutier & Cie., Tain
Delas Frères, Tournon
Paul Jaboulet Ainé, Tain

Jaboulet-Vercherre, Tain
Paul-Étienne, Père et Fils,
St. Péray
J. Vidal Fleury, Nuits
Vins Fins Salavert, Bourg

Loire

Ackerman-Laurance
Donatien Bahuaud

Blanchard & Fils
Drouet Frères
Roger Gouin
Rémy-Pannier
P. Guéry & Cie.
Co-operative Vinicole
 Les Caves de la Loire
De Ladoucette Frères
Lalanne Frères
Maison Veuve Amiot
Ets. J. M. Monmousseau
Marcel Martin

Fernand Rossignol
Société d'Exportation des
 Vins Nantais (Jean Breton)
Unifrance
Claude Verdier

Dreyfus, Ashby, New York
Crosse & Blackwell, New York
French Trade Center, Los Angeles
Louis Glunz, Chicago
Common Market Specialties, Seattle
Monsieur Henri, New York
Austin Nichols, New York
Austin Nichols, New York
Austin Nichols, New York
Bercut-Vandervoort, San Francisco
Bercut-Vandervoort, San Francisco

Dreyfus, Ashby, New York
Frank Schoonmaker, New York
Eric Lambert, New York
Winegate Imports, New York
Wine Import, New York
Stuart Imports, San Francisco
Macy's, Chicago
Bamberger's, Newark
Vintage Wines, New York
Munson Shaw, New York

André Crispin, Houston
Great Lakes Wine, Chicago
Leonard Kreusch, N.J.
Stuart Imports, San Francisco

Rioja

Bodegas Bilbainas
Bodegas Españolas Franco
Bodegas Riojanas
Compañía Vinícola del Norte España
Federico Paternina

Other Spanish Shippers

Alella, Barcelona
René Barbier
La Vinícola Ibérica
Marqués de Murrieta
Marqués de Riscal
Miguel Torres

German Shippers

The following is a list of the German Wine Export Association —Verband Deutscher Weinexporteure—which includes many of the major shippers but few of those growers who market their wines directly.

Duhr Conrad Fehres, Mosel

Jakob Gerhardt, Rheinhessen
Carl Graff, Mosel
Louis Guntrum, Rheinhessen
Arthur Hallgarten, Rheingau
Eduard Hautt, Rheinhessen
J. W. Huesgen, Mosel
Adolph Huesgen, Mosel
Weingut Ernst Jungkenn, Rheinpfalz

Langenbach & Co., Rheinhessen

F. W. Langguth, Mosel

Maximiner Stiftskellerei,
 Stephan Studart, Mosel
Stewart Chase, Milwaukee

Various regional
 distributors
Bon Vin, Houston
Dreyfus, Ashby, New York
Schenley Imports, New York
Carillon Importers, New York
Agent: J. Levine, Detroit
E. Preiss, Los Angeles
Silver Hills Products, New York

Ginday Imports, Baltimore
AAA Wine, Beverly Hills
Frederick Wildman, New York
S. S. Pierce, Boston
M. Kronheim, Washington, D.C.
Various regional
 distributors

Hooper-Richardson, Boston

EXPANDED LIST OF SHIPPERS

Rudolf Müller, Mosel	Warren Strauss, New York
Friedr. Carl Ott & Co, Würzberg	Foreign Brands, New York
Franz Reh, Mosel	German Distilleries, Ltd., New York
Balthasar Ress, Rheingau	Various regional distributors
Scholl & Hillebrand, Rheingau	International Vintage Wines, San Francisco
P. J. Valckenberg, Rheinhessen	Dreyfus, Ashby, New York
Wilh. Wasum, Rhein	Dennis & Huppert, New York
	The Hammer Co., Cleveland
Michael Weber, Mosel	Various regional distributors
Franz Winkel, Rheingau	Various regional distributors
Zentralkellerei der Winzergenossenschaften, Mosel	Leonard Kreusch, Carlstadt, N.J.
	Blenheim, Philadelphia

INDEX

Aaron, Sam, 188
Acids (acidity), in wines, 26, 27, 28; fruit acids, 17–18, 19
Adriatica, 90–91, 175
Affames, 103
Age (Spanish jug wine), 27, 96
Agents, 187–89
Alameda, Calif., 105
Alby, Jules, 177
Alcobaça, 98
Alcohol(s), 13–14, 18, 23, 27; added to wine, 130, 131; higher, 13; in pop wines, 30, 32, 34
Alcools blancs, 71
Alella, Spain, 26
Algeria, 78, 187, 216
Algiers, 216
Alicante-Bouchet, 120
Aligoté, 45, 149
Allied Grape Growers, 110, 114
Almadén, 116–17, 202, 209, 210
Aloxe, 61
Alsace, 5, 12, 23, 70–74, 135, 177, 180, 186, 213 (*see also* specific places, wines); growers and importers, 71–74
Amandières, Les, 151–52
Amontillados, 96
Angludet, Château, 146
Anjou, the (France), 69
Annheuser & Fehrs, 153–54
Antinori Bardolino, 177
Antinori Est! Est!! Est!, 177
Apéritifs, 30, 31, 33, 35, 96
Aphrodite, 103, 174
Appellations d' Origine Contrôlées (AOC), 51, 57, 67, 75, 76, 213–14, 215, 217
Apple wine, 33, 34
Aquéria, Château, 172
Arbois, 75–76
Argentina, 127, 163, 167–68
Aromatic wines, 31, 32. *See also* specific kinds, wines
Arsinoe, 103
Asher, Gerald, 158
Asti Spumante, 54
Aurora, 122, 123
Auslesen, 81, 153
Austin, Nichols, 158
Austria, 88–89, 159, 186; *heurige*, 88
Auxey-Duresses, 62
Aymonier, Henri, 171

Babeasca Nicoresti, 92
Baco Blanc, 121
Baco Noir, 120, 122, 123
Baden, 85
Bali Hai, 32
Banfi Products Corp., 25, 26, 158–59
Barbaresco, 53
Barbera, 10, 26, 53, 105, 113, 210
Barbier, René, 179
Bardolino, 26, 53, 55, 162, 176, 177
Bardolino Bertani, 162

Barenblut, 112
Barnyard reek, in wines, 16
Barolo, 53
Baroque, 117
Barsac, 2, 64
Barton & Guestier (B&G), 135, 136–37, 152, 159–61
Bas-Rhin, 71
Bass Charrington, 194
Beaujolais, 10, 23, 33, 36–37, 39–41, 62, 131, 147–48, 149, 150, 151, 160, 166, 167, 170, 175, 188, 204; buying, 40–41; described, 39; temperature for drinking, 40
Beaujolais Blanc, 151
Beaujolais Brouilly, 167, 168
Beaujolais Nouveau, 39, 41
Beaujolais Supérieur, 39, 40, 41, 150, 170, 204
Beaujolais Vallières, 151
Beaujolais-Villages, 39, 40, 41, 166, 195, 204
Beaulieu, Château, 110
Beaulieu Vineyards (BV), 110, 170, 203, 209–10
Beaumont (Pinot Noir), 110
Beaune, 61, 62, 149, 150, 151, 177
Beefeater gin, 171–72
Beerenauslesen, 81
Benicarlos, 95
Benmarl Vineyard, 211
Bergerac, 76, 77
Bergerie, La, 136
Beringer Brothers, 25, 112–13
Bernkasteler Kurfürstlay, 83
Bertrán, 27
Best buys, 2–6, 13, 37–42, 45, 46, 53–57, 62–71 *passim*, 76, 78, 80–85, 87, 88, 91, 95–97, 100, 109–10, 120–24, 131–32, 135–54 *passim*, 158–82 *passim*, 187, 189–97 (*see also* Prices; Wine Selections; specific distributors, growers, importers, places, shippers, wines); Bordeaux châteaux, 205–7; French country wines, 213–14; regionals, 37, 38–39, 41 (*see also* specific places, wines); representative wine-cellar selections, 208–12; shippers and importers and, 43, 131–32, 135ff., 158ff.; sweet wines, 217; wine tastings and, 200–4
Beverage media, 189–90
Beyerman, H. & O., 137
Bianco di Verona, 55
Bikavér, 90
Bingen's, 84
Binger Sankt Rochuspelle, 84
Birkedal Hartmann & Co., 137–38
Birnbaum, Leonard, 180–81
Bitterness, in wines, 18
Blanc de Blancs, 44, 45, 64, 115, 136, 149, 161, 166, 169
Blanc de Blanc Sauvignon, 147
Blanc Fumé, 68, 106
Blanquette de Limoux, 76

INDEX

Blayais, 65
Blends (blending), 23, 37, 130ff., 155–83 passim, 185 (see also specific kinds, places, wines); shippers and importers and, 130ff., 155–83, 185
Blue Nun, 146, 153, 201
Blue Nun Bernkasteler Riesling, 46
Blue Nun of Sichel, 46
Blue Ridge Mountains, vineyards of, 211
Blum, Bernard, 176
Boal (Bual), 100
Bodegas y Viñeros López, 163
Body, in wine, 18–19
Bohemia, wines from, 92
Bolla, 55
Bolla Soave, 169
Bonfils, Georges, 29
Bon-Sol, 161
Boone's Apple Wine, 34
Boone's Farm Strawberry Hill, 118
Boordy Vineyards, 120, 121, 211
Bordeaux, 2, 3, 4, 5, 28, 50, 51, 59–60, 61, 64–68; blanc and rouge, 43–44; château-bottled, 185, 205–7 (see also specific kinds, wines); Classed Growths, 43, 136, 137, 140, 141; co-operatives, 187; country wines, 213–14; district and township wines, 64–68 (see also specific places, wines); grapes (vines), 9, 10, 12; importers, shippers, and distributors, 130, 131, 133–48, 152, 156, 158, 159, 161, 167, 170–74, 177, 181–82; regionals, 2, 3, 9, 10, 12, 43–44 (see also specific places, wines); selections and prices by shippers (listed), 135; top châteaux (listed), 205–7
Bordeaux-Burgundy shippers, 152
Bordeaux-Côtes de Castillon, 66, 67
Bordeaux-Côtes de France, 66
Bordeaux Rouge, 213
Bordeaux Supérieur, 4, 43–44, 60, 64, 66, 67, 136, 182, 195; best regionals, 43–44; Classed Growths, 43
Borgogno, 158–59
Bottles, jug wines and, 25, 28, 29; double (magnum), 25, 28; plastic, 29
Bouchard Monopole, 150
Bouchard Père & Fils, 150, 152
Bouchet, 10, 66
Bouquet, in wines, 19
Bourgeois Supérieur, 141
Bourgogne Aligoté Grand Pavois, 152
Bourgogne-Passe-Tout-Grains, 44–45
Branaire Ducru, Château, 140
Brand-name wines, 4, 5–6, 64–65, 186, 189 (see also specific individuals, kinds, organizations, places, wines); California, 108–18; importers and shippers and, 131–32, 158–83 passim
British Columbia, 125
Brolio, 160
Brolio Chianti, 160, 161
Brolio Riserva, 38
Brouilly, 39, 40, 41
Browne Vintners, 159–60
Bucelas, 98
Buena Vista, 209, 210
Bulgaria, 91–92
Bully Hill, 210
Burgundy, 4, 5, 9, 10, 11, 24, 27, 28, 39, 42, 44–45, 50, 51, 60–62, 148–52, 185; country wines, 213–14; district and township wines, 60ff. (see also specific places, wines); grapes (vines), 9, 10, 11; regionals, 39ff., 44–45; shippers and importers and, 131–32, 135, 137, 140, 147, 148–52, 156, 160, 167, 170, 172, 176–78, 191, 193–94, 196, 197–98
Burgundy/Bordeaux shippers, 152
Buyers, 188–89
Byrrh, 31

Cabernet, 5, 90, 91, 92, 105, 121, 209
Cabernet Franc, 10, 43, 66, 69
Cabernet Mau, 182
Cabernet Sauvignon, 9, 43, 105, 109, 110, 113, 117, 177, 203, 209
Cahors, 76, 77, 215
California, 5, 9, 10, 11, 44, 45, 105–18, 132, 185 (see also specific growers, organizations, places, wines); buying wines from, 106–7ff.; and European wines compared, 105, 106–7; grapes (vines), 9, 10, 11, 105–6; and improved wine-making techniques, 6; jug wines, 3–4, 15, 24–25, 28–29; names and labels, 106; producers, 108–18; representative small cellar of wines from, 209–10, 212; small producers (listed), 106–7ff.; wines for tasting from, 202–3
"California Riesling," 11
Calvet, 135, 136, 138, 152
Calvet Latour-Montagne, 162
Calvet St. Émilion, 162
Campania, Italy, 53
Canada, 125
Canandaigua Industries, 121, 211
Canepa, John, 211
Canned wines, 29
Canova, Franco, 162
Canteloup, Château, 182
Cantemerle, Château, 137
Cantenac Brown, Château, 139
Carillon Importers, 161–62
Carmel Wine Company, 186
Carte Grise, 72
Cask odor, in wines, 17
Cassis, 31, 74, 75
Castelli Romani, 25
Castello di Meleto, 38
Catawba, 122
Cave Bel Air, 146, 147
Caves Alsaciennes, 74
Caves de la Reine Pédauque, 140
Cellarmasters Cuvée, 112
Cellars, wine. See Wine cellars
Cellar taint, in wines, 17–18
Cepa Negra ("Red Wine"), 27
Chablis, 3, 11, 24, 44, 60, 118, 131, 155, 178, 179, 202; vineyard classifications, 60
Chablis Blanc, 3, 118
Chalon, Château, 75
Chambertin, 50, 178, 179, 191
Champagne, 28, 33, 155, 160, 168, 181
Champigny, 69
Chanson Père et Fils, 177
Chapoutier, 175
Chapoutier La Marcelle, 42
Chaptalization process, 18, 80, 81
Chardonnay, 5, 11, 44, 45, 105, 106–7, 108, 109, 111, 121, 122, 209, 210. See also specific kinds
Charmant, 72
Chassagne, 61
Chassagne-Montrachet, 150
Chasselas, 71, 87
Château-bottled wines, 5, 185 (see also specific growers, kinds, places, wines); Bordeaux, 133–35, 136, 137, 138–39ff.; Bordeaux (listed), 205–7; price range, 134; shippers and, 133–35, 136, 138–48; top (listed), 205–7
Châteauneuf-du-Pape, 36, 41–42, 63; buying (listed, prices), 42
Chauvenet, F., 151–52
Chauvenet Rouge, 151
Chelois, 121, 122, 123
Chemical stink, in wines, 16
Chénas, 39, 40, 41
Chenin Blanc, 12, 68–69, 105, 106–7, 109, 111, 113, 117, 203, 210
Chevaliers de Tastevin, 165
Chianti, 7, 10, 36, 37–39, 53, 56, 131, 204; best, 38–39; bottles, 37, 38; California,

24; *governo* system, 37; importers, shippers, and distributors, 155, 159, 160, 161, 168, 169, 172, 176, 188, 203, 204; in jugs, 24, 25; *putto* neck labels, 37–38; temperature for drinking, 40
Chianti Classico, 37, 38–39, 204
Chianti dei Colli Empolesi, 38
Chianti Putto, 39
Chiaretto, 55
Chiavennasca, 54–55
Chile, 5, 127–28, 161
Chinon, 69
Chiroubles, 39, 40, 41
Christian Brothers, 108–9, 202, 203, 204, 209, 210; best buys (jugs), 3, 4, 24, 26
Cider, 33, 35
Claret, 50, 109, 111, 147, 166; best buys, 4; California, 24; in jugs, 24, 27
Classed Growths, 43, 136, 137, 140, 141. *See also* specific wines
Clos Gänsbrönnel, 177
Clos des Jacobins, 139
Clos Sainte Hune, 72–73
Clos de Vougeot, 148
Cognac, 33
Colares, 98, 100
Cold Duck, 32–33
Colli Aretini, 38
Colli Fiorentini, 38
Colline Pisane, 38
Colli Senesi, 38
Commandaria, 102–3, 174
Common Market, European, 60, 80, 187
Complete Wine Book, The (Schoonmaker and Marvel), 191
Concannon, 115–16, 210
Concord grape wines, 34, 197
Condrieu, 63
Co-operatives, 186–87
Corbières, 147, 148, 167, 213, 215
Corbières du Rousillon, 77
Corbières Supérieur, 77
Cordier, 138–39
Cordon d'Alsace, 74
Cornas, 63
Cortese, 54
Corton Charlemagne, 11
Corton Grancey, 131–32
Cos d'Estournel, 141
Cot (Malbec, Pressac), 10
Côteaux du Languedoc, 29, 77
Côteaux du Layon, 69
Côteaux de la Loire, 68, 69
Côteaux de Mascara, 78
Côteaux de Tlemçen, 78
Côte de Beaune, 60–61, 62
Côte-de-Beaune-Villages, 62, 151
Côte de Bordeaux-Saint Macaire, 65
Côte de Brouilly, 39, 40, 41
Côte Chalonnaise, 62
Côte Mâconnaise, 62
Côte de Nuits, 60–61, 62
Côte-de-Nuits-Villages, 62
Côte d'Or, 44, 60–61, 148–49, 152
Côte Rôtie, 10, 42, 63
Côtes de Bourg, 158
Côtes-Canon-Fronsac, 67
Côtes-de-Castillon, 67
Côtes de Duras, 76
Côtes-de-Francs, 67
Côtes de Fronsac, 67
Côtes du Lubéron, 77
Côtes de Provence, 74–75
Côtes de Provence Rosé, 213
Côtes-du-Rhône, 63, 136, 148, 160, 166, 167, 171, 175, 195
Côtes-du-Rhône Rouge, 3; best buy, 3
Cotnari, 92
Country wines (*vin du pays*), French, 69, 213–14; listed, prices, 213–14

Courtiers (Bordeaux wine brokers), 133 134
Cresta Blanca Vineyards, 114
Criolla, 127
Crispin Wines, 162
Crosse & Blackwell, 162–63
Crown of Crowns, 178
Crozes-Hermitage, 63
Crus Classés, 43, 136, 137, 140, 141. *See also* specific places, wines
Cruse et Fils Frères, 135, 136, 139, 152, 168, 169
Crystal d'Alsace, 72
CUNE (Compañía Vinícola del Norte España), 179
Cyprus, 102–3, 174
Czechoslovakia, 92

Dacia, 92
Dame Blanche, La, 139
Dão, 100
Deideisheimer Mariengarten, 85
De la Gardine, Château, 42
Delaware, 122, 123, 124
Del Gambia, 182
De Luze & Fils, A., 139–40, 152
Dennis & Huppert, 163
"Dessert wines," 30, 34. *See also* Pop wines; Sweet wines; specific kinds
Deutscher Qualitätswein, 81
Deutscher Tafelwein, 81
Dijon, 31
Dillon, Clarence, 136, 193
Dimyat, 91
DI's (direct imports), 187–89
Distillates, 71
Distributors, 190
District and township wines, 4–5, 50–51, 52ff. *See also* specific kinds, places, wines
DOC (*Denominazione di Origine Controllata*), 53
Domaine de Beaucastel, 42
Domaine Cordier, 198
Domaine de la Meynarde, 160
Domaine de Mont Redon, 42
Domaine de la Romanée-Conti, 178
Domaine Ropiteau-Mignon, 178
Domains (domain wines), 185. *See also* specific growers, places, wines
Dopff, 72
Dopff & Irion, 72
Dordogne, 66
Double bottle size (magnum), 25, 28
Douro, the (Portugal), 98, 99
Dreyfus, Ashby, 163–66
Dreyfus, Michel, 162, 163–66
Drouhin, Joseph, 4, 132, 151
Dry Semillon, 112
Dubonnet, 31
Dulong Importers, 166–67

Earth smell, in wines, 17
Eastern Mediterranean, 102–3; Cyprus, 102–3; Greece, 102; Israel, 103
Ecu Royal, 166
Edelzwicker, 71
Eger, 90
Einzellagen, 81
Eltviller Steinmächer, 84
Emerald Dry, 117
Emerald Riesling, 106
Emilia, Italy, 53
England, 35, 50; fruit wines from, 35
Entre-Deux-Mers, 65, 213
Erbacher Deutelsberg, 84
Eschenauer, Louis, 135, 140
Escherndorfer Kirchberg, 85
Est! Est! Est!, 53, 56, 177
Estanciero, 163
Estate-bottled wines, 5, 51, 185. *See also* specific places, wines
Etoile, l', sparkling wines of, 75

INDEX 225

European Community. *See* Common Market, European
European jug wines, 22, 23, 25–29; France, 28–29; Italy, 25–26; Portugal, 27–28; sizes, 25; Spain, 26–27
Evxinograd, 91–92
Excelsior (importers), 167–68; best buys, 168
Experts, method of wine tasting by, 13–14
Fairchild, Robert, 171
Fazi-Battaglia Verdicchio, 161, 162
Fendant grape, 87
Feteasca, 92
Fifield, William, 194
Fils de Marcel Quancard, Les, 142
Finger Lakes region, 120–24
Finos (sherries), 3, 96, 100
First Growths, 60–61, 65, 136
Fitou, 76, 77
"Flambeau d'Alsace," 72
Fleurie, 39, 40, 41
Fleury, J. Vidal, 181
Florence, Italy, 37, 38
Folle Blanche, 12, 105, 111
Fonseca, 99
Forster Mariengarten, 85
Fortia, Château, 42
Fournier, Charles, 121, 123
Fracia, 54
Fraise, 71
France, 59–77 (*see also* specific growers, importers and shippers, places, vines, wines); Bordeaux shippers, 131–32, 133–48; Burgundy shippers, 148–52; château-bottled wines, 5, 133ff., 205–7 (*see also* specific places, wines); co-operatives, 186–87; country wines, 213–14; district and township wines, 50–51, 58–77 (*see also* specific places, wines); extended list of shippers, 218–19; grapes (vines), 8–12 (*see also* specific kinds); jug wines, 28–29; legal controls over wine production in, 4, 50–51, 59–60, 213–14, 215–16 (*see also* specific classifications); *petits châteaux*, 43, 65, 66–68, 134, 135, 158; pop wines, 31–32; production and consumption of wine in, 13, 59–60, 185; regional wines, 39–45, 47 (*see also* specific regions, wines); representative small wine cellar, 208–9; rise in price of wines from, 47, 55; shippers and importers, 131–32, 133–52, 155–83 *passim*, 186–98; top Bordeaux châteaux, 205–7; wines for tasting, 203
France Vinipole, 141–42
Franconia, 85, 152, 153
Frank, Konstantin, 121–22, 123, 210
Franken Riesling, 12
Frankenwein, 85, 153
Frascati, 25, 26, 53, 55, 159, 169
Freisa, 53, 54
French Tom, and B&G, 136–37
Fronsadais, Le (France), 67
Frontignan (France), 76
Fruit acids, 17–18, 19
"Fruits de Mer-Escargots-Spécial," 74
Fruit wines, 30–32, 33–35
Fullness, in wines, 18
Fumé Blanc, 109, 113
Furmint grape, 92

Gaillac, 76
Gallo, 3, 4, 24, 34, 118, 202, 203, 204
Gamay, 10, 44–45, 87, 91, 106, 109, 110, 149
Gamay Beaujolais, 10, 105, 106, 110, 112, 115, 117, 210
Gamay Noir, 109
Gamay Noir au Jus Blanc, 10
Garneau (Joseph) Company, 168–69
Gattinara, 53
Generic wines, 4, 5–6

German Wine Export Association (*Verband Deutscher Weinexporteure*), 220
Germany, 12, 80–85 (*see also* specific places, wines); importers and, 159–60, 172, 173, 175, 178, 191, 193–94; regional wines, 45–46; shippers, 152–54; shippers (listed), 220–21; wine classifications and labels, 81–82
Gevrey, 50, 61
Gevrey-Chambertin, 50, 191, 202
Gewürztraminer, 12, 70, 72, 73, 74
Gewürztraminer Eichberg, 72
Ginestet, 135, 140–41, 172, 173
Ginestet, Bernard, 140
Gold Seal, 123
Graacher Münzlay, 83
Grand Chartrons Red and White, 143
Grand Crus, 60–61, 65, 67, 136, 141
Grand-Larose, Château, 138
Grand Pontet, 137, 160
Grand vins, 23
Granvins, 136, 193
Grape juice, spiked, 34
Grapes (grape names, grape varieties, varietal wines), 4, 5, 8–12, 44–45, 80, 105–6ff. (*see also* Wine[s]; specific kinds, places, wines); blends (*see* Blends); hybrids, 121–24; improvements, 115–16, 120–24, 146–47; noble vines, 8–12; red-wine, 8–12; rosé-wine, 11; white-wine, 11–12
Graves, 12, 36, 43, 44, 64, 66, 140, 144, 158, 159, 173, 174, 177, 194; top châteaux, 207
Graves de Vayres, 65
Gray Riesling, 106, 113
Great Growths, 60–61, 65, 67, 136, 141
Great Western, 121, 122–23, 210
Greece, 102
Grenache (Grenache rosé), 11, 63, 95, 217
Grigioni, 54
Grignolino, 53, 54, 112
Grillet, Château, 63
Grinzing, 88
Gros Plant, 12
Grosslagen, 81–85, 153
Growers, 185ff. *See also* Vineyards; specific growers, places, wines
Grumello, Italy, 54
Guild Wine Company, 114
Guiraud-Cheval Blanc, 158
Gumpoldskirchener, 88, 89

Hallgartener Mehrhölzchen, 84
Hanns Christoff Deinhard Liebfraumilch, 177, 201
Haraszthy, Agoston, 112
Harvey's of Bristol, 170, 196–97; Selections, 196–97
Hattenheimer Deutelsberg, 84
Haut Brion, Château, 136, 193, 194
Hautes-Côtes-de-Beaune, 62
Hautes-Côtes-de-Nuits, 62
Haut-Médoc, 4, 43, 64, 158, 159, 163, 170
Hearty Burgundy, 4, 118
Heitz Winery, 209, 212
Herbs, in wines, 31
Hermitage, 10, 42, 54, 63, 64, 175; Blanc, 64; Red, 166
Heublein, 110, 114, 169–70, 186–87
Hochheimer Daubhaus, 84
Hock (Hochheimer), 50, 84
Homemade wines, 35
House of Burgundy, 171
Hudson's Bay Company, 182–83
Hugo et Fils, 71–72
Hungary, 90, 170, 187
Hymettus, 102

Importers, 6, 54, 155–83, 186–87ff. *See also* specific individuals, organizations, places, wines
Inferno (Italian town and wine), 54

Inglenook, 24, 76, 110, 202, 203
International Wines (importers), 170
Iphofener Burgweg, 85
Ischia, 56
Israel, 103, 186
Issan, Château, 139
Italian Swiss Colony, 114, 202, 203
Italy, 10, 12, 13, 53–57; distributors and importers, 53–57, 156, 158–81 *passim;* district and township wines, 53–57; grapes (vines), 10, 12, 53–54; jug wines, 25–26; prices, 55; regionals, 37–39; wine consumption, 13

Jacquet, Château, 135, 144, 166
Jadot, Louis, 150–51, 172
Jaffelin Bourgogne du Chapitre, 163
Jasnières, 69
Jean Jervais, Château, 197
Jerez, Spain, 50, 94, 96, 196–97
Johannisberg, 87, 109
Johannisberger Erntebringer, 84
Johannisberg Riesling, 11, 105, 106, 109, 111, 116, 117, 122, 173, 210
Johnston (Nathaniel) & Fils, 143
Jouvet, 152
Joyce, James, 36
Juan Hernández (jug wine), 27
Jug wines, 22–29; best buys, 3–4, 24; blends, 23; bottle sizes, 22–23, 25, 28; California, 3–4, 15, 24–25, 28–29; European, 25–29; France, 28–29; Italy, 25–26; Portugal, 27–28; prices, 22–23; Spain, 26–27
Juliénas, 39, 40, 41
Jura, the, 75–76

Kabinett wines, 81, 84, 153
Kadarka grape, 90
Kaiserstuhl, 85
Kalte Ente, 32
Keo Aphrodite, 174
Keo Othello, 174
Kir (liqueur), 31
Kirsch, 71
Kirwan, Château, 135, 144
Kobrand, 171–73
Kokkinéli, 102
Korbel, 113
Kornell, Hanns, 171
Kosher wines, 34, 103, 197
Kressman, Ed., & Cie., 135, 143–44
Kreusch, Leonard, 197–98; Selections, 197–98
Kreuznacher Kronenberg, 83
Kreuznacher Steinberg, 154
Kriter, 181
Kröver Nacktarsch, 153
Krug, Charles, 3, 4, 24, 109, 112, 202, 209, 210
Kuehn wines, 73

Labels, 191–92
Labottière, 139
Lachryma Christi, 53, 56
Lafaurie-Peyraguey, Château, 138
Lafayette, Marquis de, 143
Lafite, Château, 50, 134
Lafon-Rochet, Château, 181
La Garde, Château, 140
Lalande-de-Pomerol, 66, 67
Lamberti Bardolino, 176
Lamberti Soave, 176
Lamberti Valpolicella, 176
Lambrusco, 53, 55, 56, 159
Lamoureux, Château, 140
Lancer's, 46, 99, 100
Langenbach, 178
Langguth, 159
Langoa-Barton, 137
Languedoc, 29, 76, 77
Lapelletrie, 142
La Rode, Château, 197

Latada, 28
Latin America, 127–28. *See also* specific countries, wines
Latium, Italy, 53
Latour, Louis, 130, 131–32, 178, 180
Latour Colombier, Château, 182
La Tour Martillac, Château, 135, 143, 144
La Tour de Mons, Château, 137
La Tour St. Bonnet, Château, 182
Léoville-Barton, 137
Lichine, Alexis, 152, 188–89, 193–94; Selections, 193–94
Liebfraumilch, 36, 45–46, 84, 153, 188, 201; best buys, 46
Lindos, 102
Lirac, 64
Lisbon, 27–28, 98–100
Livermore Dinner Red, 116
Livermore White, 116
Loire, the, 9, 12, 28, 44, 68–69, 135, 178, 196; shippers (listed), 219
Lombardy, Italy, 10, 53, 54–55
Lussac-Saint-Émilion, 66
Luxemburg, 179

Macération carbonique process, 146–47
Mâcon, 62, 151, 161, 171
Mâcon Blanc, 45, 62, 131, 132, 136, 151, 213
Mâcon Rouge, 29, 45, 62, 132
Mâcon Supérieur, 62
Mâcon Viré, 151
Macy's Taster Selections, 196
Madeira(s), 99–100
Madrigal, 153
Madrigal Johannisberg Riesling, 173
Magnums, 25, 28
Maire, Henri, 75–76
Mai Wein, 31
Malaga(s), 97
Malbec, 10, 76, 105, 127, 177
Malbec, Château, 177
Malleprat, 144
Malmsey, 100
Malval, Henri, 171
Manischewitz, 197
Mantinea, 102
Manzanilla sherry, 2, 96; best buy, 2
Marche, Italy, 53
Marchesini della Rovere, 26
Margaux, 4, 135, 139, 143, 144; top châteaux, 205
Margaux, Château, 140, 172, 205
Margnat, 29
Marino, 25
Markgräflerland, 85
Marquisat, Pasquier-Desvignes, 175
Marson & Natier, 178
Martini, Louis M., 4, 24, 111, 209, 210
Marvel, Tom, 191
Masson, Paul, 25, 117, 130, 160, 202, 203, 209, 210
Mateus, 46, 99, 165
Mauerweine, 85
Mavrodaphne, 102
Mavron grape, 102
Mayras, Château, 197
Media, beverage, 189–90
Mediterranean. *See* Eastern Mediterranean
Médoc, 66, 131, 135, 137, 139, 144, 158, 160, 161, 172, 174, 180, 182, 186, 194; lesser-known châteaux, 206; top châteaux, 205–6

Meiers Wine Cellars, 211
Meister-Krone, 178, 180, 201
Melin, Château, 182
Melini Chianti, 176
"Mellow Roman Country Wines," 25
"Mellow" wines, 23, 25, 33, 118
Melon grape, 68
Mendocino County, Calif., 105, 114
Mendoza, Argentina, 127, 168

INDEX

Mercurey, 62
Merlot, 10, 43, 66, 105
Merrydown (Sussex, England), fruit wines from, 35
Meursault, 61, 150, 179
Mexico, 128
Meyney, Château, 138
Mialhe, W. A., 142
Middle Europe, 90–92. *See also* specific countries, wines
Midi, the, 28, 76–77; VDQS, 205
Minervois, 77
Mirabelle, 71
Mirassou, 117–18, 202, 204, 209, 210
Mommessin, 151, 152
Monarch Wine (importers and distributors), 197
Monbazillac, 76
Mondavi (Robert) Winery, 109, 112, 171, 209, 210
Monimpex, 90, 187
Monopoles, 143
Monopolies, 186–87; state, 186–87
Monsieur Henri, 47, 173–74; Bordeaux Château Reds, 174
Montagne-Saint-Émilion, 66
Montagny, 62
Montalbano, 38
Montaña, 95, 96
Montefiascone, 56
Monterey, Calif., 105, 117–18
Monthélie, 61, 62
Montrachet, 11, 61, 179
Montravel, 76
Moore's Diamond, 124
Moravia, 92
Morey, 61
Morgenstern (Charles) & Co., 174
Morgon, 39, 40, 41
Morocco, 78, 187
Moscatel de Setúbal, 98
Mosel (Moselle), 46, 61, 81, 82–83, 152
Moselblümchen, 46, 153
Moulin-à-Vent, 39, 40, 41
Mountain Claret, 4, 111
Mountain Dry Chenin Blanc, 111
Mountain Folle Blanche, 111
Mountain Gamay Rosé, 111
Mountain Gewürztraminer, 111
Mountain Red, 24, 111
Mountain Riesling, 111
Mountain Rosé, 25
Mountain Sylvaner, 111
Mountain wines (Almadén blends), 116
Mountain Zinfandel, 41, 112
Mouton-Rothschild, Château, 134, 136
Muller, Jules, 140
Müller-Thurgau, 80, 120
Mumm, 160
Munson Shaw, 175
Murfatlar, 92
Muscadet, 68, 69, 131, 165, 166, 167, 173, 180, 213
Muscadine, 211
Muscat(s), 12, 71, 72, 76, 78, 91, 92, 97; sweet wines (listed), 217
Muscat Ottonel, 92

Nackenheim, 46
Nackenheimer Rehbach, 84
Nahe, Germany, 83, 154
Napa Gamay, 10, 105, 106, 210
Napa Rosé, 109
Napa Valley, Calif., 28, 105, 109, 110, 111, 112, 118
Napa Valley Gamay Beaujolais, 110
Napa Valley Red, 124
Napa Valley Zinfandel, 110
Naturwein, 80, 81–82
Navalle, 110
Navip, 90–91, 175

Nebbiolo, 10, 41, 53, 54–55, 105
"Négociants-Propriétaires," 132
Nemea, 102
Neszmely, Hungary, 90
Neuchâtel, 36, 87, 166
New York State, 120–24, 204; importers and, 157, 171, 186–87, 188–89ff.; representative small cellar of wines from, 209, 210–11
Niagara Winery, 211
Nierstein, 46
Niersteiner Auflangen, 84
Nipozzano, 38
Noble vines, 8–12
North Africa, 78, 187, 215, 216. *See also* specific countries, wines
North Coast County, Calif., 110
Nozzole Chianti, 172
Nuits (wines), 61

Oberemmeler Scharzberg, 83
Odors, in wines, 16–18
Oestricher Gottesthal, 84
Ogier (A.) & Fils, 42
Olivier, Château, 140, 177
Oppenheim, 46
Oppenheimer Güldenmorgen, 84
Oran, Algeria, 216
Ortenau, 85
Orvieto, 25, 53, 55–56
Orvieto Melini, 176
Othello (Cyprus wine), 103, 174

Pailhas, Château, 197
Paisano, 4
Palatinate, the, 84–85
Palmer, Château, 146
Palmes, Les, 144
Pamid grape, 91
Pampas, 163
Panadés, Spain, 96, 172, 179
Parducci, 209, 210
Parsac-Saint-Émilion, 66
Passe-tous-Grains, 10, 149
Pauillac, 64; lesser-known châteaux, 206; top châteaux, 205
Paveil de Luze, 139
Pavillon Blanc, 64
Peartree Imports, 180–82
Pécharmant, 77
Perla de Tarnave, 92
Pernand-Vergelesses, 62
Perry (pear wine), 33
Peterson, Richard, 110
Petit Chablis, 60
Petite Sirah, 10, 115, 116, 118, 210
Petits châteaux, 43, 65, 66–68, 134, 135, 158 (*see also* specific growers, places, wines); buying, 67–68
Petit Syrah, 10, 105
Petri, 24
Pfirsich-bowle, 31
Phylloxera (insect pest), 103, 127, 179
Piat Père & Fils, 151
Pick, Château, 197
Picpoul, 12
Piedmont, the (Italy), 10, 26, 53–54
Piemonte (wine), 26
Pierre Jean (shippers), 142
Piesporter Michelsberg, 83
Pineau des Charentes, 174
Pineau de la Loire, 12, 68–69, 106, 109
Pink wines, 11 (*see also* Rosé[s]); grapes for, 11
Pinot, 73, 105
Pinot Blanc, 11, 12, 45, 71, 105, 106–7, 210
Pinot Chardonnay, 11, 44, 45, 106, 109, 111, 113, 124, 147, 168, 177, 180, 210
Pinot-Chardonnay-Mâcon, 45, 62
Pinot Gris, 70
Pinot Noir, 5, 10, 44, 45, 87, 105, 108, 109, 110, 113, 117, 121, 147, 172, 177, 209

INDEX

Pinot Noir Gamay, 149
Pinot Rosé, 70
Pizay, Château, 160
Pizay-Morgon, Château, 160
Plaisir de France, 139, 198
Plastic wine bottles, introduction of, 29
Platey, Château, 197
Plavac, 91, 175
Pleasant Valley Wine Company, 120, 121, 122
PM's (push merchandise), 190
Pomerol, 43, 64, 66; top châteaux, 207
Pommard, 61, 131, 149, 150
Pontet Canet, 139
Pop wines, 30–34; alcoholic content of, 32; history of, 30–32
Port, 32, 33, 50, 99
Porto, 46, 98–99; vintage, 99
Portugal, 46, 98–100, 131, 165, 174, 182; jug wines, 27–28; rosés (pinks), 28, 46, 131, 165, 182; vinhos verdes, 98–99
Portuguese Rosé, 46, 131, 165, 182
Pouilly Blanc Fumé, 178
Pouilly-Fuissé, 11, 12, 36, 45, 62, 131, 150
Pouilly-Fumé, 68, 69, 165
Pouilly-Loché, 45
Pouilly-sur-Loire, 68
Pouilly-Vinzelles, 45
Prats Frères, 177
Preiss-Henny, 74
Premier Crus, 60–61, 65, 136
Premières Côtes de Blaye, 65, 67
Premières Côtes de Bordeaux, 139
Pressac (grape), 10
Prices, 3–4, 12, 37, 38–39, 41, 46, 47, 60–61 (*see also* Best Buys; Wine Selections; specific distributors, grapes, growers, importers, places, shippers, wines); average spending for wines, rule of thumb for, 3; best buys of the seventies, 2–6; French wines, rise in, 47, 55; importers and, 156–57, 158–82 *passim*, 192; jug wines, 22–23; regionals, 37, 38–39, 41
Prieuré-Lichine, 194
Prince d'Argent, 137, 160
Prince Blanc, 137, 160
Prince Noir, 137, 160
Prince Rouge, 137, 160
Prokupac, 91, 95
Provence, 74–75, 215
Provins, 186
Puisseguin-Saint-Émilion, 66
Puligny, 61
Puyfromage, Château, 182

Quarts de Chaume, 69
Quien & Cie., 142–43
Quincy, 68

Rainwater (madeira), 100
Rallo estates, 25
Ramisco grape, 98
Randersacker Ewig Leben, 85
Rauenthaler Steinmächer, 84
Rausan-Ségla, 140
Ravat Blanc (*formerly* Ravat 6), 121
Rayon d'Or (*formerly* Seibel 4986), 121
Red Cap Chauvenet, 151
Red wines, 9–11, 90–92, 94–100, 102–3, 105–18, 120–24, 127–28 (*see also* specific grapes, kinds, places, wines); district and township, 50–51, 53ff. (*see also* specific places, wines); grapes for, 9–11; importers and shippers and, 130–54, 155–83; in jugs, 4, 24–29; pop wines, 30–35; regionals, 36–47 (*see also* specific places, wines); for small wine cellars, 208
Reggio Emilia, 26
Regional wines, 4, 5–6, 36–47 (*see also* specific distributors, growers, places, wines); defined, 37; district and township wines and, 50–51, 53ff.; importers and shippers and, 133ff., 148–54, 155–83; prices, 37, 38–39, 41; wine tastings and, 200–4
"Région de Sèvre-et-Maine," 68
Renfield (importers), 176
Residual sugars, 18, 147
Retsina, 102
Reuilly, 68, 69
Rheingau, 83–84, 152
Rheinhessen, 45–46, 84
Rheinpfalz, 84–85
Rhine(land), 5, 28, 31, 32, 50, 51, 61, 80, 105, 106, 120, 159–60, 175, 178, 191, 193–94 (*see also* specific distributors, growers, places, wines); estate-bottled, 185; noble vines, 9; pop wines, 31, 32; shippers, 152–54
Rhine Castle, 117
Rhine Wine, 3, 24, 25
Rhône, the, 23, 28, 40, 42, 63–64, 135, 160, 168, 170, 172, 175, 178, 180, 181, 186, 191, 196, 215 (*see also* specific distributors, growers, places, wines); red-wine grapes, 10, 11; shippers (listed), 219; white-wine grapes, 11
Ricasoli, Barone, 37, 160
Richard's Wine Cellars, 211
Riesling(s), 5, 11, 12, 70, 71, 72, 80, 84, 87, 90, 120, 121, 124, 152, 168, 173, 174, 195; California, 11, 105, 106, 109, 111
Riesling Schoenenburg, 72
Rikat, 92
Rince cochon, 31
Rioja, Spain, 26, 27, 46–47, 94–95, 96, 173, 179; shippers (listed), 220
Río Negro, Argentina, 127
Riquewihr, 71–75
Riserva Ducale, 38
Rishon-el-Zion, 103
Riunite de Reggio Emilia, 26
Rochette & Cie., 42
Roc-Saint Michel, Château, 140
Romania, 92
Rosé(s), 9, 11, 46, 55, 64, 75, 95, 100, 127, 186, 210, 213; grapes for, 11; in jugs, 24, 25, 28
Rosé d'Anjou, 213
Rose de Pauillac, La, 186
Rosella, 174
Rosso di Verona, 55
Roundness, in wines, 19
Rousillon, 76, 77
Rovere Barbera, 26
Royal Médoc, 137
Rubion, 117
Rudesheimer Burgweg, 84
Rufina district, Italy, 38
Rully, 62
Ruppertsberger Hofstück, 85
Rust (town and wine), 88, 89
Rusticano, 181

Saar-Ruwer, 83
Sable-Saint-Émilion, 66
Saint-Amour, 39, 40, 41
Saint Émilion, 10, 43, 64, 65, 66, 131, 135, 137, 138–39, 140, 141, 143, 144, 158, 160, 162, 168, 170, 174, 180, 182; top châteaux, 207
Saint Estèphe, 4, 64, 138, 140, 141; top châteaux, 205
Saint George-Saint Émilion, 66
Saint Joseph, 63
Saint Julien, 64, 135, 137, 138, 140, 160; top châteaux, 205
Saint Patrice, 42
Saint Péray, 64
Saint-Roman, 62
Saint Véran, 45, 62, 167
Sales, wine, 13
Salinas Valley, Calif., 117
San Benito, Calif., 105

INDEX

Sancerre, 12, 68, 69, 178
San Giovese, 10, 11
San Gioveto, 10, 41, 106
Sangria, 31, 46–47, 95, 97, 156
Santa Clara, Calif., 105
Santenay, 61, 62, 150
Sassella, 54
Saumur, 69
Sauterne(s), 2, 12, 24, 33, 43, 64, 138, 140, 194
Sauvignon Blanc, 12, 68, 105, 109, 110, 115, 116, 210
Sauvignon Sec, 147
Savennières, 69
Savigny, 61, 62
Savigny-les-Beaune, 62
Savoie, 76
Sazerac, 163
Schloss Böckelheimer Burgweg, 83
Schloss Böckelheimer Königsberg, 154
Schoonmaker, Frank, 7, 55, 145, 188–89, 191–92, 193; Selections, 189, 191–92
Schröder & Schyler, 135, 144–45; and vintage ratings, 144–45
Scuppernong grape, 211
Seagram's, 137, 159, 160, 161
Sebastiani (growers), 113
Seeweine, 85
Segesta, 25
Segesta Sicilian, 159
Semillon, 12, 112, 115
Semillon, Château, 115
Sercial, 100
Seyssel, 63, 64, 76, 195
Seyval (*formerly* Seyve-Villard 5276), 121
Sherry, 3, 32, 33, 50, 96, 155
Sherry Wine & Spirits, 188, 196
Shippers, 5–6, 8, 54, 130–54, 185, 188 (*see also* specific places, shippers, wines); Bordeaux, 133–48; Burgundy, 148–52; Burgundy/Bordeaux, 152; listed, 218–21
Shy bearers, 9
Sichel, Peter M. F., 145–47
Sichel & Fils, 64–65, 135, 136, 145–47, 152
Sicily, 159
Siena, 37, 38
Silver Satin (pop wine), 32
Simon, Abdalleh, 158
Sipon, 175
Sipp, Louis, 73
Sipp Riesling Grand Réserve, 163
Slovin, 90–91, 175
Smell, and judging of wines, 16–18
Smith Haut Lafitte, Château, 140
Sneaky Pete, 30
Soave, 25, 26, 53, 55, 162, 176
Soave Bertani, 162
Soleil Blanc, 4, 132, 151, 166
Soleil Noir, 132, 151, 166
Sonoma Valley, Calif., 105, 113, 114
"Sophistication" of wines, 30–31, 130
Southern Burgundy, 44–45, 60, 62
Southwest, the (France), 76–77
Soviet republics, 29, 187. *See also* specific countries, wines
Spain, 46–47, 94–97, 173, 174, 196–97 (*see also* specific growers, places, wines); control laws, 95; jug wines, 26–27; major shippers, 95; shippers (listed), 220; and wine classifications, 94–95
Spanna, 54–55
Spätlesen, 73, 81, 153
Spritzer, 31
State monopolies, 186–87
Steigenberger, A., 154
Steinwein, 46, 85
Strauss, Warren B., 194–95; Selections, 194–95
Stravecchio Melini, 38–39
Straw-covered bottles, Chiantis in, 38
Sugar, 18, 146–47; added to wine to increase alcoholic content, 18, 23, 80, 81; residual, 18, 147
Sumner, George, 188–89, 195–96
Sweetness in wines, 18; in pop wines, 30–32, 33
Sweet wines, 18, 76 (*see also* Dessert wines; Fruit wines; Kosher wines; Pop wines; specific grapes, wines); French, listed, 217
Switzerland, 87, 159, 186
Sylvaner, 2, 11, 12, 45, 70, 71, 72, 80, 84, 105, 106, 111, 112, 117, 120, 152, 166, 171, 174, 180, 210
Sylvaner Domaine Voltaire, 72
Sylvaner Riesling, 109, 110, 118

Table wines, 9–12, 22, 23, 29, 51, 81. *See also* specific kinds, places, wines
Taillan, 139
Tamianka, 92
Tannin, in wines, 18, 19
Tarragona, 26, 27, 95, 96, 97
Tarragona Port, 95
Tasse d'Or award, 194
Tasting(s), wine, 7–8, 13–14, 15–19, 200–4; descriptive terms, 14, 15–19; groups (for comparison), 156, 165, 202–4; method, 13–14
Tavel(s), 11, 63, 64, 75, 172
Taylor Wine Company, 121, 122–23
Tchelistcheff, André, 110
Terrefort, Château, 142
Thomas, Gregory, 145
Thunderbird (pop wine), 32
Timothy, Brother, 108
Tinto, 168
Tokay, 90, 92
Tokay d'Alsace, 70
Touraine, 68–69
Township wines, 4–5, 50. *See also* District and township wines; specific places, wines
Trade listings, 189–90
Traminer(s), 2, 12, 70, 71, 105, 110, 112, 166
Trierer Römerlay, 83
Trimbach, F. E., 72–73
Trimoulet, 142
Trockenbeerenauslesen, 81
Tunisia, 78
Tuscany, Italy, 37, 53
Tytell Europa Wines, 197

Umbria, Italy, 53
Undurraga Riesling, 127
Unifrance, 162
United States of America: California wines, 105–18 (*see also* California); importers and shippers and, 130–54, 155–83, 186–87ff. (*see also* specific importers, shippers, wines); jug wines, 22–24; New York State and the East, wines of, 120–24; pop wines, 30–35; representative wines for small cellar, 209–12; shippers (listed), 218–21; wine consumption in, 13; wine tastings and, 200–4
United Vintners, 170

Valais, the, Swiss wines from, 87
Valdepeñas, Spain, 26, 95, 96
Valencia, Spain, 26, 27
Valpolicella, 26, 53, 55, 176, 180
Valtellina, Italy, 54
Varietal wines. *See* Grapes; specific kinds, places, wines
VDNV (*Verband Deutscher Naturwein Versiegerer*), 81–82
VDQS (*Vins Délimités de Qualité Supérieure*), 29, 51, 75, 76; listed, 215–16
Vegetable stench, in wines, 16
Verdelho, 100
Verdicchio, 53, 55

Vermouth, 31, 32, 33, 155
Verona, Italy, 53, 55
Vieille-Chapelle, Château, 181
Vienna, Austria, 88-89
Vieux Robin, Château, 135, 144
Villa Antinori, 39
Villa Armando, 25
Vin chaud, 31-32
Vin courant, 23
Vin du pays. See Country wines (*vin du pays*)
Vines. *See* Grapes; specific kinds
Vineyards, 4, 5, 8-9, 185ff. *See also* Grapes; Wine(s); specific growers, places, wines
Vin Fou, 75-76
Vin gris, 70
Vinho Verde, 98-99, 100, 182, 195
Vinho Vida, 182
Vinifera Wine Cellars, 122, 210
Vin jaune, 75
Vin ordinaire, 22, 23, 29, 51
Vino Rustico, 25
Vino Santo, 102
Vinprom, 91
Vins de paille, 75, 217
Vin Supérieur de Tunisie, 78
Vintages, prices and, 132
Visp, 87
Voigny, Château, 140
Volnay, 61
Vouvray, 68-69, 180

Wachau, Austria, 88
Wachenheimer Schenkenbohl, 85
Wagner, Philip M., 120
Wan Fu, 64-65, 146
Wehlener Münzlay, 83
Wente Bros., 115, 210
White Mountain (N.H.) Vineyards, 211
White Pinot, 12, 106-7, 110
White Riesling, 11, 106
White wines, 9-11, 53-58, 80, 90-92, 94-97, 98-100, 105-18, 120-24 (*see also* specific kinds, places, wines); district and township, 50-51, 53ff.; grapes for, 11-12; importers and shippers, 130-54, 155-83 (*see also* specific importers, shippers, wines); in jugs, 3, 23-29; pop wines, 30-35; regionals, 36-47 (*see also* specific regions, wines); for small cellars, 208, 209
Wholesalers, 190
Widmer Wine Cellars, 122, 123-24, 210
Wildman (Frederick) & Sons, 178-80, 188
Wile (Julius) Sons & Co., 176-78
Willm, A., 74
Wiltinger Scharzberg, 83
Wine(s), 2-19 (*see also* Red wines; White wines; specific distributors, grapes, growers, kinds, places, wines); agents and buyers, 187-88; alcohol in (*see* Alcohol[s]); best buys of the seventies, 2-6 (*see also* Best buys; Prices); brand names, 4, 5-6 (*see also* Brand-name wines; specific kinds); buying in quantity, 13; château-bottled, 5 (*see also* Château-bottled wines; specific wines); classifications, 5, 50-51 (*see also* specific classifications, wines); co-operatives and monopolies, 186-87; district and township, 4-5, 50-51, 52ff.; general information, 2-19; generic, 4, 5-6; grapes for (*see* Grapes); importers, and shippers and, 5-6, 8, 130-54, 155-83, 186-87ff.; looking for and discovering of, 2, 7-19; new techniques in making, 6, 115-16, 120-24, 146-47 (*see also* specific individuals, processes, wines); regional (*see* Regional wines); shippers (listed), 218-21; "sophistication" of, 30-31, 130; "style" of, 8; tasting and judging, 7-8, 13-14, 15-19, 200-4; trade listings, 189-90
Wine and Food Society, 165
Wine-based drinks, 30-35. *See also* specific kinds, wines
Wine cellars, small, stocking of, 208-12; 50-bottle, 210; reds, 208, 209; representative American wines, 209-12; special case, 210-12; 25-bottle, 209-10; whites, 208, 209
Wine Imports of America, 182
Wine Selections, 189-97; Harvey, 196-97; Kreusch, 197; Lichine, 193-94; Macy's Taster, 196; Schoonmaker, 189, 191-92; Strauss, 194-95; Sumner, 195-96; Tytell Europa, 197
Wines of France (Lichine), 194
Wine tasting. *See* Tasting(s), wine
Wine Tour of France, A (Wildman), 179
Winkler Honigsberg, 84
Woodiness, in smell and taste of wines, 17
Woodruff, in May Wine, 31
Würzburger Himmelspforte, 85

Xynister, 103

Yago, 27, 96, 173
Yago Sant'Gria, 47, 173
Young wines, 23, 28
Yquem, Château, 115
Yugoslavia, 90-91, 175

Zeller Schwartze Katz, 153
Zeltinger Münzlay, 83
Zinfandel, 2, 11, 24, 41, 209, 212; best buy, 2; California, 24, 105, 106, 109, 110, 112, 113, 118; grapes, 11; in jugs, 24
Zwicker, 71